BETTER HOMES AND GARDENS® BOOKS

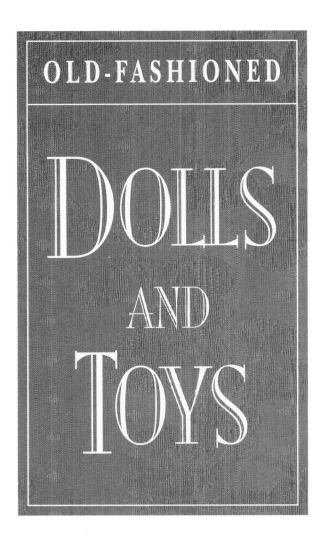

OLD-FASHIONED

DOLLS
AND
TOYS

BETTER HOMES AND GARDENS® BOOKS
Des Moines, Iowa

OLD-FASHIONED DOLLS AND TOYS

Editor: Sara Jane Treinen

Associate Art Director: Linda Ford Vermie

Project Manager: Jennifer Speer-Ramundt

Photographer: Peter Krumhardt

Contributing Writers: Patricia Wilens,
   Linda Stueve, Eve Mahr

Contributing Illustrator: Chris Neubauer

Publishing Systems Text Processor: Paula Forest

BETTER HOMES AND GARDENS® BOOKS

An Imprint of Meredith® Books

President: Joseph J. Ward

Vice President and Editorial Director: Elizabeth P. Rice

Executive Editor: Connie Schrader

Art Director: Ernest Shelton

Art Production Director: Randall Yontz

WE CARE!

The editorial department at Better Homes and Gardens® Books assembled this collection of projects for your crafting pleasure. Our staff is committed to providing you with clear and concise instructions so that you can complete each project. We guarantee your satisfaction with this book for as long as you own it. We welcome your comments and suggestions. Please address your correspondence to Better Homes and Gardens® Books Editorial Department, 1760 Locust Street, Des Moines, IA 50309-3023.

Welcome to the wonderful world of doll and toy crafting! We wish you the greatest pleasure as you use this book and hope this collection of sweet and charming playthings will take you back to some of your fondest childhood days. Among the 51 featured projects are many soft dolls made from an assortment of fabrics, constructed from wood, and others using a variety of crafting materials. Use your imagination and skills so each of your toys possesses your distinctive flair and reflects your love and respect for handmade treasures.

Table of Contents

How To Use This Book

For the beginner as well as the experienced doll- or toymaker, *Old-Fashioned Dolls and Toys* provides complete instructions, full-size patterns, and tips for successful crafting for each project in this book. We compiled the following information to help you understand the presentation of the material. It would be beneficial to read through it before you start any of the projects.

GENERAL SUPPLIES

Each project begins with a list of supplies that are required to complete the project. General supplies that are essential to the ongoing activities of crafters are intentionally omitted; these include tracing paper, pins, needles, sewing threads, pencils, rulers, and scissors. You will need to have these supplies on hand for the projects in this book.

MATERIALS LIST

The items in the materials list are all the supplies that are needed to complete the project or projects shown in the photograph. Sometimes we divided the list, making one list for the doll body and another list for the doll clothing or accessories (see Rachel on pages 36 and 37 or Vincent and Victoria on pages 58–62). Use the heading for each list as a guide, and before you begin, look further in the instructions for an additional list of materials for other parts of the project.

When actual yardage is given, that yardage assumes a 44- or 45-inch fabric width. It allows for the longest pattern piece to be cut either on the length or the crosswise grain of the fabric. The exception is when nap fabrics, such as fur, are needed. Then it is important to cut the pattern pieces following the nap of the fabric. In these cases, arrows are shown on the pattern pieces to designate the direction of the pile or fur.

For fabric collectors who have lots of fabric scraps, the yardage may not be important. Use the scraps and your imagination to create dolls that have their own character and personality and reflect your ingenuity.

For projects that call for wood materials, we listed dimensions of lumber, but this should not preclude the use of lumber scraps.

Decorative laces, trims, embroidery floss, buttons, carpet or button threads, glues, and special cutting tools are listed when we felt it influenced the charm or character of the project. Substituting other supplies, such as dental floss for tan or white carpet thread or felt instead of wool, will not hinder the success of your crafting. In the same way, to trim your projects use your scraps of laces, ribbons, braids, or other embellishments rather than purchasing them.

PREPARING THE PATTERNS

All the patterns in this book are full-size and include ¼-inch seam allowances unless noted otherwise. Sometimes you will need to join two pattern pieces together to make one complete pattern. The instructions are specific when this occurs. You can either trace these patterns separately and tape them together after you cut them out, or you can lay the tracing paper over each piece and join them together as you trace.

Oftentimes there are fabric or wood pieces that have no patterns. These pieces are basic squares, rectangles, or circles. These pieces are included in the "cutting" directions and do not require pattern pieces.

CUTTING THE MATERIALS

Each type of fabric or wood has its own cutting instructions. When there are no traced patterns to use, simply use a ruler or compass to draw the dimensions directly onto the material. For sewing projects, the fabric measurements include ¼-inch seam allowances unless noted otherwise in the instructions.

The cutting instructions include directions for cutting all the materials for the projects in the photograph. For example, when two dolls are in the photo, the cutting instructions include all the pieces that are required to make both dolls unless the instructions indicate otherwise. When pattern pieces such as arms, legs, or bodies are used for more than one doll or toy, each full-size pattern indicates how many pieces it is necessary to cut to make one doll. Before you begin to gather and cut your materials, determine if you want to make all or part of the project. Then carefully read through the directions, making notes to adjust the materials list and cutting instructions, based on your decision.

SEWING FABRICS

Since most of the fabric projects require sewing two fabric pieces together "with right sides facing," this type of construction is always assumed. The directions are explicit when it is necessary to sew pieces together with the wrong sides facing.

Pattern pieces are drawn with ¼-inch seam allowances; all cutting instructions include ¼-inch seam allowances. Sew all pieces together using ¼-inch seams unless the instructions note otherwise.

PATTERN PIECES

All pattern pieces are drawn with a solid line for cutting and a short dashed line for sewing. Long dashed lines indicate the dashed line is placed on the fold of the fabric before cutting out the piece. These lines are marked with the word "fold."

The pattern pieces frequently have markings that are useful for following the sewing directions. Among the markings that are found on the patterns, the most common is the X that is used to designate eye placements, the positions for jointing arms and legs to the body, and other instructions for special assembly. Topstitching lines, embroidery and painting lines, and placement positions for pockets, ears, and other details on the dolls and toys are marked with straight lines inside the pattern pieces. Small and large dots along the sewing lines are usually in pairs and designate special sewing instructions.

EMBROIDERY STITCH DIAGRAMS

Backstitch

Outline Stitch

Running Stitch

Straight Stitch

Satin Stitch

French Knot

Lazy Daisy Stitch

Long-and-Short Stitch

DOLLMAKING TECHNIQUES

As you begin your adventures in dollmaking, you'll discover lots of your own tips and techniques. Write them down and keep a notebook for a handy reference. Many of our tips are included with the directions with each doll so they are available to you as you are working. Here are some additional guidelines that we noted as we assembled this collection.

FABRIC SELECTIONS

Doll bodies and their clothing can be made from an assortment of fabrics. Muslin, felt, cottons, wool, fur, silk, upholstery, lamé, osnaburg, and knits are among the fabrics we used in this collection. Cutting the Fabrics lists the fabrics we used to make the doll shown in the photograph. Check the materials list to review the fabric suggestions.

The weight, weave, texture, and design of the selected fabrics influence the fun and look of the finished project. Closely woven and light- and medium-weight fabrics are easier to work with, especially when a project has narrow seams and important details. Textured fabrics, such as velvet and corduroy, add interest to dolls and toys. These fabrics can be used for both bodies and clothing. Make sure the weight of these fabrics is suitable for the size of the project. Because the projects in this book are relatively small, use fabrics with small designs rather than large ones. Whatever you choose, the fabrics should work for the intended use of your doll. If your doll is for child's play, select fabrics that are closely woven and suitable for narrow seams.

Acrylic felt comes in lots of colors and is washable. Because it's a nonwoven fabric, it's easy to work with and does not unravel. It has no grain—you can cut pieces in any direction. When sewing, you can sew seams with the wrong sides facing to create seams on the right side that add an interesting dimension to both doll bodies and clothing. It's a great fabric for lots of crafts projects because pieces can be glued together. When

sewing, set the machine for 8 to 10 stitches per inch to avoid weakening the seams. Finger-press felt seams or press felt on the wrong side to avoid shininess on the right side.

FACIAL FEATURES

All of the dolls in this book have either painted or embroidered faces. With few exceptions, the faces have simple lines that are easy to produce. Add the features onto the face before you sew the head pieces together. Use dressmaker's carbon paper or a water-erasable pen to transfer the face pattern onto the fabric.

Use acrylic paints and a fine-tip artist's paintbrush. Acrylics dry fast and will not delay your doll construction. It is a good idea to practice painting the face on a scrap of fabric to develop the skills for brush strokes and to get a sense for the amount of paint you need on the brush. Marking pens are available in lots of colors. Use them for fine lines such as eyebrows and lips.

When embroidering the face, do not cut out the pattern piece until after the face is stitched. Draw the whole face (or body) pattern piece onto the fabric and transfer the facial features. Allow enough fabric around the piece so you can place it in an embroidery hoop. Diagrams for the embroidery stitches are on page 7. For fine lines (outline stitches), use one or two strands of embroidery floss. For satin stitches and French knots use two strands of floss. The doll instructions indicate the number of strands to use. Feel free to experiment with your stitching to obtain the finished look you want for your doll. When all the stitching is completed, remove the hoop, cut out the piece, and proceed with the construction.

STUFFING DOLLS

The most popular material for stuffing dolls and toys is polyester fiberfill. It's easy to use, it's clean, lightweight, washable, and nonallergenic. To fill tiny spaces, such as hands or feet, pull off small pieces and stuff them into the part with your fingers. Use the eraser end of a pencil to push the fiber into these tight spaces. Use small pieces to stuff around curves and fill out the seams. After filling these spaces, finish stuffing the rest of the project. Stuff the doll or toy with the amount of firmness that you desire.

To help make a doll or toy sit better, use plastic filler beads to stuff the lower part of the body. These beads are clean, sold in bags, and available in crafts and fabric stores. Avoid the use of sand or seeds that might have bug infestations when stuffing projects. The redheaded twin dolls on page 70 and the frog doll on page 96 use these beads so these dolls sit nicely on pint-size chairs or on a shelf.

TRIM EMBELLISHMENTS

One of the delights in creating dolls and toys is that you discover many uses for the odds and ends of trims that are in your workbasket. Scrap pieces of laces, handkerchiefs, old pillowcase trims, appliqués, and doilies make useful items when sewing doll clothing. The instructions indicate the width and yardage of the trim pieces for each of the projects in this book. Use these measurements as a guide to make use of decorative trims you already have before purchasing others. Watch out for trims that do not match the care instructions for the rest of the doll.

PURCHASED ACCESSORIES

As you are making your doll, you will come up with playful ideas to complete its character by using accessories that you can buy. Browse through the miniature departments in doll and crafts stores. Here you'll find hats, shoes, baskets, and lots more that can be painted or trimmed with ribbons and laces, dried or silk flowers, and beads or buttons that add special touches to the finishing of your project. Dollhouse miniatures—chalkboards, picture frames, fruits and vegetables—are charming additions.

TURNING TUBES WITH EASE

When making dolls or other projects that require a narrow strip of fabric to be sewn together and turned right side out, follow this easy method.

1. Cut string or bias tape 2 or 3 inches longer than the length of the fabric strip. Place the string atop the right side of the fabric so it extends beyond both edges of the strip. Make an overhand knot in one end of the string to keep it from slipping through the seam.

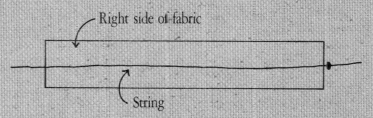

2. With right sides facing, fold the fabric in half with the string running down the center of one side of the strip. Sew the seam, encasing the string in just *one* narrow edge (the end with the knot). Do not sew the string in the long seam.

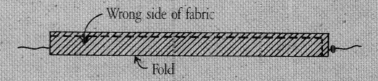

3. Gently pull on the unsewn end of the string and the fabric will slide through the tube and turn right side out. Trim the string from the seam; press.

Doll Hairstyling Tips

All projects include the directions for styling the doll's or toy's hair in the fashion that is shown in the photograph. The following information provides some additional guidelines for using fabrics, yarns, and natural fibers to design hairstyles and helpful tips about these materials. When one of our dolls requires a hair product you cannot find, write and request a catalog from the suppliers listed on page 158. These folks will be most willing to help you find the right product for your doll or toy.

When selecting the materials for styling hair, consider how the doll will be used. A child's doll requires sturdy construction with durable materials that will withstand lots of love and affection. Delicate fibers arranged in lifelike styles are well worth the investment in time and effort for shelf-dolls.

FABRIC HAIR

Cotton and knit fabric strips are an ideal choice for children's toys. They make a bushy head of hair and can be sturdily attached to the doll's head. One method of using fabric is to tear long narrow strips, ½ to ¾ inch wide, along or across the fabric grain. Cut these strips into pieces that are 3 to 4 inches long for a short bob. Tie a knot in the center of each short piece. Hand-sew the knot of each piece to the head. Then trim the strips to the desired length.

For a less scrappy look, cut the strips with pinking shears. Layer a couple of short strips together, pinch the center together to resemble a bowknot, wrap thread around the pinched center to secure the bow, and sew lots of bows to the head.

Cutting fabric circles and turning them into "yo-yos," a technique often used during the 1930s for assembling patchwork coverlets, is a clever way to cover heads of dolls. Cut lots of 4-inch-diameter circles from fabric scraps. To make one yo-yo, double-thread a needle with sewing thread and tie a knot in the ends of the threads. With the wrong side of a circle facing, fold the circle edges under ¼ inch to the wrong side; at the same time, hand-sew small running stitches around the circle, through the folded fabric edge. Pull on the thread to gather and draw the outside edges of the circle to the center, keeping the wrong side of the fabric hidden inside the yo-yo. Tightly pull the thread to leave a small center opening; knot the thread to secure the gathers. Flatten the circle, keeping the gathered edge centered on one side of the yo-yo. Hand-sew the yo-yos to the doll, overlapping them to cover the head. To make braids, thread lots of yo-yos onto two separate long strings; tack one end of each string to each side of the head.

YARN HAIR

Versatility and ease of styling make yarn one of the most widely chosen hair mediums. Yarns are readily available in a diverse range of colors and textures. Don't discard your old sweaters. They can be unraveled for fabulous doll hair. Rachel, our cover doll, utilizes this method, which is described on page 36. If you don't have a sweater that you want to tear apart, look for old sweaters at garage sales as an inexpensive source. Or, if you are a knitter, knit a swatch from the yarn you want to use. Dampen the swatch with cool water; set it aside to dry or tumble it dry in the dryer. When the swatch is unraveled, you will have wavy yarn that's great for hair.

Precut rug yarn is quick and easy to use for short hairstyles and bangs. To make a wig, position the precut strands of yarn in a row on a sheet of typing or notebook paper. For stability, tape both edges of the yarn to the paper. Machine-sew down the center of the yarn, between the cut edges, through the paper. Gently remove the tape and paper from the yarn. Depending on the size of the doll's head, you may need to prepare several strips. To attach the strips to the head, begin winding the strips at the top of the head; then wind them around the sides. Overlap the yarn strands for a full head of hair. Hand-sew the strips to the head using the sewing-machine stitches as a guide.

Braids, ponytails, and hair buns are fun and easy to make with yarns. But first you need to form a wig. The technique for creating a yarn wig is similar to the precut yarn strip method previously described.

Select the yarn you wish to use and cut strands of yarn that are extra long for styling. As a general rule, determine the length of one braid or ponytail, then measure the head from the center of the forehead to the center back of the neck. Add these two measurements; then cut the yarn twice as long as the sum. Remember, you can always trim tresses that are too long. Measure the length of the part for your hairstyle. For braids and ponytails at the sides of the head, the part will run down the center of the head, from the top of the forehead to the nape. Draw the line onto the paper and cut enough pieces of yarn so they cover the line when taped to the paper. Machine-sew the yarn to the paper; remove the tape and paper. Lay the wig over the head; glue or hand-sew the wig in place. Braid or make ponytails with the long strands of yarn, tacking or gluing the yarn to the sides of the head as necessary.

For a full head of shoulder-length or longer hair, measure the part from the center of the forehead to the crown. When the wig is placed on the doll, the hair will fall across the back of the head. Evenly distribute the strands with your fingers and glue them to the head.

For bangs, wrap yarn around a strip of cardboard that measures the width of the doll's forehead. Remove the bundle from the cardboard strip and tie a knot around the center of the bundle. Tack the knot to the center of the forehead. Then cut the loops on opposite sides of the bundle. Arrange the bangs and trim the yarn ends as desired.

Embroidery floss, pearl cottons, and crochet threads are more delicate fibers that can be used like yarn to create more sophisticated hairstyles, and are useful materials when crafting small dolls.

WOOL AND FLAX HAIR

Wool fibers make wonderful doll hair. These fibers have a close resemblance to human hair in their crimp, shine, and texture. These fibers are now packaged for dollmaking and are widely available in crafts and fabric stores.

Packaged wool roving is dyed in a range of natural hair shades and is available in straight and braided (curly) crepe. Roving is so versatile that professional results can be achieved with minimal effort. A roving wig can be made using the same method as for yarns. Curly crepe wool is processed by braiding it over twine. When pulled and fluffed apart, the crepe wool becomes beautiful wavy hair.

Raw wool is perfect for ladies and gentlemen of distinction. The Uncle Sam doll on page 42 is easily groomed with bits of wool that are hot-glued to the face and head. Styling of the hair is easy when working with wool roving; it has a natural crimp and spreads easily across the head. Start with pieces of wool that are longer than the finished hairstyle. Then trim the style to the desired length.

Curly roving also can be hot-glued directly to the doll head. Pull both ends of the roving to expose the twine. Remove the twine from the fibers to separate the ends for adequate head coverage. Glue one strip of the roving from the forehead to the nape of the neck. Glue the second strip onto one side of the head, then take the strip under the chin (do not glue it) and glue it to the opposite side of the head. Cut the second strip under the chin. Fluff and finger-comb the roving between the glued sections to blend the strips together. Trim and style the hairdo as desired.

Due to its fine texture, flax makes beautiful, lifelike hair for both large and small dolls. Use the wig method described for yarn hair for best results. Florence, the long-legged angel on page 82, has flaxen braids.

Picture Puzzle Blocks

These six-in-one block puzzles were great favorites during Victorian times. Use pastoral scenes or illustrations from favorite fairy tales to make fun-time games for little folks on rainy days. Or you can use wrapping paper, greeting cards, calendars, or your child's own artwork to make one-of-a-kind picture puzzles. Just glue a picture onto wooden blocks in a few easy steps. Keep turning the blocks over and glue pictures to adjacent sides. Cover all six sides if you want a real brainteaser.

GENERAL INSTRUCTIONS

1. Reproduction prints can be obtained from many sources. We used pictures from the children's storybook *A Day in the Country*, published by Merrimack Publishing. You may choose to cut up a calendar or to purchase old prints from flea markets or antiques shops.

2. Determine the picture area of each of the six prints that you want for your puzzles as follows: To fit the blocks, the width and length of each print image must be divisible by 1½ inches. For example, if your print is 10 inches wide, you will need to trim the print to 9 inches so it will fit onto six 1½-inch blocks. In the same manner, trim each print to fit the length. The puzzle on the opposite page has an image area of 9x6 inches and requires 24 blocks.

3. Draw a grid of 1½-inch squares on the back of each print. Working on a protected surface, use the crafts knife and the ruler to cut the squares apart. Place the squares from each print in a separate envelope.

PREPARING THE BLOCKS

1. Lightly sand all sides of each block to remove rough edges.
2. Wipe each block with the tack cloth.

ASSEMBLING THE BLOCKS

1. Working with one print at a time, lightly coat the back of a few paper squares and one side of an equal number of blocks with the rubber cement. (The paper squares are easier to align with the edges of the blocks if you work on only a few at a time. While the cement is tacky, you can lift and move the paper until it is centered on the block.)

2. Press the paper squares onto the blocks. When the cement is dry, use your fingers to rub off and peel away any excess. Fasten all the paper squares cut from one picture in the same manner.

3. Glue each of the 1½-inch squares of a second picture to another side of each of the blocks. Continue in this manner until all six sides of the blocks are covered with the six pictures.

4. When the rubber cement is thoroughly dry, spray the blocks with the polyurethane varnish.

R·A·G·G·E·D·Y K·I·D·S

When *Raggedy Ann Stories* first was published in 1918, the cloth doll was sold to complement her narrative adventures. Quickly the doll became as popular as the stories. Perpetual favorites of children and collectors, the identifying features of the raggedy family remain constant— painted-on smiles and triangle noses, and striped leggings under pinafores and trousers. Our 15-inch-tall twins, with tousled hair made of torn fabric scraps, are captivating versions of this beloved tradition.

PREPARING THE PATTERNS

Trace the full-size patterns on pages 16 and 17 onto tracing paper. Cut out the patterns.

◆

CUTTING THE FABRICS

The cutting instructions for pieces that have no patterns include ¼-inch seams.

From muslin, cut:
- Four bodies
- Four collars
- Four pantaloons
- Eight arms

From striped fabric, cut:
- Four legs

From red print fabric, cut:
- Two 1½x22-inch apron ruffle and waistband strips
- One 4x12-inch apron skirt
- One 1½x8-inch apron neck strap

From solid blue fabric, cut:
- Four pants
- Two 1½x7-inch straps

From black scraps, cut:
- Eight shoes

From plaid fabric, cut:
- One bodice front
- Two bodice backs
- Two 6½x5½-inch dress sleeves
- One 6x29-inch dress skirt
- One shirt back
- Two shirt fronts
- Two 5½-inch squares for shirt sleeves

From solid red fabric, tear lots of:
- ¾x3½-inch strips for hair

GENERAL INSTRUCTIONS

The instructions are for sewing one doll body. Repeat these instructions to make the second doll. The clothing directions for each doll are given separately.

FACE

1. Lay one muslin body atop the pattern on page 16. With the black marker, trace the eyes, eyebrows, eyelashes, and smile.
2. With the rust marker, trace the nose, oval mouth, and freckles.
3. Apply powder blush to the cheeks.

ARMS

1. Sew the arms together in pairs, leaving the tops open for stuffing.
2. Clip curves; turn the arms right sides out.
3. Firmly stuff the arms up to the topstitching line. Line up the seams and sew across the topstitching line of each arm. (See the topstitching tip on page 134.) Leave the upper arms unstuffed.
4. Using ⅛-inch seams, sew the arms, with the thumbs pointing up, to the body front between the dots.

LEGS

1. Sew the center fronts of the shoes together in pairs from the top of the shoe to the dot. Press the seams open.
2. Sew the tops of shoes to the bottoms of legs.
3. Fold the legs in half and sew the remaining foot and leg seams, leaving the tops open.
4. Clip curves; turn the legs right sides out. Firmly stuff the legs to the topstitching line.
5. Pinch each leg so the back leg seam is centered and sew across the topstitching line.
6. Lightly stuff the upper legs. Sew the legs to the body front between the dots.

BODY

1. Press under a ¼-inch seam along the bottom edge of the other body piece for the body back.
2. Sew the body pieces together, leaving the bottom edges open.
3. Clip the head and neck curves; turn the body right side out and firmly stuff with fiberfill.
4. Hand-sew the body opening closed

HAIR

1. Tie a knot in the center of each torn rectangle.
2. Hot-glue the knot of each rectangle to the head.
3. Trim the ends of the rectangles to shape the hair around the face.

GIRL'S PANTALOONS

1. Sew the center seams of the pantaloons together in pairs; press seams open.
2. Sew assembled pairs together at the side seams.
3. Press under ¼ inch along the waistline edge

and 1¼ inch along the leg opening edges.
4. Sew elastic just below the folded edge at the waist and just below the raw edge of each leg opening, stretching the elastic as you sew.
5. Sew the inner leg seams.

GIRL'S COLLAR

1. Cut the slit in one collar piece.
2. Sew one slit and one unslit collar piece together.
3. Clip the curves. Trim seams to ⅛ inch; turn and press. Slip-stitch the slit closed.
4. Overlap and sew a snap to the collar fronts or tack them together after dressing the doll.
5. Cut the red satin ribbon in half and tie one piece into a bow. Tack the bow to the neckline edge of the collar.

GIRL'S DRESS

1. Sew bodice front to bodice backs at the shoulder seams. Press seams open.
2. Press under ⅓ inch along the neckline edge and ¼ inch along the center back edges. Topstitch close to the folds.
3. Gather one of the 6½-inch sides (5½-inch for boy's sleeves) of each sleeve to fit the armholes. Pull up the gathers and sew the sleeves in place.
4. Press under wrist edge ¼ inch, then ¾ inch for the sleeve hems. Sew the elastic on the wrong side just below the second fold, stretching as you sew.
5. Sew the underarm and side seams of the bodice.
6. Sew the 6-inch sides of the skirt piece together.
7. Lapping one bodice back over the other ¼ inch, gather and sew the skirt to fit the bodice waist.
8. Turn skirt hem under ¼ inch twice; machine- or hand-sew in place.
9. Sew snaps at neckline and waist, or dress the doll and slip-stitch the bodice opening closed.

GIRL'S APRON

1. Press under ¼ inch on one of the long edges of the 22-inch-long ruffle strip. Topstitch close to the folded edge.
2. Gather the opposite edge of the strip to fit the 12-inch side of the apron skirt; sew the ruffle to the apron. Press the seam toward the apron; topstitch close to the seam.
3. Press under ¼ inch on the sides of the apron and ruffle; topstitch in place. Gather the remaining edge of the apron to measure 3½ inches.
4. Press under ¼ inch on all raw edges of the waistband strip. Fold the strip in half with the wrong sides facing; press.
5. Center and pin the apron in the middle of the waistband, encasing the raw edges of the apron between the folded edges of the waistband; leave the ends free for the apron ties. Topstitch along the ties and across the waistband.
6. Finish the neck strap the same as the pant strap (see Boy's Pants, Step 3, on page 16). Loop the strap around the neck; tack it to the waistband.

BOY'S PANTS

1. Repeat steps 1-3 for Girl's Pantaloons on page 15, except press edge under ¼ inch for the leg hem.

2. Fold pleats on the front and back of the pants, folding each pleat away from the center seam; tack in place.

3. For the straps, fold under ¼ inch on all edges of both 1½x7-inch strips. Fold each strip in half, wrong sides together, and topstitch the folded edges together.

4. Slip the pants on the doll. Adjust the straps and tack them in place. Sew the heart buttons over the front pleats.

BOY'S SHIRT

1. Repeat steps 1-3 and 5 of Girl's Dress, page 15.

2. Press under ¼ inch for bottom hem and topstitch in place.

3. Sew buttons to left front. Roll each sleeve back 1 inch two times to make cuffs; press.

4. Dress doll. Sew snaps to shirt fronts or slipstitch fronts together.

BOY'S COLLAR

1. Repeat the instructions for the Girl's Collar on page 15.

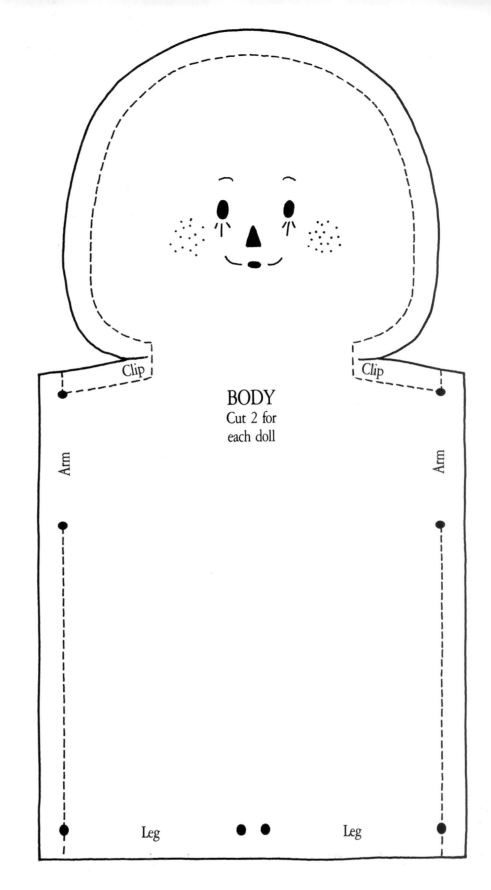

BODY
Cut 2 for
each doll

Clip

Arm

Leg

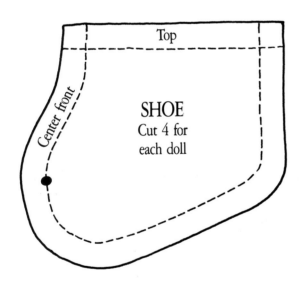

Top

Center front

SHOE
Cut 4 for
each doll

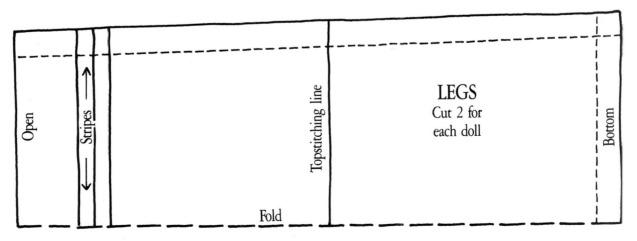

Open

Stripes

Topstitching line

LEGS
Cut 2 for
each doll

Bottom

Fold

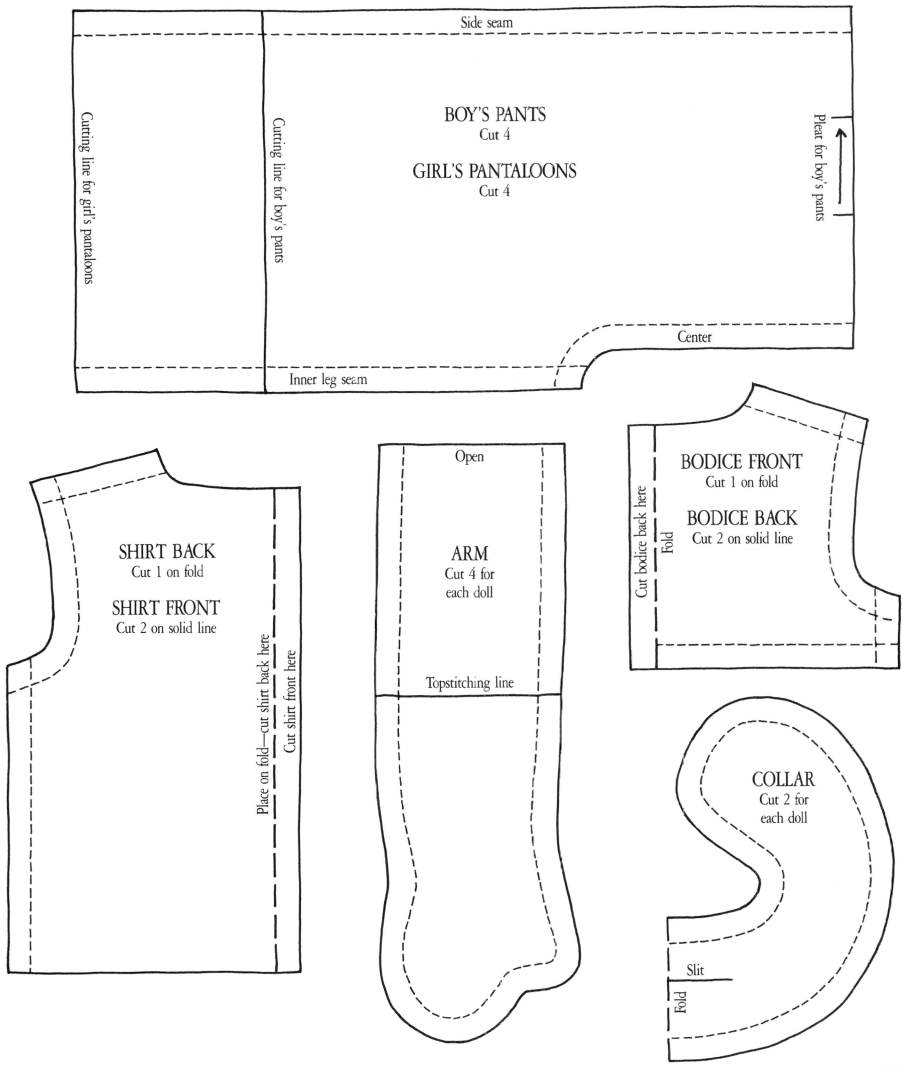

Side seam

BOY'S PANTS
Cut 4

GIRL'S PANTALOONS
Cut 4

Cutting line for girl's pantaloons

Cutting line for boy's pants

Pleat for boy's pants

Center

Inner leg seam

SHIRT BACK
Cut 1 on fold

SHIRT FRONT
Cut 2 on solid line

Place on fold—cut shirt back here

Cut shirt front here

Open

ARM
Cut 4 for
each doll

Topstitching line

BODICE FRONT
Cut 1 on fold

BODICE BACK
Cut 2 on solid line

Cut bodice back here

Fold

COLLAR
Cut 2 for
each doll

Slit

Fold

17

Rufus & Rowena

No wild hares here. This prim and proper couple blends the best of old and new, combining the costumes of turn-of-the-century children with the fanciful features of long-legged, long-eared bunnies. Both dolls stand 28 inches tall.

Catnip & Catspurr

Make these felines from the same full-size patterns as their hare-raising cousins. Use tea-dyed muslin for their bodies and buttonhole twist for their whiskers to add old-fashioned charm to the up-to-date charisma of their pen-drawn smiles.

GENERAL INSTRUCTIONS

The following instructions are for sewing one doll body. Repeat these directions to make the second doll. The clothing instructions for each doll are given separately.

ARMS AND HANDS

1. Sew the short end of one arm to the wrist of one hand with the thumb pointing to the left. Make another arm/hand unit in the same manner. Then make two more units with the thumbs pointing to the right. Sew the units together in pairs, leaving openings at the tops of the arms. Clip the curves and turn each arm right side out.

2. Firmly stuff each hand and arm to about 1 inch below the opening. Baste the tops of each arm together with the seams at the sides.

LEGS

1. Sew the short end of one leg to the top of one foot with the toe pointing to the left. Make another leg/foot unit in the same manner. Then make two more units with the toes pointing to the right. Sew the units together in pairs, leaving openings at the top of each leg. Clip the curves and turn each leg right side out.

2. Firmly stuff each foot. Insert one 5-inch-long dowel into each leg. Firmly stuff 1 inch above the dowel. Insert another 5-inch-long dowel. Crease the legs so the seams run up the center front and center back. Baste the tops of each leg together.

HEAD AND BODY

1. Trace the facial features onto one head piece; sew that head piece to one body piece for the front. Stitch the second head piece to the second body piece for the back.

2. Pin the arms to the body front between the small dots, matching the raw edges and placing the arms so the thumbs point toward the center of the body. Pin the body back to the body front. Sew the body pieces together, leaving openings between each set of dots at the side and legs.

3. Clip curves and turn the body right side out. Firmly stuff the head.

4. Turn the leg openings of the body under ¼ inch. Insert the legs into the openings so that the toes are pointing forward. Hand-sew the openings closed, securing the legs.

5. Stuff the body. Sew the side opening closed.

EARS

1. Sew ear pieces together in pairs, leaving each open at the bottom. Trim seams, clip curves, and turn each ear right side out.

2. Press under the bottom edge of each ear ¼ inch. Make a box pleat along each bottom edge, following the directions of the arrows, so the width is about ½ inch.

3. Sew the ears to the head between the dots.

FINISHING THE DOLL

1. Use the pen to draw the facial features. Brush the cheek areas and insides of the ears with powder blush.

2. For whiskers, thread a needle with a single strand of buttonhole twist. Take a tiny stitch at the base of the nose, leaving a 2-inch tail. Clip the thread on the needle, leaving another 2-inch tail. Tie the tails in a knot. Make two sets of whiskers on each side of the nose.

ROWENA'S SKIRT

1. Fold the waistband in half lengthwise. Stitch across each short end. Turn the waistband to the right side and press; set aside.

2. Press under ¼ inch on one long edge of the skirt. Press the same edge under ½ inch. Stitch close to the first fold for the hem. Pin the short edges of the rectangle together. Starting 3 inches from the unfinished long edge, stitch the short edges of the rectangle together.

3. Gather the raw edges of the skirt to fit the waistband. Stitch the raw edges of the waistband to the skirt through all fabric thicknesses.

4. Place the skirt on the doll and tack the waistband closed at the center back of the doll.

ROWENA'S HAIR BOW

1. Sew the two hair bow pieces together, leaving a 1-inch opening on one long edge for turning. Turn the bow right side out. Gather the center.

2. Turn the 2-inch edges of the bowknot under ¼ inch. Wrap the bowknot around the gathers of the hair bow and tack it in place.

3. Place the bow between the doll's ears and tack it in place.

FINISHING ROWENA

1. To fashion the body to resemble a blouse bodice, hand-sew a 3-inch piece of flat lace around each wrist over the seam. Hand-sew a 4-inch piece of flat lace around the neckline at the seam line. With the remaining lace, make a V-shape neckline from the shoulders to the center front of the body.

2. Sew the ¼-inch buttons to the center front of the dress inside the V shape.

RUFUS'S KNICKERS

1. Fold the waistband in half lengthwise. Stitch across each short end. Turn the waistband to the right side and press; set aside.

2. Stay-stitch along the V-shape sewing lines at the bottom edge of each knickers piece. Cut along the solid line between the stitching. Turn the cut edges under along the stay-stitched lines and top-stitch the edges in place.

3. Sew the knickers pieces together at the center front seam. Sew the center back seam, leaving an opening above the dot. Sew the inside leg seams. Turn the knickers right side out.

4. Gather the top edge of the knickers to fit the waistband. Stitch the unfinished edges of the waistband to the knickers.

5. Fold each leg band in half lengthwise and stitch across each short end. Turn the bands to the right side and press. Gather the bottom of each leg opening to fit each leg band. Stitch the unfinished edges of each leg band to each knickers leg. Slip the knickers on the doll. Tack the ends of the waistband together. Tack the ends of the leg bands together.

FINISHING RUFUS

1. Fold the necktie in half lengthwise. Stitch around the tie, leaving a 3-inch opening.

2. Turn the tie right side out and press. Hand-sew the opening closed. Tie it around the doll's neck.

3. Sew a ½-inch-diameter button to each leg band atop the edges where the band joins.

MATERIALS FOR CATNIP AND CATSPURR

Note: Gather all the supplies cited in the materials list on the *opposite* page, except for the fabrics for the bodies, arms, skirt, knickers, hair bow, and necktie. The fabrics for these items are listed below

⅓ yard of small print fabric for bodies and arms

1 yard of coordinating small print fabric for skirt, knickers, hair bow, and necktie

◆

PREPARING THE PATTERNS

Follow the instructions for Preparing the Patterns for Rufus and Rowena, *opposite.*

◆

CUTTING THE FABRICS

Follow the instructions for Cutting the Fabrics for Rufus and Rowena, *opposite.* Cut the body and arm pieces from the small print fabric; cut the skirt, knickers, hair bow, bowknot, and necktie from the coordinating small print fabric. *Note:* There are no ear patterns for Catnip and Catspurr.

GENERAL INSTRUCTIONS

Repeat the directions for making Rufus and Rowena, *opposite,* to make Catnip and Catspurr. Do not follow the instructions for the Ears. The ears for the cats are parts of the head pattern.

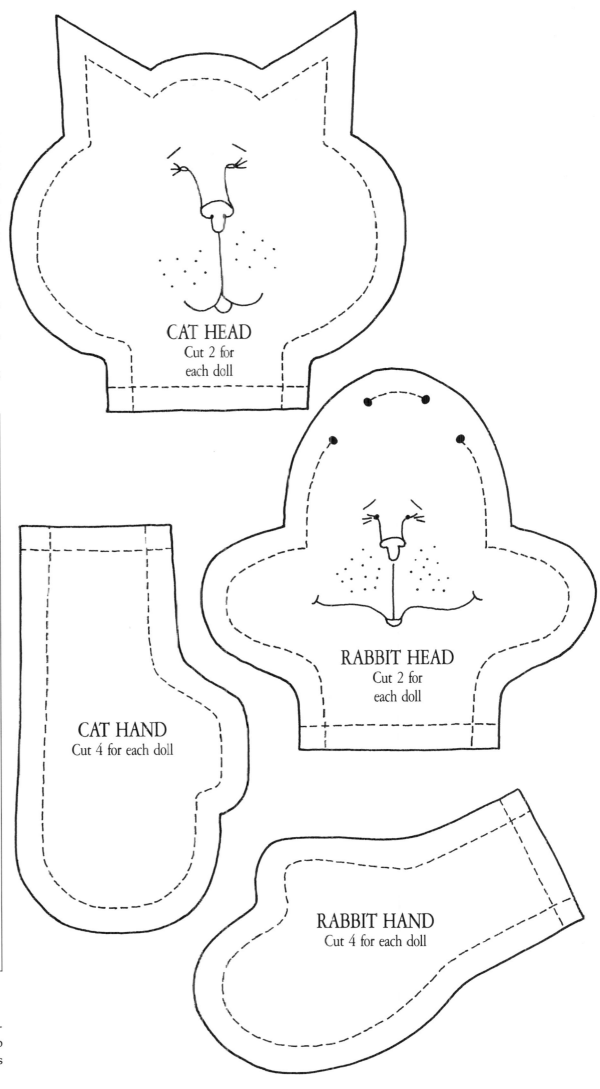

CAT HEAD
Cut 2 for
each doll

RABBIT HEAD
Cut 2 for
each doll

CAT HAND
Cut 4 for each doll

RABBIT HAND
Cut 4 for each doll

21

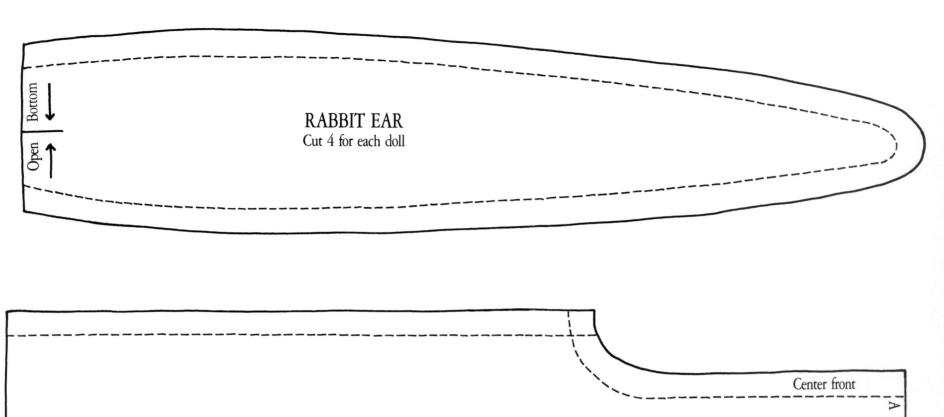

RABBIT EAR
Cut 4 for each doll

Bottom

Open

KNICKERS
Cut 2 for each boy doll

Center front

A

Stitch before cutting

RABBIT FOOT
Cut 4 for each doll

B

Center back

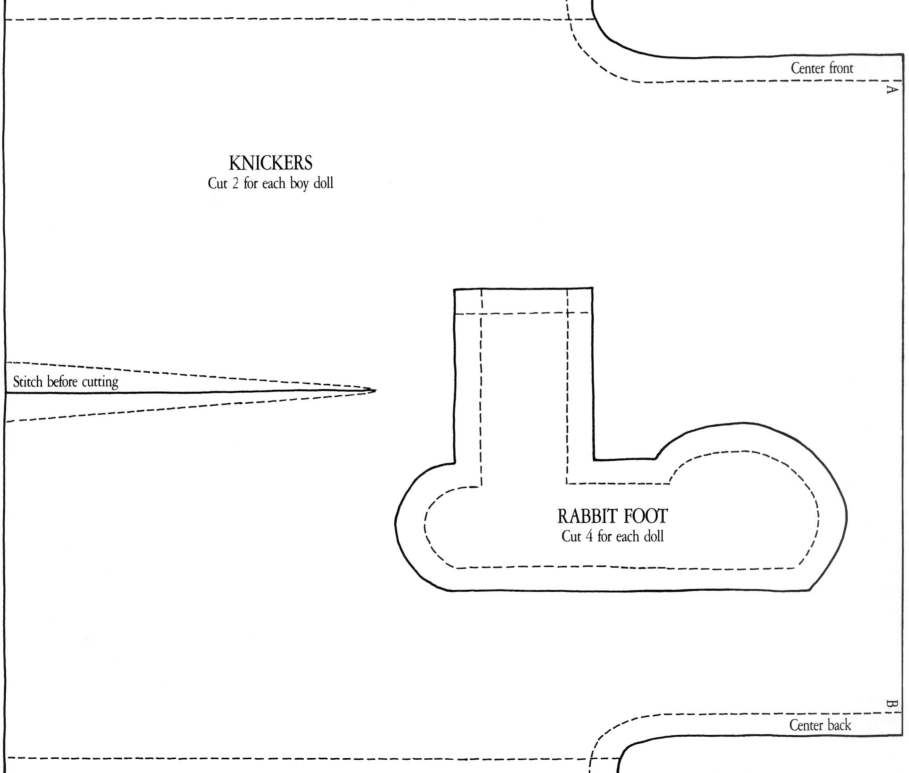

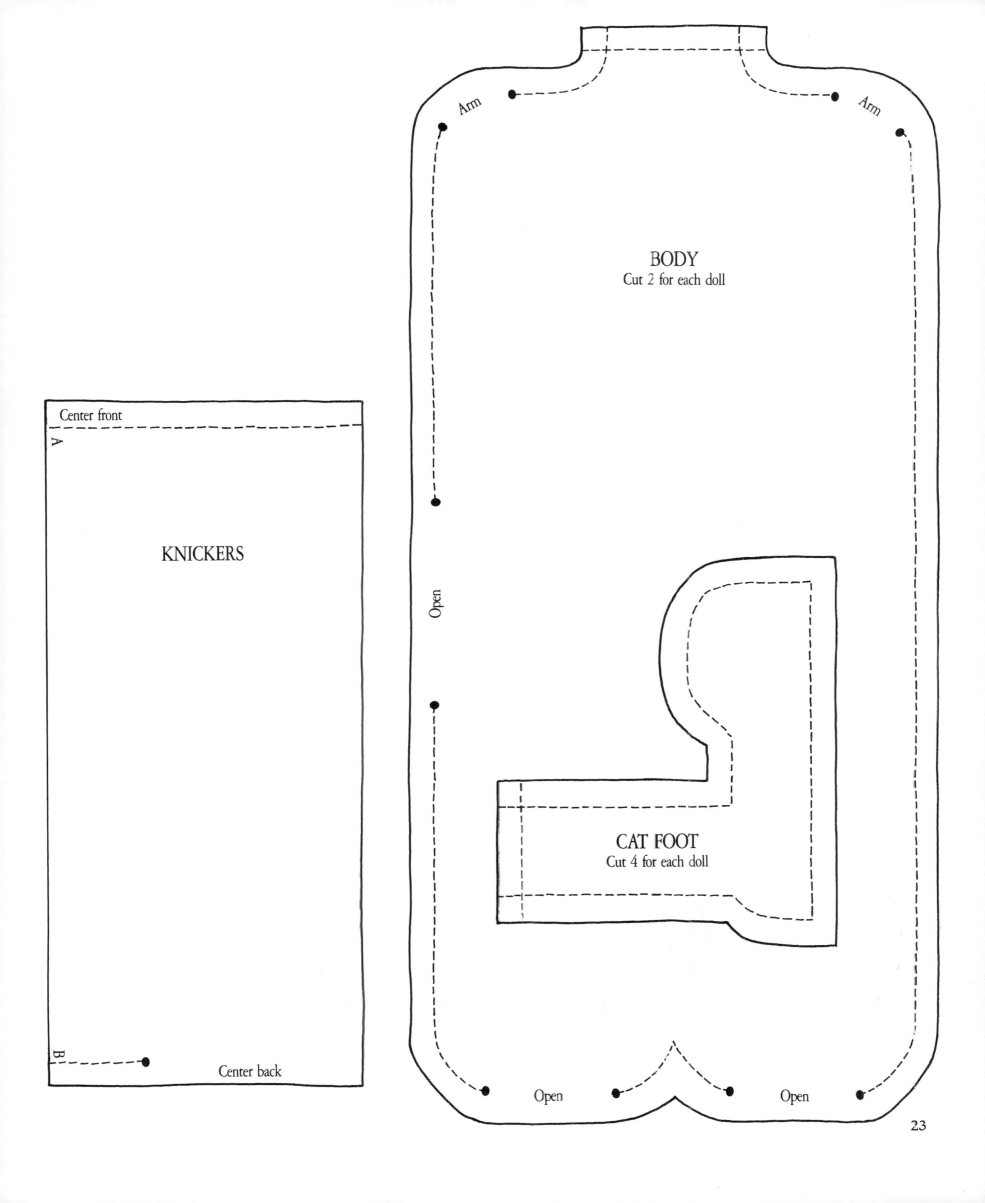

KNICKERS

Center front

A

B

Center back

BODY
Cut 2 for each doll

Arm

Arm

Open

CAT FOOT
Cut 4 for each doll

Open

Open

23

Nursery Rhyme Pull Toys

Hey diddle, diddle,
The cat and the fiddle,
The cow jumped over the moon;
The little dog laughed
To see such sport,
And the dish ran away with the spoon.

Humpty Dumpty
Sat on a wall,
Humpty Dumpty
Had a great fall,
All the king's horses and all the king's men,
Couldn't put Humpty together again.

These brightly painted wooden pull toys capture the whimsy of two favorite Mother Goose rhymes that were first published in England around 1760. The "Hey diddle, diddle" toy is about 11 inches long, and "Humpty Dumpty" measures 10 inches long.

PREPARING THE PATTERNS

Trace the patterns, *opposite*, onto tissue paper. Transfer the patterns to the pine using the graphite paper.

◆

CUTTING INSTRUCTIONS

Use the band saw to cut out the designs and bases as listed *below*. Bevel the upper edges of each base with the block plane or sandpaper.

For cow design, cut:
◆ One cow-moon pattern
◆ One 3⅛x10⅞-inch base

For Humpty Dumpty design, cut:
◆ One Humpty Dumpty pattern
◆ One 3⅛x10-inch base

GENERAL DIRECTIONS

1. Sand all pieces with fine-grit sandpaper before painting them.
2. When painting, thoroughly clean brushes after each color.
3. Paint one side of a design; then paint the other side. Allow the paint to dry before proceeding to the next color.

PAINTING THE COW

1. Use the No. 4 brush to paint the cow white and the moon bright yellow.
2. Use the No. 000 brush to paint bright blue on the collar and cow's eyes; pink on the muzzle, udders, and insides of ears; bright yellow on the bell; red oxide on the eyelashes and eyebrows of the moon and around the bell; orange on the dots on the collar; and black on the tail, forehead, and hooves. Also paint black spots around the eyes and ears, in the center of the eyes, and on the body as shown in the photo on page 24.
3. Use the No. 000 brush and light gray paint to outline the cow and to give texture to the tail and forehead. Apply bright red paint diluted with water to the nose and corners of mouth and as accents on the ears and udder. Use the same diluted paint to outline and paint accents on the moon. Paint a dot of white on each eye; add white accents to the hooves and nose. Use the marker to outline the entire design.

THE COW'S BASE

1. To prepare the base for the wheels, use the drill to make two holes to fit the axle pegs in each long side of the base 2 inches from each short end.
2. To prepare the base for the cow, use the ⅛-inch bit and drill two holes vertically all the way through the base. Center the holes between the long sides, one 2⅜ inches from the front edge of the base and the other 8 inches from the front edge.
3. Use the No. 8 brush to paint the base dark blue.
4. Use the No. 000 brush to paint bright yellow stars on the top and sides of the base.

FINISHING THE COW

1. Attach the cow to the base by inserting a screw through each of the holes in the bottom of the base and into the front and back feet of the cow.
2. Lightly spray the cow, moon, and base with wood finish; allow the wood finish to dry.
3. Attach the wheels as directed on the package.
4. Center an eye screw in the front edge of the base. Tie one end of a 2-foot length of twine into the eye. Knot the opposite end of the twine.

PAINTING HUMPTY DUMPTY

1. Use the No. 4 brush to paint peach on the face and hands and bright red on the bricks.
2. Use the No. 000 brush to paint bright red on the bow tie and its band; white on the top portion of the wall, the socks, shirt cuffs, front of the shirt, and collar; orange on the jacket and sleeve; bright blue on the pants; red oxide on the eyelashes and eyebrows; and light gray between the bricks.
3. Referring to the photo on page 25, use the No. 000 brush to outline and to accent clothing with light gray paint. Use a sponge to apply light gray paint to the top of the wall. Use bright red paint diluted with water to paint the cheeks and lips. Also use the diluted paint to outline the fingers and head.
4. Use the marker to outline the entire design.

HUMPTY DUMPTY'S BASE

1. To prepare the base for the wheels, use the drill to make two holes to fit the axle pegs in each long side of the base 2 inches from each short end.
2. To prepare the base for the wall, with a ⅛-inch bit, drill two holes vertically through the base, centered between the long sides, one 2⅞ inches from the front edge of the base and the other 6⅜ inches from the front edge.
3. Use the No. 8 brush to paint the base black.
4. Use the No. 000 brush to randomly paint light gray paving bricks on the top of the base as shown in the photo.

FINISHING HUMPTY DUMPTY

1. Attach the bottom of the wall to the base by inserting a screw through each of the holes in the base and into the bottom of the wall.
2. Lightly spray the Humpty Dumpty and base with wood finish; allow the wood finish to dry.
3. Attach wheels as directed on the package.
4. Center an eye screw in the front edge of the base. Tie one end of a 2-foot length of twine into the eye. Knot the opposite end of the twine.

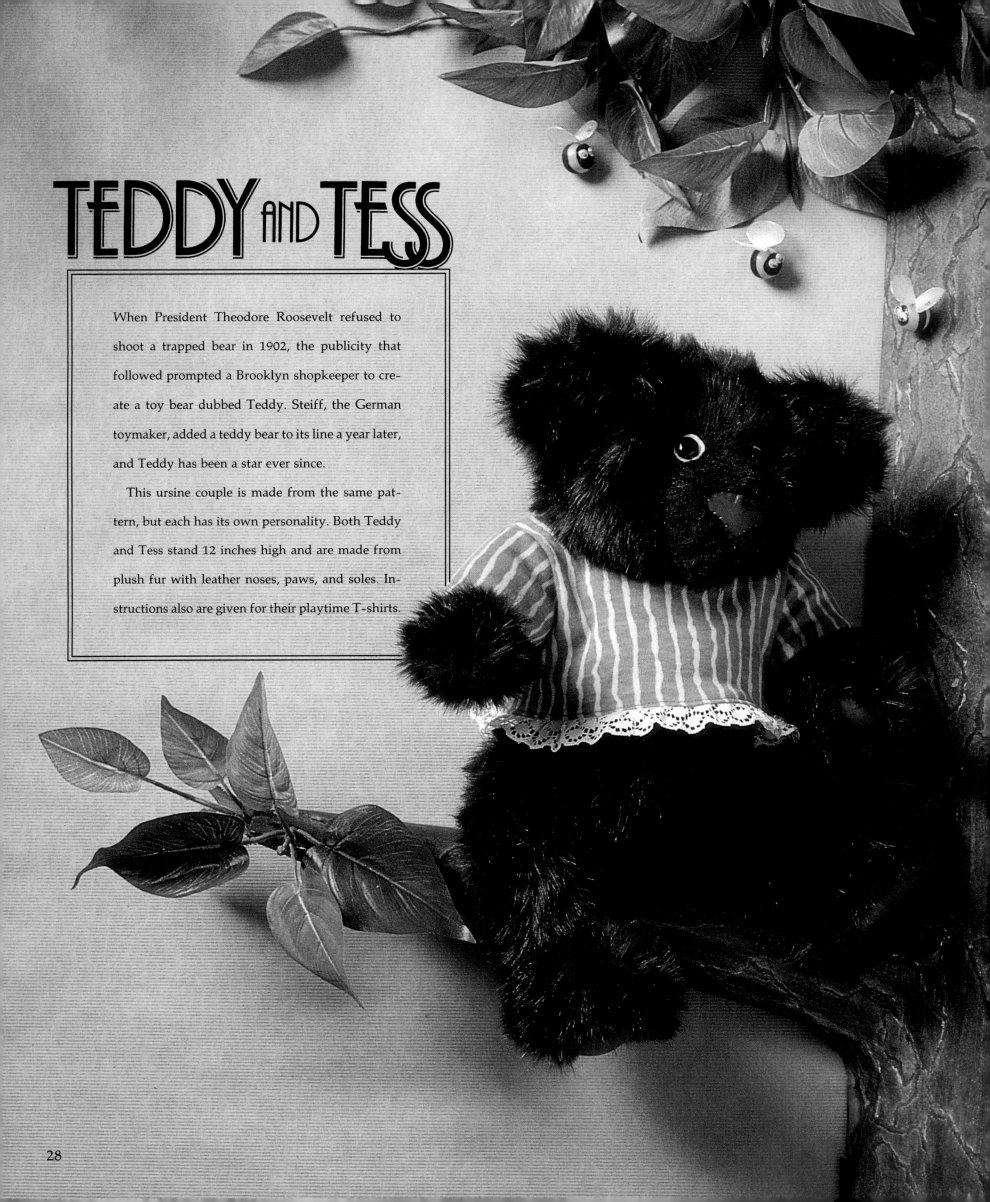

TEDDY AND TESS

When President Theodore Roosevelt refused to shoot a trapped bear in 1902, the publicity that followed prompted a Brooklyn shopkeeper to create a toy bear dubbed Teddy. Steiff, the German toymaker, added a teddy bear to its line a year later, and Teddy has been a star ever since.

This ursine couple is made from the same pattern, but each has its own personality. Both Teddy and Tess stand 12 inches high and are made from plush fur with leather noses, paws, and soles. Instructions also are given for their playtime T-shirts.

GENERAL INSTRUCTIONS

1. After cutting, transfer the X placement markings to the pile side of the fabric using brightly colored tailor's tacks (see the tip box on page 31). The remaining construction markings can be transferred to the wrong side of the pile.

2. Before sewing fur pieces together, brush the pile away from the seam lines. After sewing, use a straight pin to pull the pile from the seam. This technique blends the fur and conceals the seams. Trim the pile remaining in the seam allowances to reduce the bulk.

3. Firmly stuff the bear with fiberfill. As you sew openings closed, continue to add fiberfill to make the body firm.

HEAD

1. Pin and sew the head pieces together along the center front seam from the dot at the tip of the nose to the neck edge. Referring to the drawing, *below,* pin and baste the gusset to the head pieces, matching the nose dots. Pivot the gusset at the small dots and ease the pieces together around the curve of the head. Machine-stitch the gusset and head pieces together. Clip the curves; turn the head right side out.

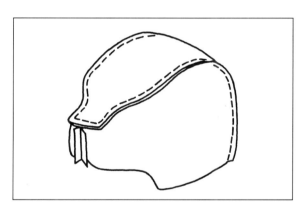

2. Stuff the head with fiberfill. Hand-sew running stitches ¼ inch from the neck edge using a double strand of button thread. Pull the threads to close the neck opening; knot the threads.

3. Trim the pile to ⅛ inch from the tip of the nose to the muzzle line. Center the leather nose between the large and small dots on the head gusset pattern and hand-sew it to the bear's face.

4. Using six plies of floss, embroider the mouth with two straight stitches following the mouth markings on the head pattern. (See stitch diagram on page 7.)

5. To attach each eye, double-thread the dollmaker's needle with buttonhole thread. Begin sewing at the back of the head at the base of the neck. Bring the needle out at one of the X eye placements on the front of the head. Thread a glass eye onto the needle and return the needle to the back of the neck. Pull the threads to indent the eye; knot to hold the eye in place.

6. Glue a white felt circle behind each eye.

EARS

1. Sew the ears together in pairs, leaving the bottom edges open. Clip the curves; turn the ears right side out. Fold the bottom edges to the inside and hand-sew the openings closed.

2. Position the ears on the head following the placement lines; blindstitch in place.

ARMS AND LEGS

1. Sew the leather paws to the inner arms along the straight edge. For each arm, sew matching inner and outer arms together leaving openings between the dots. Clip the curves and turn the arms right side out.

2. Sew the legs together in pairs, leaving openings as marked. Referring to the drawing on page 108, pin and baste the leather soles to the bottom of the legs. Sew the soles in place. Clip the curves; turn the legs right side out.

BODY

1. Sew each body front to a body back at the side seams. Pin the two sections together and sew the center front and center back seams. Clip curves; turn the body right side out.

2. To joint the body, snip a hole at each X just large enough for the joint stem to fit into each inner arm and leg and into the body marks.

3. Insert the joint into one of the legs through the snipped hole. Push the stem of the joint into the corresponding hole on the body. Inside the body, apply the washer and clasp to the stem. Tightly snap the pieces together. In the same manner, attach the remaining leg and each arm.

4. Firmly stuff the legs, arms, and body. Hand-sew the openings on the arms and legs closed.

FINISHING

1. Center the head on the body, matching the center front seams. Using a double strand of button thread, blindstitch the head to the body, adding additional fiberfill in the neck as you work. Sew around the neck one more time.

2. Brush all seams to blend the fur.

SHIRT

1. Sew the two shirt pieces together at the shoulder seams. Sew the short ends of the neckband together. Fold the band in half lengthwise with wrong sides together. Pin and sew the band to the neck edge, stretching slightly to ease the fit.

2. Pin and sew the sleeves to armhole openings, stretching slightly to ease the fit. Sew the underarm and side seams.

3. Turn under each sleeve edge ¼ inch twice. Hand-sew the hem. Sew the shirt hem in the same manner. For Tess's shirt, pin and sew the top edge of the lace to the bottom edge of the shirt.

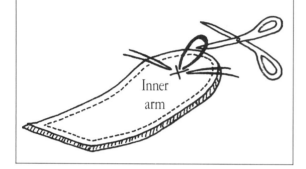
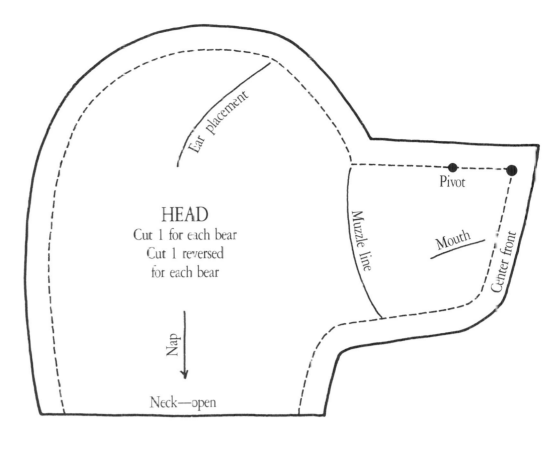

HEAD
Cut 1 for each bear
Cut 1 reversed
for each bear

Ear placement

Pivot

Muzzle line

Mouth

Center front

Nap

Neck—open

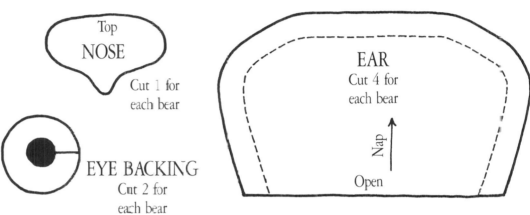

Top
NOSE
Cut 1 for
each bear

EYE BACKING
Cut 2 for
each bear

EAR
Cut 4 for
each bear

Nap

Open

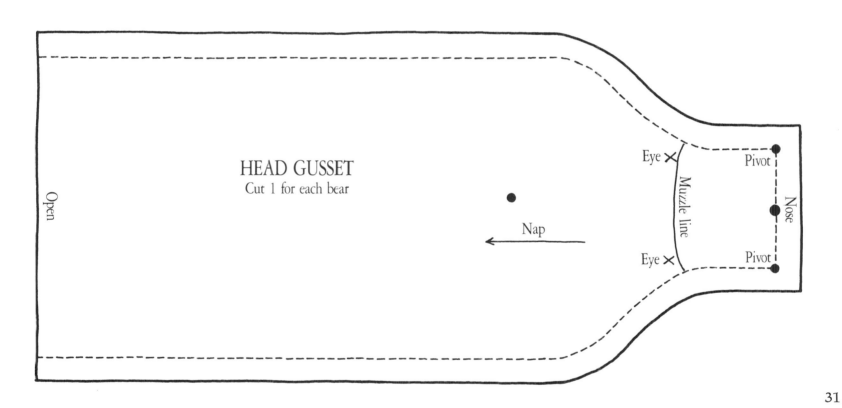

HEAD GUSSET
Cut 1 for each bear

Open

Nap

Eye ✕

Muzzle line

Eye ✕

Pivot

Nose

Pivot

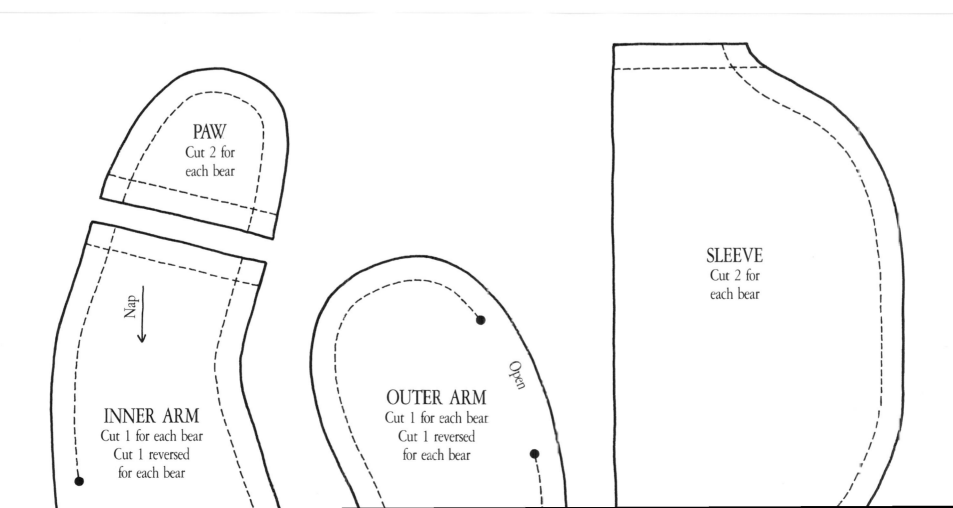

PAW
Cut 2 for
each bear

Nap

INNER ARM
Cut 1 for each bear
Cut 1 reversed
for each bear

OUTER ARM
Cut 1 for each bear
Cut 1 reversed
for each bear

Open

SLEEVE
Cut 2 for
each bear

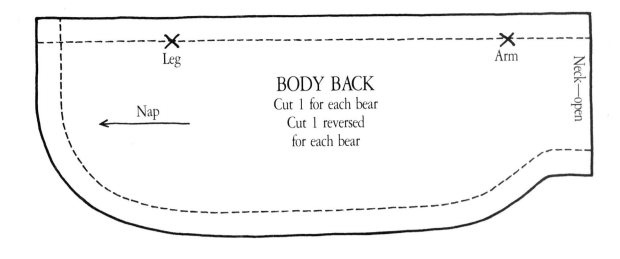

BODY BACK
Cut 1 for each bear
Cut 1 reversed
for each bear

Leg

Arm

Neck—open

Nap

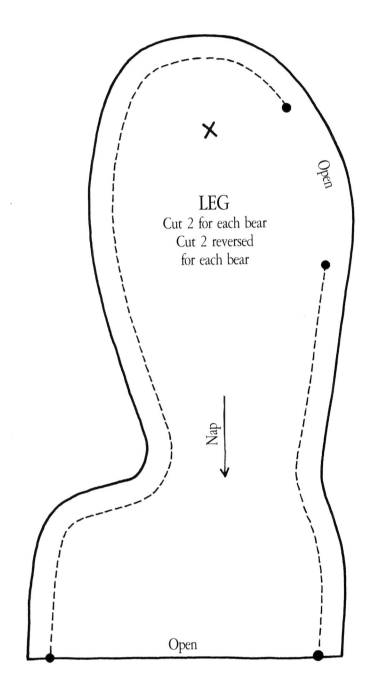

LEG
Cut 2 for each bear
Cut 2 reversed
for each bear

Open

Nap

Open

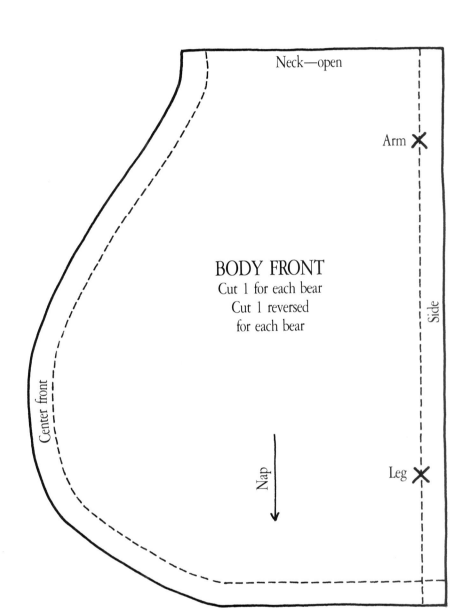

Neck—open

Arm

BODY FRONT
Cut 1 for each bear
Cut 1 reversed
for each bear

Center front

Side

Leg

Nap

Rachel

Charming Rachel embodies our

favorite heroines of romantic

Victorian novels. Imagine a young

miss running through heather-strewn

meadows to meet a gallant

sweetheart, hat in hand and hair

flying behind her.

Her lace-trimmed dress, wavy hair of

mohair yarn, and dainty embroidered

features make Rachel the vision of

the lovely, refined English rose for

whom men pine in *Wuthering Heights*,

Adam Bede, and *A Tale of Two Cities*.

Rachel measures 25 inches from the

top of her curly head to the toes of

her dainty little slippers. Her dress

and vest of cream-color batiste are

embroidered and embellished, adding

to her sweetness and idealistic charm.

MATERIALS FOR
RACHEL'S BODY

½ yard of muslin

Pale gray, black, camel, pale green,
peach, and salmon embroidery floss

Polyester fiberfill

Off-white button thread

Old sweater in desired hair color or
one 50-yard skein of mohair yarn

½ yard of ¼-inch-wide ribbon

One 4x18-inch piece of cardboard

◆

PREPARING THE PATTERNS

Trace the full-size head, body, and leg
patterns on pages 38 and 39 onto tracing
paper. Cut out the patterns.

◆

CUTTING THE FABRIC

From muslin, cut:
◆ One head (back)
◆ Two bodies
◆ Four legs

EMBROIDERING THE FACE

1. Trace the head pattern onto muslin, transferring the facial details. Do not cut out.

2. Referring to the stitch diagrams on page 7, and using two strands of floss, satin-stitch the pupils with black, the irises with pale green, the upper lip with salmon, and the lower lip with peach. Using one strand of floss, outline-stitch the eyebrows with pale gray, the line above the pupils with black, the nose with camel, and the lip line with salmon. Cut out the embroidered head.

LEGS

1. Sew the legs together in pairs; leave the tops open. Clip the curves; turn the legs right sides out.

2. Firmly stuff each leg to the bottom topstitching line. Matching the front and back seams in the center of each leg, pin the seams together and topstitch across the line. (See the box on page 134 for tips on topstitching using the zipper foot.) Stuff lightly to the second topstitching line. Pin seams together and topstitch on that line. Lightly stuff the tops of the legs. Baste the top of each leg closed. Set the legs aside.

HEAD AND BODY

1. Sew the embroidered head to one body piece; sew the head back to the second body piece. Press

36

the seam allowances toward the head. Sew the assembled front and back pieces together, leaving the bottom and shoulder seams open between the dots; clip the curves and turn right side out. Turn bottom edge under ¼ inch.

2. Stuff each arm through the shoulder openings to the topstitching line. Topstitch across the lines. Finish stuffing the upper arms; slip-stitch the openings closed.

3. Stuff the head and the remainder of the body with enough fiberfill to firmly support the head.

4. Insert the top leg seams into the body, spacing them ¼ inch apart at the center of the body. Hand- or machine-stitch the bottom edges of the body together, securing the legs.

5. Shape the chin according to the directions in the tip box, *below.*

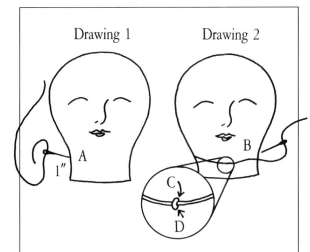

Drawing 1   Drawing 2

HOW TO SHAPE THE CHIN

With a knotted strand of button thread, and referring to Drawing 1, sew two tiny backstitches at the head side seam about 1 inch above the bottom of the neck at the A mark. Referring to Drawing 2, extend the thread across the face and insert the needle into the opposite side of the head at B. Bring the needle back out at the center of the chin at C. Form a loop by holding the thread under the needle. Tug on the thread to shape the chin. When the chin is established, secure the thread by taking the needle over the thread and into the head at D. The detail drawing shows the stitching at the center of the chin. Return the needle to the B position and secure the thread with two tiny backstitches. Then extend the thread across the back of the head and shape the back neckline in the same manner. Cut and bury the tail of the thread inside the doll.

HAIR

1. For curly hair, unravel enough of the sweater to make about 40 yards of yarn. For straight hair use mohair or other fine yarn.

2. For bangs, loosely wrap yarn around your middle finger eight times. Tie a piece of yarn around the bundle and slide the bundle off the finger. Cut the loops opposite the tie. Position the bundle so the yarn ends extend onto the doll's forehead. Tack the bundle in place.

3. Wrap the sweater yarn 25 times around the 18-inch length of the cardboard. Remove the bundle from the cardboard and spread it to measure 3 inches wide down the center. Place a piece of paper under the center of the bundle and machine-sew across the center of it, through yarn and paper, to make the part. Pull the paper away from the yarn and cut the loops on each side of the part. Position the yarn on the head with one end of the part at the top head seam. Hand-sew the hair in place along the part. Finger-comb the hair to distribute the strands. Tack the hair to the sides of the face and along the back neckline.

4. Cut the same piece of cardboard to measure 4x16 inches. Wrap yarn 15 times around the 16-inch length of the cardboard. Remove the yarn from the cardboard and spread the bundle to about 1 inch; stitch and cut the loops as directed in Step 3, *above.* Position the bundle at the top of the head, behind the bangs; hand-sew in place. Gather this bundle into a loose ponytail at the back of the head and secure it with a ¼-inch-wide ribbon bow. (See the photo, *below,* for the hairstyle on our doll.) Trim the hair even.

MATERIALS FOR RACHEL'S CLOTHING

⅞ yard of cream-colored batiste

⅓ yard of peach broadcloth

⅔ yard of white scalloped-edge eyelet

Scrap of light-colored print fabric

2 yards of 1½-inch-wide lace

2 yards of ½-inch-wide pregathered lace

⅔ yard of ⅛-inch-wide elastic

Two ⅜-yard pieces of ⅛-inch-wide ribbon or narrow lace trim for heart

Pale yellow-green embroidery floss

Peach, light blue, and yellow pearl cotton

Two 4-mm pearl beads

Scraps of kidskin leather or suede cloth

Scrap of beige yarn

One sheer knee-high nylon stocking

One 5/16-inch-diameter button

Polyester fiberfill

◆

PREPARING THE PATTERNS

Trace the full-size clothing patterns on pages 39–41 onto tracing paper. Cut out the patterns.

◆

CUTTING THE FABRICS

The vest fronts and bib will be cut from batiste after they are embroidered. The socks and shoes will be cut from the fabrics after they are sewn together. The cutting instructions for pieces that do not have patterns include ¼-inch seams.

From batiste, cut:
◆ One vest back
◆ Two bodice fronts
◆ One bodice back
◆ One 13x30-inch skirt

From broadcloth, cut:
◆ Two bloomers

From eyelet, cut:
◆ One 11x24-inch petticoat, keeping the scalloped edge along the 24-inch side

From scrap of print fabric, cut:
◆ Two hearts

EMBROIDERING BIB AND VEST

1. Trace one bib and two vest fronts onto the batiste. Transfer the embroidery designs onto the pieces, flopping the design on one of the vests.

2. Use three plies of yellow-green floss to work lazy daisy stitches over the teardrop shapes and outline stitches over the straight lines. Use light blue pearl cotton to work French knots over the solid black dots around the cluster flowers; use peach or yellow pearl cotton to work French knot centers. For the three large flowers on the bib, use yellow pearl cotton to satin-stitch the flower center. Work long-and-short stitches with peach pearl cotton for the inner petals and with yellow pearl cotton for the outer petals.

3. Cut out the bib and vest fronts.

SOCKS

1. Cut the elastic top off the knee-high stocking; discard the elastic. Lay the stocking flat, creating folds along the sides. Pin the pattern along one folded edge of the stocking with the top of the pattern on the cut edge. Sew around the pattern on the stitching line. Make another sock in the same manner by flopping the pattern and placing it along the fold on the opposite side of the stocking. Cut out the socks, leaving ⅛-inch seams.

2. Turn the socks right sides out and slip them onto the doll's legs. Place the seam of each sock over the back leg seams.

SHOES

1. Trace two shoe patterns onto folded kidskin or suede cloth. Sew on stitching lines. Cut ⅛ inch from stitching at heels and toes. Cut on cutting line along the instep. Turn shoes right sides out.

2. Use the beige yarn scrap to make a French knot on the toe of each shoe. Slip shoes on feet, adding small pieces of fiberfill to fill out toes. Tack top and heels of the shoes to each foot.

BIB

1. Stay-stitch around the bib on the stitching line. Clip to the stitching around the neckline and at points. Press under all edges ½ inch. Cut a piece of ½-inch-wide lace to fit around the neckline and baste it in place. Topstitch close to the folded edge around the entire bib.

2. Place the bib onto the doll. Overlap the ends of the bib at the back of the neck and tack them in place. Tack the bottom bib corners to the body.

BLOOMERS AND PETTICOAT

1. Press under the bottom edge of each bloomer leg ¼ inch. Cut two 4½-inch pieces of 1½-inch-wide lace. Lap the top edge of the lace over the right side of the bottom edge of each bloomer leg. Topstitch the lace in place.

2. Sew the center seam of one bloomer to the center seam of the second bloomer. Sew the remaining two center seams together.

3. Press under the waist edge ¼ inch. Cut a 5-inch piece of elastic. Sew the elastic on the wrong side, close to the fold, stretching the elastic as you sew.

4. Sew the inside leg seams. Slip the bloomers onto the doll.

5. Sew the 11-inch edges of the petticoat together. Turn under the unscalloped 24-inch edge ¼ inch. Cut a 5-inch piece of elastic. Sew the elastic on the wrong side, close to the fold, stretching the elastic as you sew. Slip the petticoat onto the doll.

LACE SLEEVES

1. Cut five 6-inch lengths of 1½-inch-wide lace. Sew the lace strips together, topstitching the top edge of one strip to the bottom edge of another to form a 6x7½-inch rectangle.

2. Cut the rectangle in half to make two 3x7½-inch rectangles. Sew the 7½-inch edges of each rectangle together using ⅛-inch seams. Turn the sleeves right side out. Slip sleeves onto arms.

DRESS BODICE

1. Sew bodice back to bodice fronts along shoulder seams. Stay-stitch around seam line of the neck edge. Clip curves and press the neck edge under at the stitching. Turn center front edges under ¼ inch. Topstitch ⅛ inch from the folded edge around the center fronts and neckline.

2. Turn each sleeve edge under ½ inch. Cut two 3-inch pieces of elastic. Sew one elastic piece on the wrong side, ¼ inch from each fold, stretching it as you sew. Sew underarm and side seams.

3. Fold the tucks as marked on the bodice front and back. To secure the tucks, topstitch along the folded edge. Tack the front edges of the bodice together at the waistline so the folded edges just meet. Set the bodice aside.

DRESS SKIRT

1. Sew the 13-inch edges of the skirt together for the center back seam. Press under one long edge of the skirt ⅛ inch. Press under the same edge 1 inch. Sew in place for hem.

2. Cut a 30-inch piece of 1½-inch-wide lace. Beginning at the center back seam, topstitch the lace to the right side of the skirt atop the hem. Turn under the ends of the lace at the seam.

3. Gather the remaining long edge of the skirt to fit the bodice waistline. With the skirt seam at the center back of the bodice, distribute the gathers evenly. Stitch the skirt to the bodice.

4. Slip the dress onto the doll.

VEST

1. Turn the two long diagonal edges of the back vest under ¼ inch. Cut an 11-inch piece of the ½-inch-wide lace. Position the straight edge of the lace under the edge of the fold, making a small tuck in the lace where the edges come to a point. Topstitch the lace in place. Stay-stitch around the neckline on the seam line. Clip the curves. Turn under the neckline edge. Topstitch ⅛ inch from the fold.

continued

2. Turn under all edges of each front vest piece ¼ inch. Cut two 16-inch pieces of ½-inch-wide lace. Pin the straight edges of the lace under the folds around each of the vest pieces, easing the lace at the corners. Topstitch the lace in place.

3. Lap the finished shoulder edge of the vest fronts over the vest back at the shoulder seams, keeping the armhole edges even. Topstitch the pieces together at the shoulder seams.

4. Slip the vest over the doll's head. Tack the point of the vest back to the center back waist of the dress. Lap the left front of the vest over the right front, matching the upper Xs. Sew on the button, stitching through both layers at the right-hand X. Tack the other pair of Xs together; then tack these Xs to the front bodice waist.

FINISHING

1. Sew pearl beads at the sides of the face near the hairline for earrings.

2. Sew the heart pieces together, leaving an opening between the dots. Clip curves and turn the heart right side out. Stuff lightly and blindstitch the opening closed. Fold the ⅛-inch-wide ribbons or narrow lace in half. Tack the fold of the ribbon to the bottom of the heart. Tack the heart between the hands.

3. Cross the doll's legs and tack them together at the ankles.

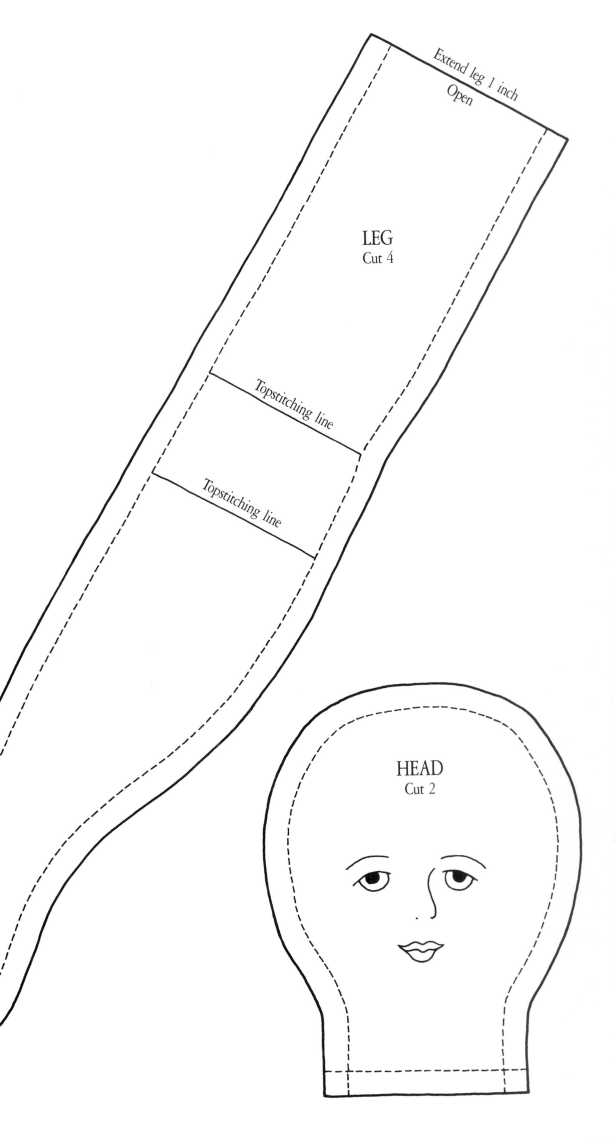

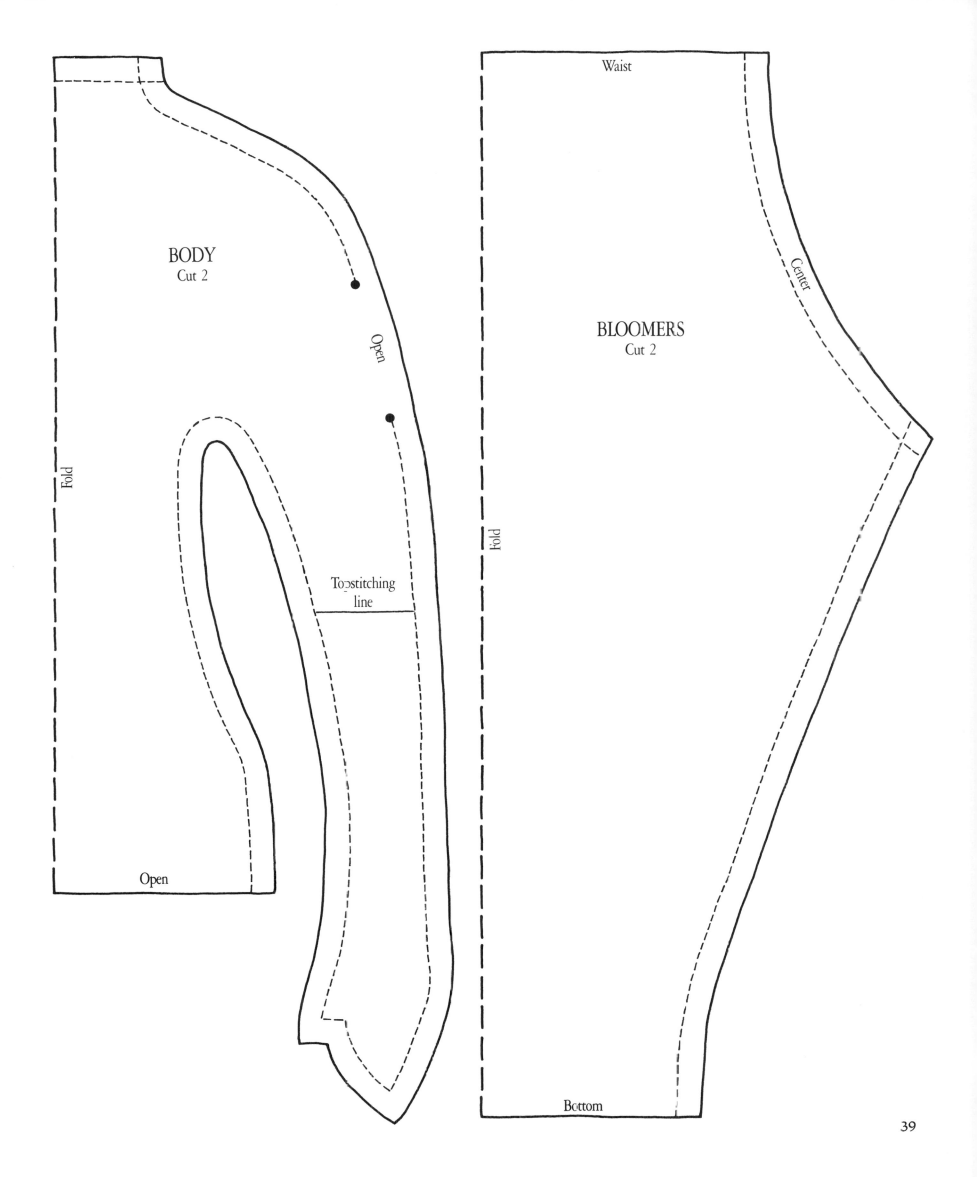

BODY
Cut 2

Fold

Open

Open

Topstitching
line

BLOOMERS
Cut 2

Waist

Center

Fold

Bottom

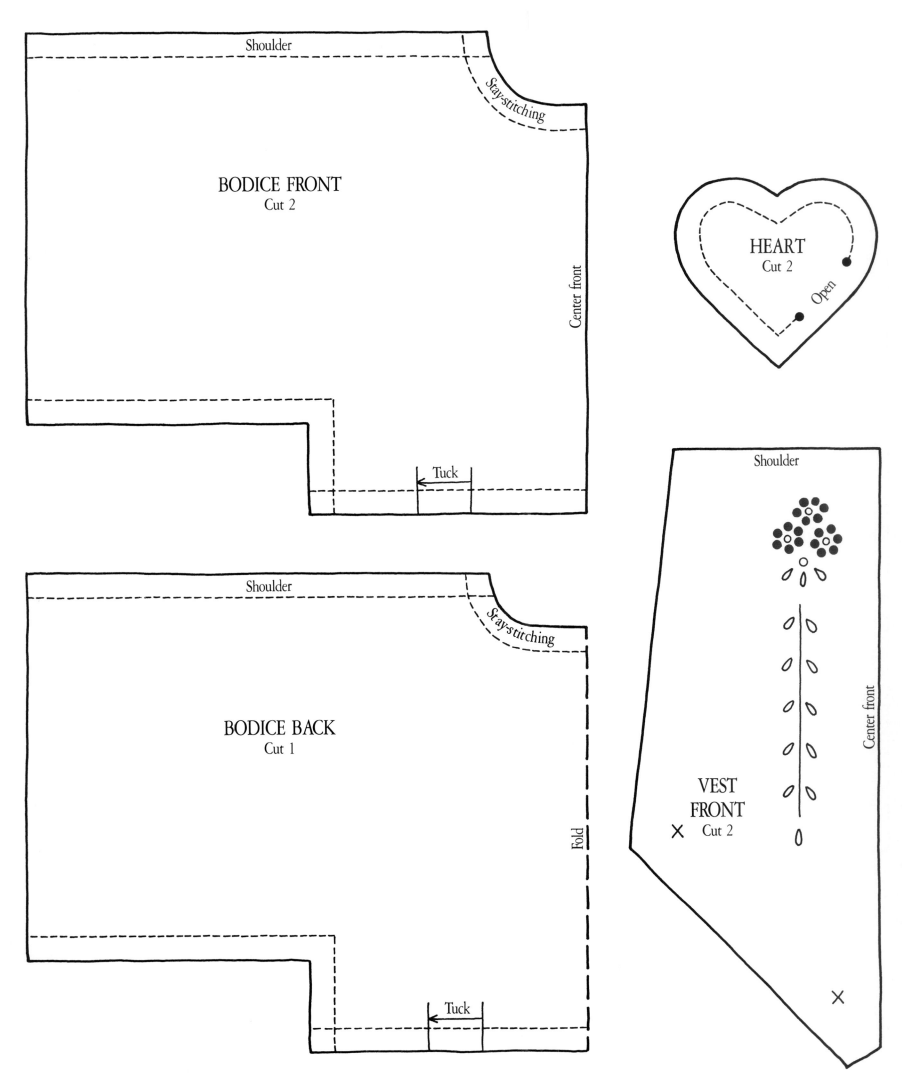

BODICE FRONT
Cut 2

Shoulder

Stay-stitching

Center front

Tuck

HEART
Cut 2

Open

Shoulder

BODICE BACK
Cut 1

Stay-stitching

Fold

Tuck

VEST FRONT
Cut 2

Center front

40

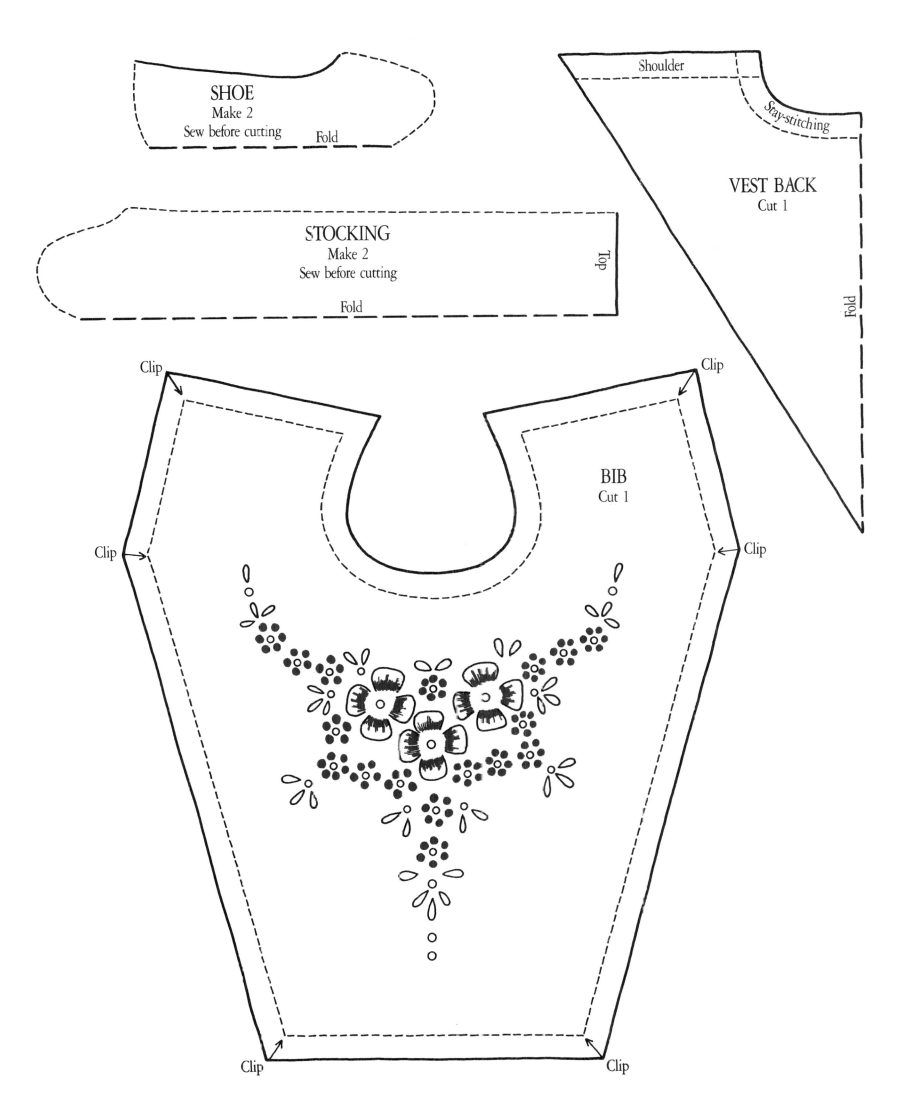

SHOE
Make 2
Sew before cutting
Fold

STOCKING
Make 2
Sew before cutting
Fold
Top

VEST BACK
Cut 1
Shoulder
Stay-stitching
Fold

BIB
Cut 1

Clip
Clip
Clip
Clip
Clip
Clip

41

UNCLE SAM

Beat the drums, sound the trumpets—here comes the Fourth of July parade with Uncle Sam in the lead! For lovers of Americana, no doll collection is complete without the bearded fellow in the stovepipe hat who is the symbol of U.S. independence and tough-mindedness. Our flag-waving version stands approximately 16 inches tall and wears a coat and mock vest of dark blue wool to complement his red-stripe muslin trousers. With the aid of fabric paint, his hat is a salute to the red, white, and blue.

MATERIALS FOR UNCLE SAM

⅓ yard of muslin

¼ yard of navy wool

Eight tea bags

Polyester fiberfill

Antique white, brown, blue, barn red, black, and medium gold acrylic paints

Artist's paintbrush with a pointed tip

Pine-colored stain

Clear matte-finish varnish

Sheep's wool for hair and beard

Hot-glue gun

One 4-inch twig for the flagpole

PREPARING THE PATTERNS

Trace the full-size patterns on pages 44 and 45 onto tracing paper. Cut out the patterns.

CUTTING THE FABRICS

Before cutting out the pattern pieces, cut out a 9x12-inch rectangle from the muslin. Tea-dye the rectangle as directed in the tip box on page 125.

From undyed muslin, cut:
- One head back
- Two head fronts
- Two legs
- One hat brim
- One hat top
- One 1⅝ ×3¼-inch flag

From tea-dyed muslin, cut:
- Two hands
- Two pants

From navy wool, cut:
- Two bodies
- Four arms
- Two 2⅜x3½-inch coattails

BODY

1. Sew the two body pieces together, leaving the bottom edges open. Clip the curves; turn the body right side out and stuff firmly.
2. Turn the bottom edge of the body under ¼ inch and baste in place. Set the body aside.

LEGS

1. Sew each leg together, leaving the top open. Clip the curves; turn the legs right side out. Firmly stuff the legs to the topstitching line. For each leg, align the seam with the center back fold and hand-sew the leg closed on the topstitching line. (The seam will run up the center front of the leg.)
2. Insert the legs into the body and topstitch across the ¼-inch fold of the body, through all fabric thicknesses, to close the opening and secure the legs. (See the tip for topstitching using the zipper foot on page 134.)

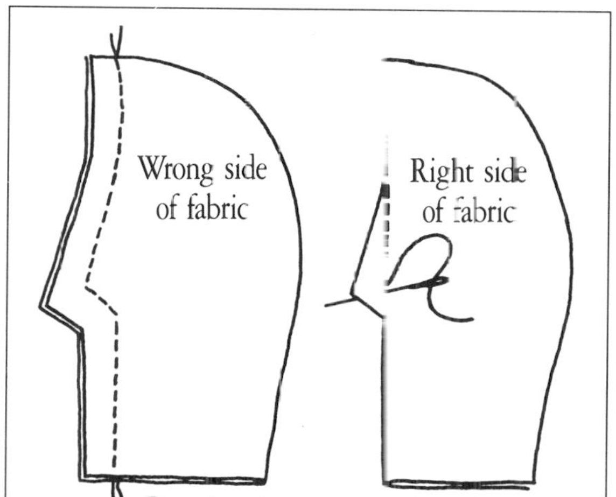

Drawing 1 Drawing 2

HEAD

1. Referring to Drawing 1, *above*, sew the two head front pieces together along the center front seam. Clip the seam at the points and finger-press the seam open. With *wrong* sides together, form the nose by machine- or hand-sewing along the top-stitching line (see Drawing 2, *above*).
2. Sew the head front to the head back, leaving the bottom open for turning. Clip the curves; turn the head right side out and stuff firmly.
3. Turn the neck edge under ¼ inch. Center the head on the body and hand-sew in place.

ARMS

1. Stay-stitch on the seam line between the dots of the open edge of each arm. Then, sew arms together in pairs along the outside curve only; clip the curves and finger-press the seams open. Turn the arms right side out.
2. Press under the top edge of each hand ¼ inch. Lay the ¼-inch fold on the wrist edge of each arm, matching the dots. Topstitch the hands to the arms. Turn the arms to the wrong side.
3. Sew the inside arm seam and around the hand of each arm. Clip the curves and trim the seam around the thumb to ⅛ inch. Turn the arms to the right side; firmly stuff the arms.
4. Turn the open edge of each arm under ¼ inch, clipping the curve to the stay stitching. Position each arm on the body shoulders. Hand-sew the arms to the body.

HAT

1. Sew the side and top seams of the hat, leaving the bottom edges open. Turn the hat right side out. Press the hat so the side seam and edge on the fold are at the sides.
2. Insert the hat through the slit in the hat brim. Aligning the bottom edges of the hat with the edges of the slit, sew the hat and brim together, using ⅛-inch seams. *Note:* It may be necessary to ease excess fullness in the hat brim as you stitch. Keep the fullness at the hat sides.
3. Lightly stuff the top of the hat.
4. Position the hat on the head so the brim seam is about ½ inch above the eyebrow markings. Use hot glue to secure the hat in place.

PANTS

1. Sew the two pants pieces together along the V-shape leg seam. Cut open along the cutting line. Sew the side seams. Turn the pants right side out.
2. Turn the bottom edges of the pants legs under ¼ inch and hem. Press under the waist edge ½ inch. Set the pants aside.

PAINTING THE DOLL

1. Dilute each color of paint with water (1 part water, 4 parts paint) before applying.
2. Follow the line markings on the pattern to paint the eyes, eyebrows, and mouth brown; paint the detail on the coat (body front) medium gold; and paint the boots black.
3. Referring to the photo, *opposite*, paint barn red vertical stripes on the hat and pants. Paint a ¼-inch-wide blue hatband just above the brim seam. Paint antique white stars on the hatband.
4. Paint red horizontal stripes on the flag. Paint a rectangular blue field in the upper left-hand corner of the flag. Add small white dots to the blue field for stars.

FINISHING

1. When all the paint is dry, slip pants on the doll and hand-sew the waist edge to the doll body waistline.
2. Press under all the edges of the coattail rectangles ¼ inch and topstitch in place. Hand-sew the tails in place at the back waist, just above the top of the pants.
3. Use a scrap piece of muslin to wipe a light coat of pine-colored stain over the head of the doll and a heavier coat over the hat. Wipe any excess stain from the fabric with a paper towel.
4. Glue sheep's wool to the side and back of the doll's head and the chin.
5. Varnish both sides of the flag. When the varnish is dry, glue the flag to the twig (pole) and whipstitch the stick to the doll's left hand.

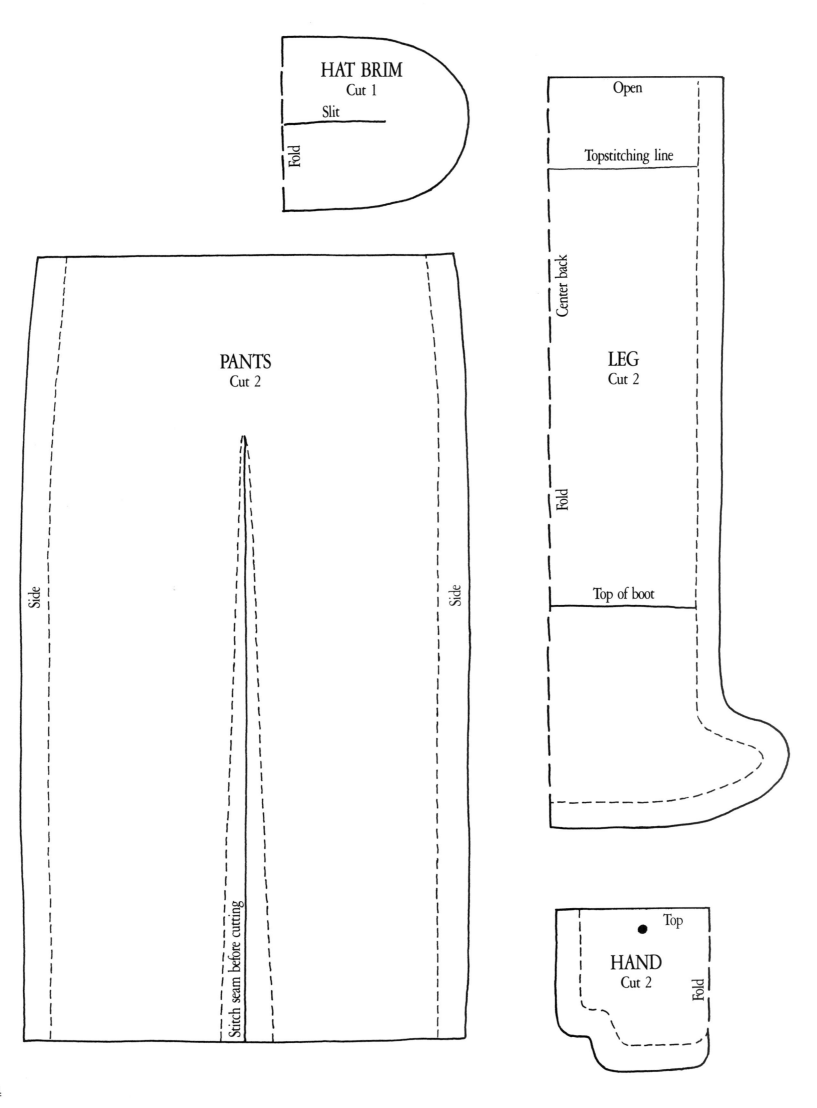

HAT BRIM
Cut 1

Slit

Fold

Open

Topstitching line

Center back

Fold

LEG
Cut 2

Top of boot

PANTS
Cut 2

Side

Side

Stitch seam before cutting

Top

HAND
Cut 2

Fold

44

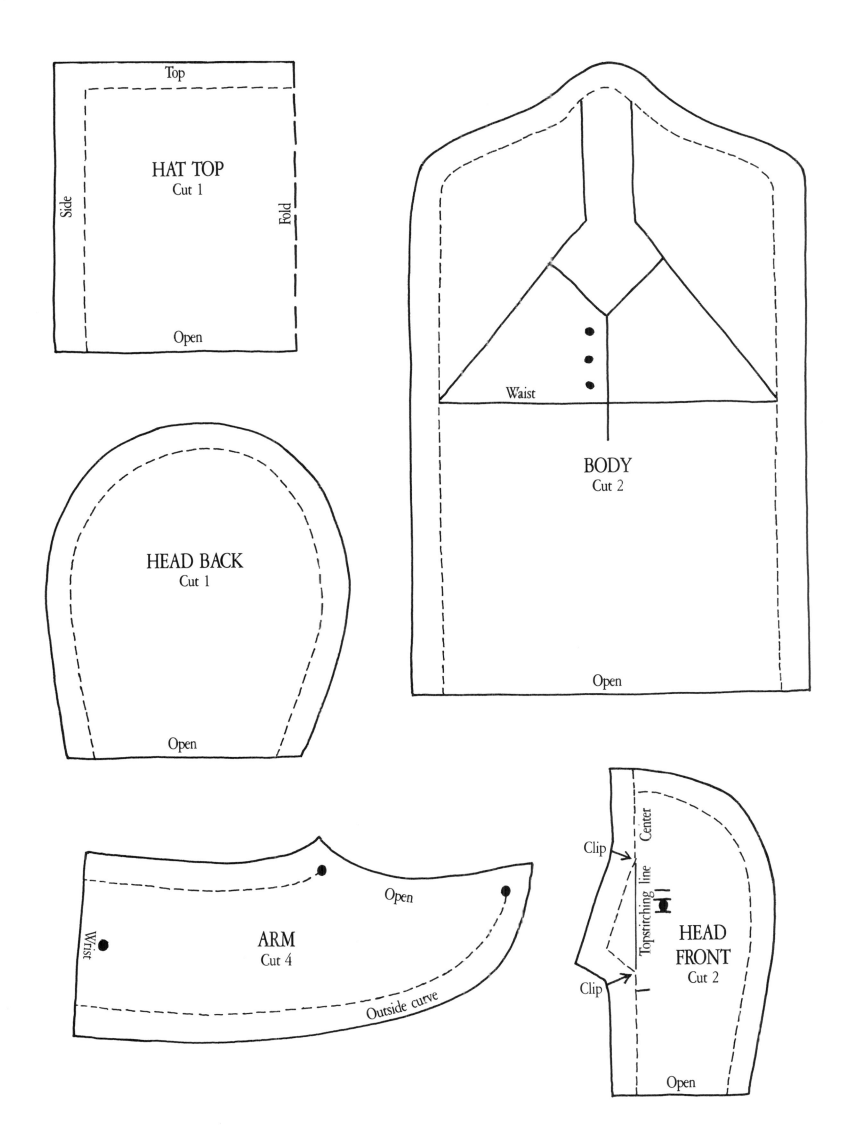

HAT TOP
Cut 1

Top

Side

Fold

Open

HEAD BACK
Cut 1

Open

BODY
Cut 2

Waist

Open

ARM
Cut 4

Open

Wrist

Outside curve

HEAD FRONT
Cut 2

Clip

Center

Topstitching line

Clip

Open

OLD MACDONALD'S FARM

With a cluck-cluck here, and a moo-moo there, here a bleat, there a neigh, everywhere an oink-oink . . . Old MacDonald had a farm and you can, too. Cut a barnyard of critters from 1-inch-thick pine, using full-size patterns for each of the five animals, the barn, and the farmer. Each figure is painted with bright acrylic paints and jigsawed to make thought-provoking playtime fun. The animals are 2½ to 4½ inches tall, the farmer stands 6 inches high, and the barn is 8 inches in height.

46

MATERIALS FOR OLD MACDONALD'S FARM PUZZLES

2-foot length of 1x10-inch pine board for barn and all figures

For the barn: burgundy red, gray, raw sienna, gold, yellow, and burnt sienna acrylic paints

For Old MacDonald: bright blue, white, peach, mustard, red-orange, raw sienna, burnt sienna, gray, light blue, bright green, yellow, and bright red acrylic paints

For the hen: white, bright red, yellow, raw sienna, gray, and black acrylic paints

For the cow: white, black, pink, mustard, bright green, burnt sienna, bright blue, yellow, gray, and bright red acrylic paints

For the goat: raw sienna, peach, bright blue, white, olive green, black, yellow, and bright red acrylic paints

For the horse: white, pink, bright blue, burnt sienna, black, yellow, gray, and bright red acrylic paints

For the pig: pink, black, white, bright blue, light gray, and bright red acrylic paints

Nos. 2 and 8 flat paintbrushes

No. 0000 round paintbrush

Scroll saw

Graphite paper

No. 1 technical pen

Clear-finish wood spray

Sandpaper

◆

PREPARING THE PATTERNS

Trace the full-size patterns, *opposite* and on pages 50 and 51, onto tracing paper. Do not cut out the patterns.

CUTTING THE PUZZLES

1. The heavy lines on the patterns are the cutting lines for the puzzle pieces. The remaining lines are the picture elements of the puzzles and define the painting areas.

2. Before cutting out the puzzles, use graphite paper to trace *all the lines* for each figure to the pine. Use the scroll saw to cut around each figure. *Do not* cut the puzzle pieces at this time.

3. If you want to paint both sides of the puzzles, turn over the puzzles, flop the tracings, and trace the details of the figures. It is not necessary to trace the lines for the puzzle pieces on this side of the pine.

4. Use the scroll saw to cut the pieces of each puzzle following the heavy lines you traced in Step 2.

5. Sand all edges of each piece.

GENERAL INSTRUCTIONS FOR PAINTING

1. Paint one side and the edges of a figure with one color; then paint the other side. Allow the paint to dry and clean brushes thoroughly before proceeding to the next color.

2. Small details have been omitted from the patterns. To add those to the figures, refer to the photographs on pages 46 and 47.

3. When painting is complete, spray each piece with several coats of clear finish.

PAINTING THE BARN

1. Use the No. 8 brush to paint the barn siding burgundy red and the silo gray.

2. Use the No. 0000 brush for steps 2–4. Paint the door hinges, door handle, hayloft opening, and a ⅛-inch-wide strip under the roof gray.

3. Paint silo bands, door frame, sign, hayloft frame, and barn roof raw sienna.

4. Paint the hay gold.

5. Use the No. 2 brush to paint raw sienna bricks on the silo.

6. Use the No. 0000 brush to paint yellow highlights on the hay and burnt sienna highlights on the silo bands, roof, hayloft frame, door, and bottom edges of the hay.

7. Use the pen to outline the silo bands, roof, hayloft, sign, door, and hinges. With a ruler and pen, draw lines ½ inch apart for barn boards. Use the pen to add "nails" to the silo bands, barn boards, and sign, and to letter Old MacDonald's Farm on the sign.

PAINTING OLD MACDONALD

1. Use the No. 2 brush to paint the overalls bright blue.

2. Use the No. 0000 brush for steps 2–10. Paint bright blue eyes, white eyeballs and pupils, and peach hands and face.

3. Paint a mustard hat and a red-orange shirt.

4. Paint the pail, shoelaces, and shoe soles raw sienna. Dilute the raw sienna with water and paint a woven pattern on the hat.

5. Paint the boots, pail bands, and pail highlights burnt sienna.

6. Paint the hair, eyebrows, eyelids, and mustache gray.

7. Paint light blue highlights on the overalls.

8. Paint bright green plaid lines on the shirt.

9. Paint yellow buttons on the overalls.

10. Paint the hatband bright red. Dilute some bright red with water and paint the cheeks and highlights on the hands and ear.

11. Use the pen to outline the hatband, face, hair, shirt, overalls, pail, and shoes and to accent the hat pattern. Draw stitches on the overalls and shoes with the pen. Make dots on the pail for nails.

PAINTING THE HEN

1. Use the No. 8 brush to paint the body, wings, and tail white.

2. Use the No. 0000 brush for steps 2–6. Paint the comb and face bright red.

3. Paint the beak, eye, and feet yellow.

4. Paint the neck and toenails raw sienna.

5. Paint gray feathers on the wings and highlights around the body, neck, and comb.

6. Paint the eyeball black.

7. Use the pen to outline the entire design.

PAINTING THE COW

1. Use the No. 8 brush to paint the head, body, and legs white.

2. Use the No. 0000 brush for steps 2–11. Paint the hooves, end of tail, line between the body and tail, and body spots black.

3. Paint the nose, udder, and inside the ears pink.

4. Paint the horns mustard.

5. Paint the collar bright green.

6. Paint burnt sienna stripes on the horns.

7. Paint bright blue eyes.

8. Paint yellow dots on the collar.

9. Paint gray accents around the ears, legs, and end of tail.

10. Paint pupils and the accents on the tail and hooves white.

11. Dilute some bright red with water and paint accents inside the ears, on the nose, and on the udder.

12. Use the pen to outline the mouth, whisker dots, collar, legs, udder, and pupil of eye.

PAINTING THE GOAT

1. Use the No. 8 brush to paint the head, body, and legs raw sienna.

2. Use the No. 0000 brush for steps 2–9. Paint the horn, muzzle, and inside the ear peach.

3. Paint the halter bright blue.

4. Paint the eyeball and an accent on the horn white.

5. Paint the iris of the eye olive green.

6. Paint the hooves and pupil of the eye black.

7. Paint yellow buttons on the halter.

8. Dilute some bright red with water and paint the mouth, tip of the nose, and accents on the ears and horn.

continued

Old MacDonald's Farm

9. Paint short white strokes to create fur tips at the back edge of the tail, lower legs, and under the neck. Paint a white stripe on each hoof and a white dot to highlight the eye.

10. Use the pen to outline the entire design, to draw eyelashes, whisker dots, and stitches on the halter, and to accent the fur tips. Draw short lines perpendicular to the edges of the horn.

PAINTING THE HORSE

1. Use the No. 8 brush to paint the head, body, and legs white.

2. Use the No. 0000 brush for steps 2–9. Paint the muzzle and inside the ears pink.

3. Paint the halter and outer area of the eye bright blue.

4. Paint the mane, tail, forelock, and spots burnt sienna.

5. Paint the nostril, center of eye, and hooves black.

6. Paint the buttons on the halter yellow

7. Paint the accents on halter, mouth, ears, mane, tail, forelock, and legs gray.

8. Dilute some bright red with water and paint accents on the muzzle and ears.

9. Paint white accents on the hooves and eye.

10. Use the pen to outline the halter, mouth, mane, ear, forelock, tail, and legs.

PAINTING THE PIG

1. Use the No. 8 brush to paint the head, body, and upper legs pink.

2. Use the No. 0000 brush for steps 2–6. Paint the hooves, tail, and nostrils black.

3. Paint the eyeball and accents on the nose, tail, hooves, and pupil of the eye white.

4. Paint the iris of the eye bright blue.

5. Paint the accents on the tail light gray.

6. Dilute some bright red with water and paint the cheek and highlight the mouth, nose, ears, and edges of the body.

7. Use the pen to outline the entire design.

PAINTING THE SHEEP, DUCK, CAT, AND ROOSTER

Using the painting style that's already established, paint the additional animals on this page.

Calico Cat & Gingham Dog

No duel between this calico cat and gingham dog. Playful mee-ows and bow-wow-wows create an air of backyard friendship. Use any old-fashioned bits of print, calico, or plaid fabrics to make this nursery rhyme duo in "an hour or so." They share the same body, legs, and head pattern pieces. Both stand 7½ inches tall and are 8¼ inches long from the front of their faces to the tip of their tails.

GENERAL INSTRUCTIONS

1. The instructions are for sewing one animal. Repeat these directions to make the second one.
2. Firmly stuff these animals. Use a sewing-machine setting of 10 to 12 stitches per inch when sewing the body, head, and leg pieces together.

BODY

1. Fold the body piece in half lengthwise. Sew the body together, leaving the neck edge open. Clip the curves; turn the body right side out.

54

2. Firmly stuff the body with fiberfill, stopping ¼ inch from the neck edge. Add the fiberfill a little at a time and pack well after each addition.
3. With a double-threaded needle, sew running stitches ¼ inch from the neck edge. Pull up the threads to close the opening; knot to secure.

LEGS

1. Fold the legs in half lengthwise. Sew each leg together along the side and top seams, leaving the foot edge open. Diagonally clip the corner seams; turn each leg right side out.
2. Hand-sew the tops of the legs to the body between the Xs with the leg side seams facing the tail end of the body.
3. Stuff the legs to ¼ inch from the opening.
4. With a double-threaded needle, sew running stitches ¼ inch from the foot edge. Pull up the threads to close the opening. Flatten the gathered edge to shape the bottom of the foot; knot the threads to secure.
5. Center and use hot glue to fasten a cardboard innersole to the bottom of each leg. The cardboard sole will be slightly larger than the bottom of the foot.
6. Loosely wrap a strip of quilt batting around the bottom of each leg two times. Pin a foot cuff to the bottom of each leg so that the cuff covers the batting and is even with the cardboard sole. Overlap the cuff at the center back seam of each leg. Hand-sew a cuff to each leg.
7. Position the felt sole on the bottom of each foot. Hand-sew the sole to the cuff, easing to fit.

HEAD

1. Cut circles of muslin that match the circumference of the eyes. Glue a muslin circle to the back of each eye with a drop of crafts glue.
2. Use a small dab of crafts glue to position the eyes, nose, and eyebrows on one of the head pieces. Use the pattern as a guide for placement.
3. Use the carpet thread and straight stitches to sew the eyes, nose, and eyebrows to the head. (See the stitching guide *above, right.*)
4. For the front of each cat ear, pin the inset to an ear piece as marked and machine-zigzag in place. Sew the calico ears together in pairs. Clip curves; turn each ear right side out. Fold pleats in each ear as marked and tack in place.
5. Sew the chin dart in both head pieces; press dart to one side. For the cat head, baste the ears between the small dots on the front head, keeping the raw edges even. *For both animals:* Sew the head pieces together, leaving an opening between the dots at the top of the head. Clip the curves; turn the head right side out.
6. Firmly stuff the head with fiberfill and hand-sew the opening closed.
7. Press under ¼ inch on the bottom of each dog ear and ear lining piece. Matching muslin with gingham fabric pieces, sew the ears together in

pairs, leaving the bottoms open. Clip the curves; turn each ear right side out and hand-sew the openings closed. Fold and tack a ¼-inch pleat in each ear. Hand-sew the left ear along the placement line. Hand-sew the right ear to the back of the head ¾ inch down and parallel to the top of the head. Tack the tip of the ear at the X above the eyebrow.
8. Hand-sew the center back of the head to the body; sew around the head two times.
9. Tack the tongue to the underside of the face over the chin dart.

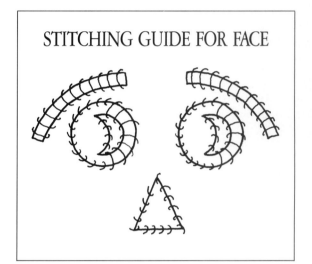

STITCHING GUIDE FOR FACE

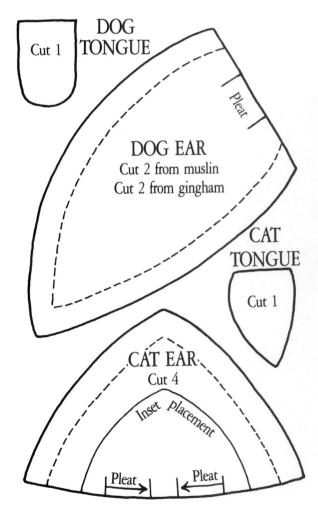

DOG TONGUE
Cut 1

DOG EAR
Cut 2 from muslin
Cut 2 from gingham

Pleat

CAT TONGUE
Cut 1

CAT EAR
Cut 4

Inset placement

Pleat   Pleat

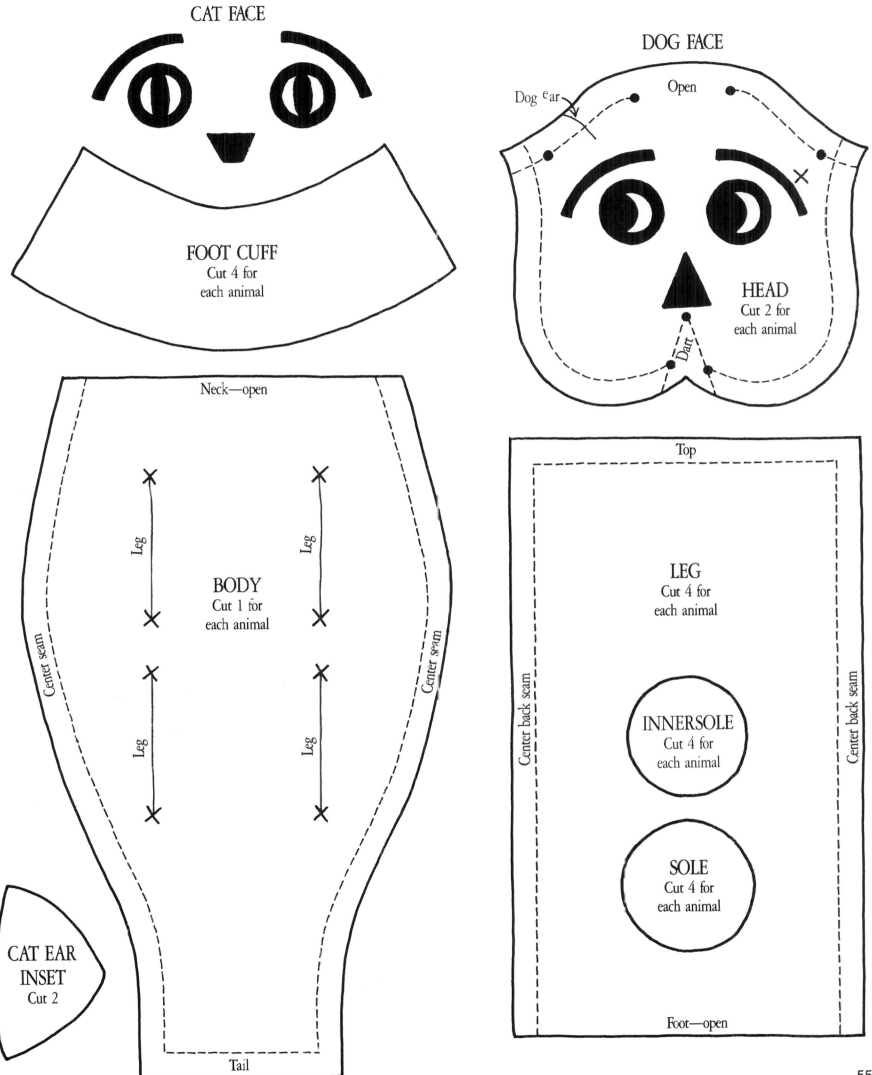

CAT FACE

DOG FACE

Dog ear

Open

HEAD
Cut 2 for
each animal

Dart

FOOT CUFF
Cut 4 for
each animal

Neck—open

Top

Leg

Leg

Center seam

Center seam

BODY
Cut 1 for
each animal

Leg

Leg

LEG
Cut 4 for
each animal

Center back seam

Center back seam

INNERSOLE
Cut 4 for
each animal

CAT EAR
INSET
Cut 2

SOLE
Cut 4 for
each animal

Tail

Foot—open

55

Vincent

Victoria

In make-believe, even dolls have playmates. Vincent, in a Little Lord Fauntleroy outfit with velveteen breeches, becomes a master puppeteer with his hobbyhorse marionette. Sweet Victoria, in lace-trimmed pantaloons, has a floppy toy kitten. Both dolls stand approximately 20 inches tall in their vinyl shoes. Full-size patterns and instructions are given for both dolls, including the clothing and hairdos, as well as their play toys. See the basketful of kittens on page 61; such a litter would thrill the cat fanciers in your life.

GENERAL INSTRUCTIONS

The following instructions are for sewing either doll. Only the head patterns are different and only the boy doll has ears.

EMBROIDERING THE FACES

1. Use carbon paper to transfer the facial features to one of the matching felt head pieces. For the girl doll, mark the Xs on the second head piece also. Do not transfer the head placement line.

2. Color the eye and eyebrow areas onto the felt with the dressmaker's chalk.

3. Referring to the stitch diagrams on page 7, and using one ply of dark brown floss and outline stitches, embroider the outlines of the eye shapes. Randomly stitch long and short straight stitches to fill in the eyebrows. Stitch two tiny short stitches for the nostrils. For the girl only, use one ply of medium brown floss and straight stitches to make eyelashes.

HEAD

1. Machine-sew the embroidered head to the matching second head, leaving the top open. Turn the head right side out and stuff it firmly with fiberfill to within ½ inch of the top.

2. To shape the nose, first cover one wooden bead with glue. Insert it into the head down to the nose position, keeping it close to the felt so it slightly protrudes through the fabric.

3. Hand-stitch a gathering thread around the top edge of the head opening. Pull the thread to close the opening; knot the thread to secure the gathers.

4. To shape the bridge of the nose, thread the dollmaker's needle with a double strand of white thread; knot the end. Insert the needle at the inside corner of one eye, through the fiberfill inside the head, and bring the needle out at the inside corner of the second eye. Pull the thread to create the bridge. Repeat the stitch one more time. Secure the thread.

5. Glue the felt pupil of each eye in place. Cut a piece of black buttonhole or quilt thread long enough to go around each pupil and glue it around the edges of the pupil. Use the toothpick to dab a highlight of white acrylic paint in the upper corner of each pupil.

6. Glue the upper and lower lips in place. Thread the dollmaker's needle with a double length of pink thread. Insert the needle into the back of the head and come out at one corner of the mouth. Take a small stitch and return the needle to the back of the head. Tighten the thread to form a slight dimple at the corner of the mouth. In the same manner, stitch a dimple on the other side of the mouth. Using the same procedure, make a tiny stitch between the upper and lower lips to create a slight indentation between them.

7. To shape the jawline on the girl doll only, thread the dollmaker's needle with flesh-color thread. Insert the needle into one of the upper Xs, take it through the head and come out at the upper X on the back side of the head. Pull the thread firmly. Repeat the stitch one more time and secure the thread. Connect the lower Xs on the face in the same manner.

8. Brush the cheeks with blush.

9. For the boy only, sew ears together in pairs, leaving openings as marked. Turn right side out.

10. Turn open edge of each ear under ⅛ inch. With flesh-color thread, backstitch around each ear on the topstitching line. Hand-sew each ear to the side of the head, positioning the bottom of the ears at the Xs.

BODY

1. Sew two body pieces together, leaving the top and bottom edges open; clip curves and turn right side out.

2. Lightly stuff the upper portion of the neck with fiberfill. Pin the back of the head to the front of the neck, using the head placement line as a guide. Hand-stitch the head in place. (Do not sew the head seam created in Step 1 of the Head to the neck. This seam creates a chin line for the doll when the head is sewn to the neck.) Sew the open edge at the top of the neck to the back of the head.

3. Finish stuffing the body through the bottom opening. Hand-sew the opening closed.

LEGS

1. Trim ¼ inch around the edge of the foot sole pattern. Cut two of this pattern from poster board. Center and glue one felt sole to each poster board sole. Clip the felt curves and glue these edges to the opposite side of the poster board.

2. Sew the legs together in pairs, leaving openings as marked; trim seams, clip curves, and turn right side out. Turn the bottom edge of each leg under ¼ inch and baste in place. Lightly stuff the feet with fiberfill. Pin, then hand-sew a sole to each foot.

3. Stuff the legs with fiberfill through the side openings. Hand-sew the openings closed.

4. Thread the dollmaker's needle with a double length of dental floss. Referring to the drawing, *below,* insert the needle through one leg at the X,

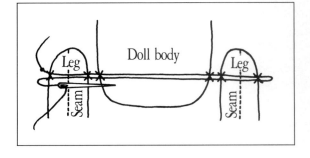

through the body between the lower Xs, and through the second leg at the X. Take the needle back through the legs and body. Tighten the thread to pull the legs against the body. Repeat this stitching sequence three more times. Knot the thread to secure it.

ARMS

1. Sew the arms together in pairs, leaving an opening between the dots. Trim the seams around the fingers to ⅛ inch, clip curves, and turn the arms right side out. Firmly stuff the arms with fiberfill and hand-sew the openings closed.

2. With flesh-color thread, hand-sew short running stitches along the topstitching line between the two attached fingers.

3. Attach the arms to the shoulders, matching the Xs, following the sewing sequence for attaching the Legs in Step 4 on page 58.

VICTORIA'S HAIR

1. To make four 12-inch-long curls, pull off a 26-inch length of the roving fleece and divide it lengthwise into four pieces. Wrap each piece around a wooden dowel. Space the roving so each wrap slightly overlaps the previous one and the roving extends along the length of each dowel.

2. To make four 10-inch-long curls, pull off a 24-inch piece of fleece and divide it into four strips. Wrap each strip around a dowel so it measures 10 inches long.

3. Gently pour water over the fleece to dampen. Place the wrapped dowels on a cookie sheet and bake in a 225-degree oven for 20 minutes. Cool, then slide the curls off the dowels.

4. Center the curls on the 2x7-inch muslin strip, laying them side by side and parallel to the 2-inch edges. Group them, keeping the 10-inch curls and the 12-inch curls together as shown in the drawing, *below*. Baste the curls to the muslin, sewing through the center of the strip.

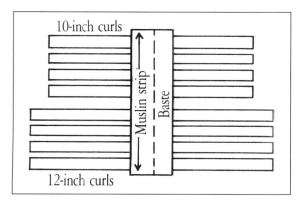

5. With the fleece side up, fold the muslin piece in half along the basting line. Machine-sew, through all thicknesses, ⅛ inch from the basting thread. Cut away any excess muslin along the short edges. Trim the long edges of the muslin ½ inch from the stitching.

6. Using the stitching line as the center part of the hair, glue the muslin strip with the longer curls to the top of the head, beginning ¾ inch above the eyebrows; let the glue dry. Spread glue from the top portion of the back of the head to the neckline. Arrange the curls so they cover the head without overlapping and extend below the shoulders. Press them into the glue. Tack the curls to the face sides and around the base of the neck.

VINCENT'S HAIR

1. Pull out five 4- to 6-inch strips of fleece and use your fingers to smooth them flat. Lay the strips across the head from front to back, placing one longer strip at the center and two or more shorter strips over each ear. Add additional strips for a fuller head of hair.

2. Shape a wig by smoothing and blending the strips together with your fingers and the tip of a needle, using the needle like a one-toothed comb.

3. Gently remove the wig, keeping the strips together. Cover the head with glue and lay the wig back on the head, pressing it into the glue. Trim the wig to the desired length and shape. If desired, spray the wig with hair spray to hold it in place.

MATERIALS FOR VICTORIA'S CLOTHING

½ yard of muslin for dress and pantaloons

6x12-inch piece of white knit ribbing for socks

6x20-inch piece of lightweight ecru vinyl for shoes

⅝ yard of ¾-inch-wide ecru gathered lace for pantaloons

1½ yards of ½-inch-wide ecru flat lace for dress

⅓ yard of ½-inch-wide white gathered lace for socks

¾ yard of ½-inch-wide ecru ribbon for shoes

⅔ yard of ⅞-inch-wide ribbon for hair

⅔ yard of narrow ecru cording for shoes

⅔ yard of pearl cotton for pantaloons

Three snaps; elastic sewing thread

Tapestry needle

Poster board; rubber cement

◆

PREPARING THE PATTERNS

Trace the full-size patterns for Victoria's clothing on pages 65–67 onto tracing paper. Cut out the patterns.

◆

CUTTING THE FABRICS

The cutting instructions for pieces that have no patterns include ¼-inch seams.

From muslin, cut:
- Two bodice backs
- One bodice front
- Two back facings
- One front facing
- Two pantaloons
- One 9x12-inch bodice for shirring
- Two 7x10-inch sleeves
- One 2x16-inch collar
- One 10½x25-inch skirt

From knit ribbing, cut:
- Two socks with folds parallel to ribs

From vinyl, cut:
- Two shoe tops
- Two shoe soles
- Two shoe heels

From poster board, cut:
- Two shoe soles
- Two shoe fillers
- Two shoe heels

continued

PANTALOONS

1. Sew the inside leg seam of each piece together. Turn one leg right side out; slip it into the other pantaloons leg, matching the seams. Sew the center seam, leaving an opening above the dot on one side for the center back. Turn the pantaloons right side out. Press under the seam allowances for the back opening and topstitch in place.

2. For the waistline casing, press the top edge under ⅛ inch. Press it under again ¼ inch and topstitch close to the double-folded edge. Thread pearl cotton onto a tapestry needle and run it through the casing for a drawstring.

3. Turn each leg edge under ⅛ inch. Turn edges under again ¼ inch and topstitch the hem. Sew ¾-inch-wide lace around the bottom of each leg.

4. Slip the pantaloons onto the doll with the opening at the back. Pull the drawstring so the pantaloons fit around the waist; tie the drawstring into a bow.

BODICE

1. For shirring, use a pencil to lightly draw 19 lines, ⅝ inch apart, parallel to the 9-inch edge of the 9x12-inch bodice rectangle. Fill a sewing machine bobbin with elastic thread. Machine-stitch on each line, pulling the fabric on both sides of the presser foot to keep it flat. When shirring is completed, center the fabric bodice front on the elastic thread (wrong) side of the shirred rectangle. Pin and sew the two pieces together around all edges. Cut away the excess shirred fabric.

2. Sew bodice backs to bodice front at shoulders.

3. Sew back facings to front facing at shoulders.

4. Sew facing around the neck and center back openings; clip curves, turn the facing to the inside, and press. Press under the raw edges of the facing ¼ inch; topstitch along the fold.

5. Designate one 7-inch edge of each sleeve rectangle as the armhole edge. Using elastic thread in the bobbin, sew three rows of shirring, ¼ inch apart. Begin the first row 3¾ inches from the armhole edge of each sleeve.

6. Run a gathering thread across the armhole edge of each sleeve and gather each sleeve to fit an armhole opening of the bodice. Sew the sleeves to the bodice. Sew the sleeve and bodice side seams.

7. Press under the bottom edge of each sleeve ⅛ inch. Press the edge under again ¼ inch and topstitch the hem. Sew ½-inch-wide lace around the bottom edge of each sleeve.

DRESS COLLAR

1. Using elastic thread in the bobbin, sew two 16-inch-long rows of shirring, ¼ inch apart, down the center of the collar strip.

2. Fold the strip in half and sew the long edges together, leaving an opening at the center for turning; press the seam open.

3. Refold the strip so the seam and shirring are centered on opposite sides of the strip. Sew across both short ends.

4. Turn the collar right side out. Pin it around the bodice neckline, overlapping half of the collar on the bodice, and lining up the edges of the collar with the center back openings. Hand-stitch the collar in place.

SKIRT

1. Designate one 25-inch edge of the skirt rectangle as the top. Using elastic thread in the bobbin, sew four rows of shirring, ⅜ inch apart. Begin the first row 3½ inches from the top.

2. Sew the short edges of the rectangle together, leaving an opening 1½ inches from the top. Press under the seam allowance for the opening; topstitch around the opening. Press under the bottom edge of the skirt ⅛ inch. Press the edge under again ¼ inch and topstitch to hem. Sew ½-inch-wide lace around the hemmed edge.

3. Run a gathering thread around the top edge and pull up the gathers to fit the bodice. Sew the skirt to the bodice, matching the center back openings.

4. Sew three snaps to the back of the bodice. Slip the dress onto the doll.

SOCKS

1. Sew the curved edge of each sock together, leaving the tops open; turn right side out.

2. Slip one sock over each foot with the seam at the center back. Turn down the top of each sock. Cut the ½-inch-wide gathered lace in half. Sew one piece of lace to the top edge of each sock.

SHOES

1. Sew the back edges of each shoe top together. Open the seams and use rubber cement to glue the seam allowances to the inside of the shoe.

2. Position the poster-board soles inside the shoes. Match the dots at the toe and heel seams. Apply rubber cement to the wrong side of the notched seam allowances of the shoe tops and to the bottom edges of the soles. Fasten the vinyl edges to the soles. Use rubber cement to glue the shoe fillers inside the shoes. Trim about ⅛ inch from the edges of each vinyl sole; glue them to the bottoms of the shoes.

3. Glue the poster-board heels to the backs of the soles. Then glue the vinyl heels over them.

4. Glue narrow cording around the bottom of each shoe to cover the joinings of the shoe top and sole.

5. Cut or punch ⅛-inch-diameter holes in each instep flap at the O marked on the pattern. Cut the ½-inch-wide ribbon in half. Thread each ribbon through the holes in the shoes. Slip shoes onto the doll and tie the ribbons into bows.

FINISHING

1. Tie the ⅞-inch-wide ribbon into a bow; tack it to the back of the head at the nape of the neck.

MATERIALS FOR VINCENT'S CLOTHING

¼ yard of muslin for shirt

¼ yard of velveteen for pants

6x12-inch piece of knit ribbing for socks

6x20-inch piece of lightweight vinyl for shoes

1 yard of ⅜-inch-wide flat lace for shirt

½ yard of ¼-inch-wide velvet ribbon for tie

Four shirt buttons

Two ⅜-inch-diameter metal buttons for pants

Three small snaps

Two hooks and eyes

Two 6-mm beads for shoes

⅔ yard of narrow cording for shoes

Poster board

Rubber cement

◆

PREPARING THE PATTERNS

Trace the full-size patterns for Vincent's clothing on pages 65–68 onto tracing paper. Cut out the patterns.

◆

CUTTING THE FABRICS

From muslin, cut:
- ◆ One shirt front
- ◆ Two shirt backs
- ◆ Two back facings
- ◆ One front facing
- ◆ Two sleeves
- ◆ Two collars

From velveteen, cut:
- ◆ Two pants
- ◆ 2x13½-inch waistband

From knit ribbing, cut:
- ◆ Two socks with folds parallel to ribs

From vinyl, cut:
- ◆ Two shoe soles
- ◆ Two shoe heels
- ◆ Two shoe tops

From poster board, cut:
- ◆ Two shoe soles
- ◆ Two shoe fillers
- ◆ Two shoe heels

SHIRT

1. To make the tucks, fold the shirt front along the pleat lines. Stitch through both fabric thicknesses on the sewing lines. Press the pleats toward the center front. Sew the shirt front to the shirt backs at the shoulders.

2. Repeat steps 3 and 4 of the Bodice instructions at *left*.

3. Sew top edge of each sleeve to an armhole. Press under the bottom edge of each sleeve ⅛ inch. Press the edge under again ¼ inch and top-stitch the hem. Sew ⅜-inch-wide lace around the wrist edge of each sleeve.

4. Hem the bottom edge of the shirt in the same manner as Step 3, *above.*

5. Sew shirt buttons at the Xs on the center front of the shirt. Sew snaps down the back opening. Slip the shirt onto the doll.

COLLAR

1. Sew the two collar pieces together, leaving an opening between the dots. Clip curves, turn, and press. Hand-sew the opening closed.

2. Baste lace around the outer edges of the collar. Topstitch around the entire collar, sewing through the edge of the lace.

3. Sew a hook and eye at the neck. Place the collar around the doll's neck and fasten.

4. Tie the velvet ribbon into a small bow; tack it to the center front of the collar.

PANTS

1. Repeat Step 1 of the Pantaloons instructions on page 60.

2. Fold the waist pleats on the front of the pants only; topstitch atop the 1-inch fold lines to secure the pleats. Sew one long edge of the waistband to the top edge of the pants, leaving ¼ inch extended beyond each edge at the back opening. Fold the waistband under, keeping right sides together, and stitch the ¼-inch seams across the short ends at the center back. Clip the seams. Turn the waistband right side out. Press the unstitched edge of the waistband under ¼ inch and blindstitch it over the waist seam.

3. Press under the bottom edge of each leg ¼ inch and topstitch. Turn the same edge under ¾ inch and hem.

4. Sew a hook and eye to the back waist opening. Sew a metal button onto the waistband above each pleat. Put the pants on the doll.

SOCKS

1. Repeat the instructions for Victoria's Socks on page 60, omitting the lace.

SHOES

1. Repeat steps 1–4 of Victoria's Shoes on page 60.

2. Slip the shoes onto the doll. Sew beads at the Xs on the outside flap of each shoe. Cut or punch a ⅛-inch-diameter hole over the dot in the other flap. Button the holes over the beads.

MATERIALS FOR VICTORIA'S KITTEN

¼ yard of children's sleepwear fleece

Two 4-mm black beads

Small scrap of black felt for the nose

⅓ yard of ¼-inch-wide ribbon

Small bell

Black sewing thread

Black button thread

Polyester fiberfill

Plastic filler beads

◆

PREPARING THE PATTERNS

Trace the full-size patterns on page 69 onto tracing paper. Cut out the patterns.

◆

CUTTING THE FABRICS

From fleece, cut:
◆ Two bodies
◆ Two tails
◆ Four ears
◆ Two heads

BODY

1. Sew body pieces together, leaving an opening between the dots. Clip the curves and turn the body right side out.

2. Lightly stuff the paws with fiberfill; fill the body with plastic filler beads. Hand-sew the opening closed.

3. Use a double strand of black button thread to stitch through the feet at the toe markings.

HEAD

1. Sew the head pieces together, leaving an opening between the dots. Clip the curves and turn the head right side out. Lightly stuff the head with fiberfill and hand-sew the opening closed.

2. For the eyes, thread a needle with a double strand of black sewing thread. Insert the needle at one of the Xs and bring it out at the other X, catching the fiberfill inside the head. Thread a bead on the needle and take the needle back through the head to the first X, pulling gently to shape the nose. Thread the other bead on the needle. Repeat the stitch and secure the thread. Use a single strand of black button thread and straight stitches for the mouth and eyebrows. Cut a nose from black felt, using the nose on the face pattern as a guide. Glue the nose to the face.

3. For the whiskers, thread a needle with black button thread. Make a knot in one end, leaving a 1½-inch tail. Insert the needle at one of the dots near the nose. Bring the needle out at a dot on the other side of the nose, pulling slightly to shape the face. Knot the thread, securing it close to the fabric. Cut the thread, leaving a 1½-inch tail. Make two more sets of whiskers.

4. Sew the ear pieces together in pairs, leaving openings as marked. Trim the seams to ⅛ inch and turn the ears right side out. Turn the raw edges of the ears under ⅛ inch and hand-stitch the ears to the head.

5. Tack the back of the head to the body at the X.

TAIL

1. Sew the tail pieces together, leaving an opening as marked. Trim the seam to ⅛ inch and turn the tail right side out. Do not stuff the tail.

2. Turn the unfinished edges of tail under ⅛ inch and hand-stitch it to the underside of the body at the placement line.

3. Slip the ribbon through the bell and tie the ribbon around the neck.

MATERIALS FOR VINCENT'S HORSE MARIONETTE

1¼-inch-diameter 6-inch-long cardboard tube for the body and head

5-inch-long coat hanger cardboard tube for the neck

4-inch square of poster board for the feet

Light, medium, and dark purple fabric scraps

Scrap of black felt

Four 15-mm wooden beads

Yellow acrylic paint

Black pearl cotton

Two wooden Popsicle sticks

Crafts knife

Hammer and nail

Stapler and staples

Polyester fiberfill

Crafts glue

Hot-glue gun

◆

PREPARING THE PATTERNS

Trace the full-size patterns on page 68 onto tracing paper. Cut out the patterns.

◆

CUTTING THE FABRICS

The cutting instructions for pieces that have no patterns include ¼-inch seams.

From light purple, cut:
◆ One 4½x5-inch body
◆ One 3x4½-inch head
◆ One 3½-inch-square muzzle
◆ One 2½-inch-diameter head

From poster board, cut:
◆ Four feet

From medium purple, cut:
◆ One upper leg
◆ Two lower legs
◆ Four ears

From dark purple, cut:
◆ One upper leg
◆ Two lower legs

From black felt, cut:
◆ Two ½x⅜-inch eyelashes

PREPARING THE PIECES

1. For the neck, cut the ends of the coat hanger tube at 30-degree and 60-degree angles as shown in the drawing *above right.*
2. Using the yellow acrylic paint, paint the neck tube, four feet, and four beads. Set aside to dry.

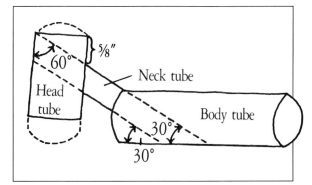

BODY AND HEAD

1. Cut the 1¼-inch-diameter cardboard tube into one 4-inch length for the body and one 2-inch length for the head.
2. Measure and mark ⅝ inch from one cut edge of the head tube. Cut a hole at the mark that is large enough for inserting the neck tube.
3. Use the crafts glue to glue the 4½x5-inch fabric rectangle around the body tube. Glue the excess fabric at the open ends inside the tube.
4. Glue the 3x4½-inch fabric rectangle around the head tube in the same manner. Locate the cardboard hole, cut a small hole in the fabric, and push the raw fabric edges into the tube, clipping as necessary.

LEGS

1. Fold and sew the long edges of each upper leg piece together. Turn the legs right side out. Press each piece so the seam is centered between the two folds (back side). Topstitch the legs on the topstitching lines. Stuff both ends of each leg piece with fiberfill. Turn the unfinished edges under ⅛ inch. Run a gathering thread around each edge. Pull gathers tightly to close.
2. Fold and sew the edges of each lower leg piece together, leaving openings as marked; turn right side out. Press the edge of each opening under ⅛ inch. Run a gathering thread around one opening and pull firmly to close; knot to secure gathers. Stuff each lower leg firmly with fiberfill. Gather and close the remaining edge.
3. Referring to the drawing in the box on page 63, and the photo on page 56, attach the medium purple lower legs to the dark purple upper legs by sewing a bead between the two pieces. Attach the dark purple lower legs to the medium purple upper legs in the same manner.
4. Place the unstuffed sections of the upper legs over the ends of the body tube. Use crafts glue to glue them in place. Glue the poster-board feet to the bottom of the legs with a hot-glue gun.

HEAD ASSEMBLY

1. For the muzzle, fold the 3½-inch square in half and sew the long edges together. Turn the piece right side out and lightly stuff. Sew across both open ends. Fold the muzzle piece in half, matching the short ends. With black pearl cotton, make

two French knot nostrils along the fold. (See the stitch diagrams on page 7.) Apply glue to the inside edges of the bottom of the head tube. With the muzzle folded in half, slip the short ends into the bottom of the tube to glue the muzzle in place.
2. Run a gathering thread around the edge of the head circle. Fill the center of the circle with fiber-fill and, at the same time, pull the thread just enough to contain the stuffing and shape the circle to fit inside the top of the head tube. Secure the gathering thread. Apply glue to the inside edges of the top of the head tube. Glue the stuffed circle into the head, placing the gathered side inside the tube.
3. Sew the ears together in pairs, leaving openings as marked. Trim the excess fabric and turn the ears right side out. Turn the unfinished edges under ⅛ inch and hand-stitch closed. Make one tiny pleat at the center of each ear. Hot-glue the ears to the top of the head tube.
4. Clip one long edge of each eyelash strip four times to fringe. Glue the eyelashes to each side of the face, slightly spreading the clipped edges.
5. Insert the end of the neck that was cut at a 60-degree angle into the hole in the back of the head. Glue the other end into the front of the body tube.

FINISHING

1. For the tail, cut eight 4x⅛-inch strips from each purple fabric. Bunch all of the strips together at one end; glue them to the top inside edge of the back end of the body tube.
2. Cut a 12-inch length of pearl cotton. Loop it twice around the head tube about ¼ inch above the muzzle. Tie the thread securely; clip the ends.

STRINGING THE HORSE

1. Punch a small hole through each foot at the dot. Use a hammer and nail to punch small holes in each end of the Popsicle sticks. Lay one stick on top of the other, crisscrossed, forming a right angle intersection. Use hot glue to glue the sticks together at the intersection.
2. Cut a 26-inch length of pearl cotton; fold it in half. Loop it around the body behind the front legs and tie a knot close to the top of the body. Knot the ends of the thread together; staple this knot to the underside of the intersection of the sticks.
3. Cut four 15-inch lengths of pearl cotton. Thread one end of each length through the holes in the feet, knotting the thread on the underside of each foot. Referring to the drawing on page 63, thread the other ends through the matching holes in the Popsicle sticks.
4. Adjust the thread so the legs hang straight. Knot the threads and cut off any ends.

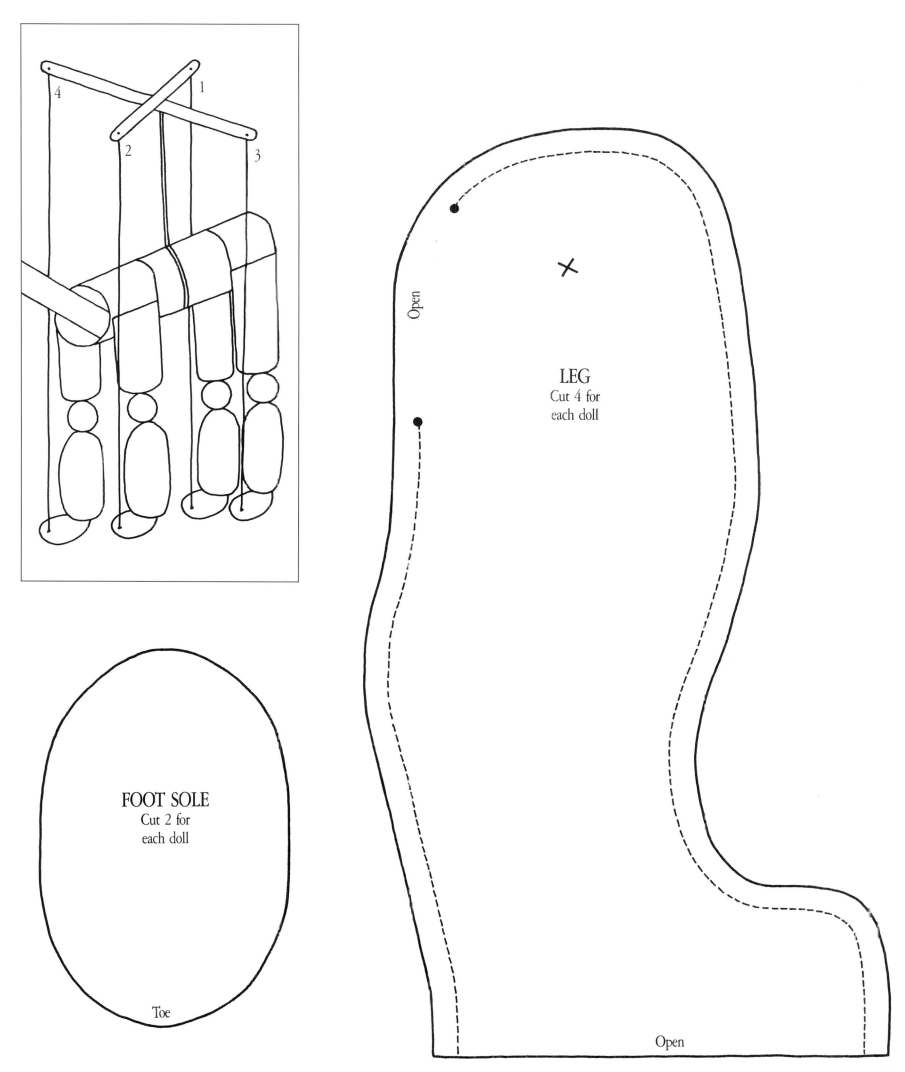

LEG
Cut 4 for
each doll

Open

Open

FOOT SOLE
Cut 2 for
each doll

Toe

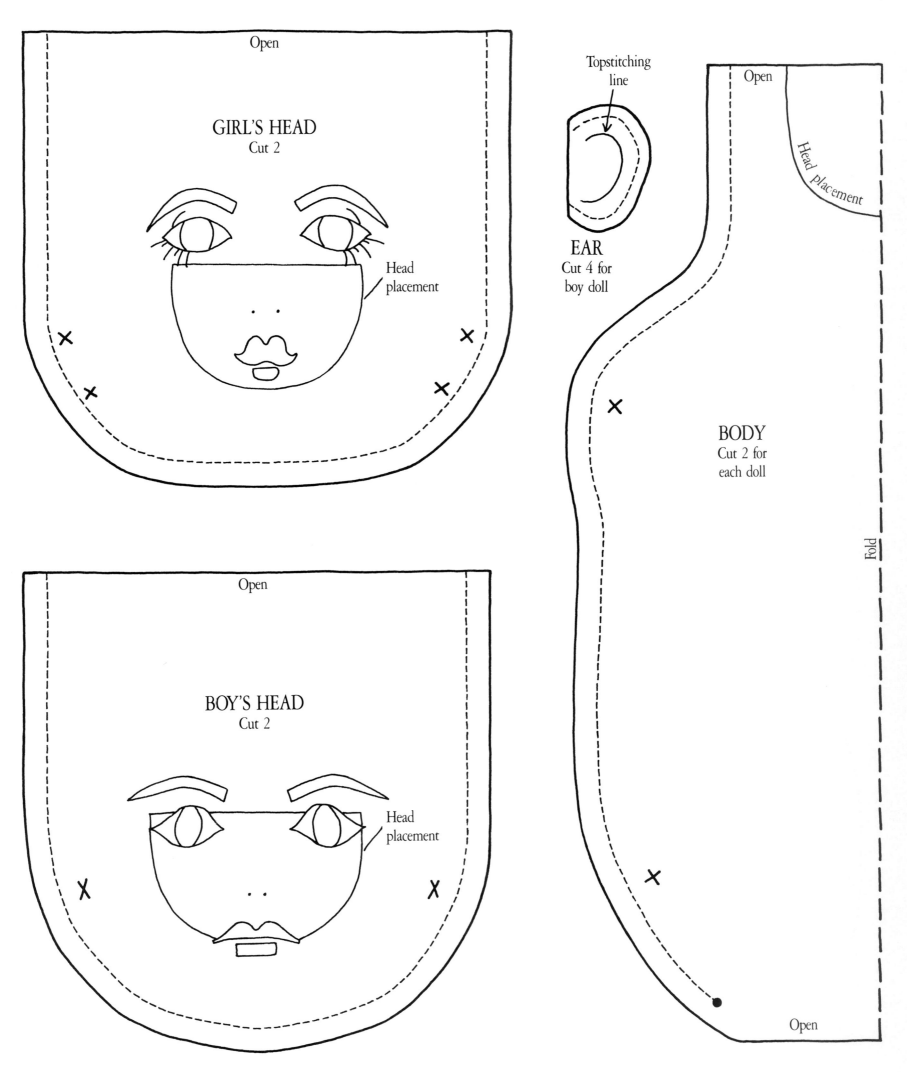

GIRL'S HEAD
Cut 2

Open

Head placement

BOY'S HEAD
Cut 2

Open

Head placement

Topstitching line

EAR
Cut 4 for boy doll

Open

Head placement

BODY
Cut 2 for each doll

Fold

Open

64

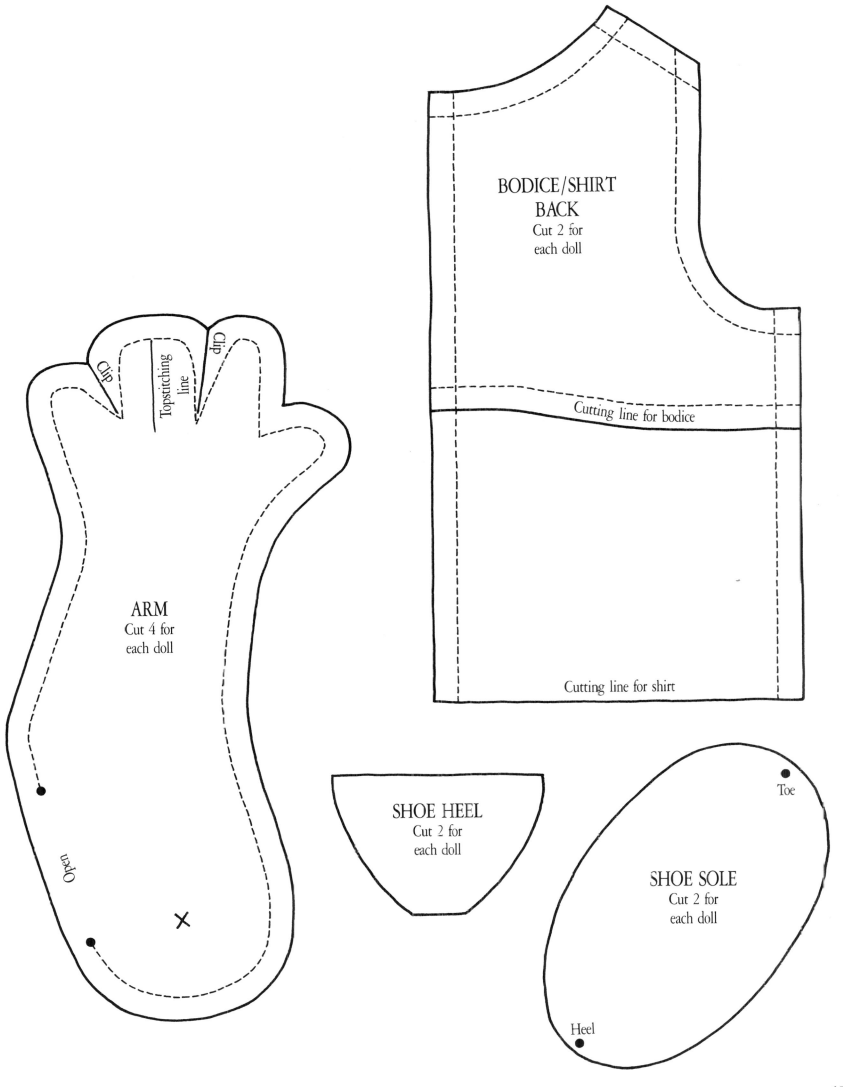

ARM
Cut 4 for
each doll

Clip

Topstitching line

Clip

Open

BODICE/SHIRT
BACK
Cut 2 for
each doll

Cutting line for bodice

Cutting line for shirt

SHOE HEEL
Cut 2 for
each doll

SHOE SOLE
Cut 2 for
each doll

Toe

Heel

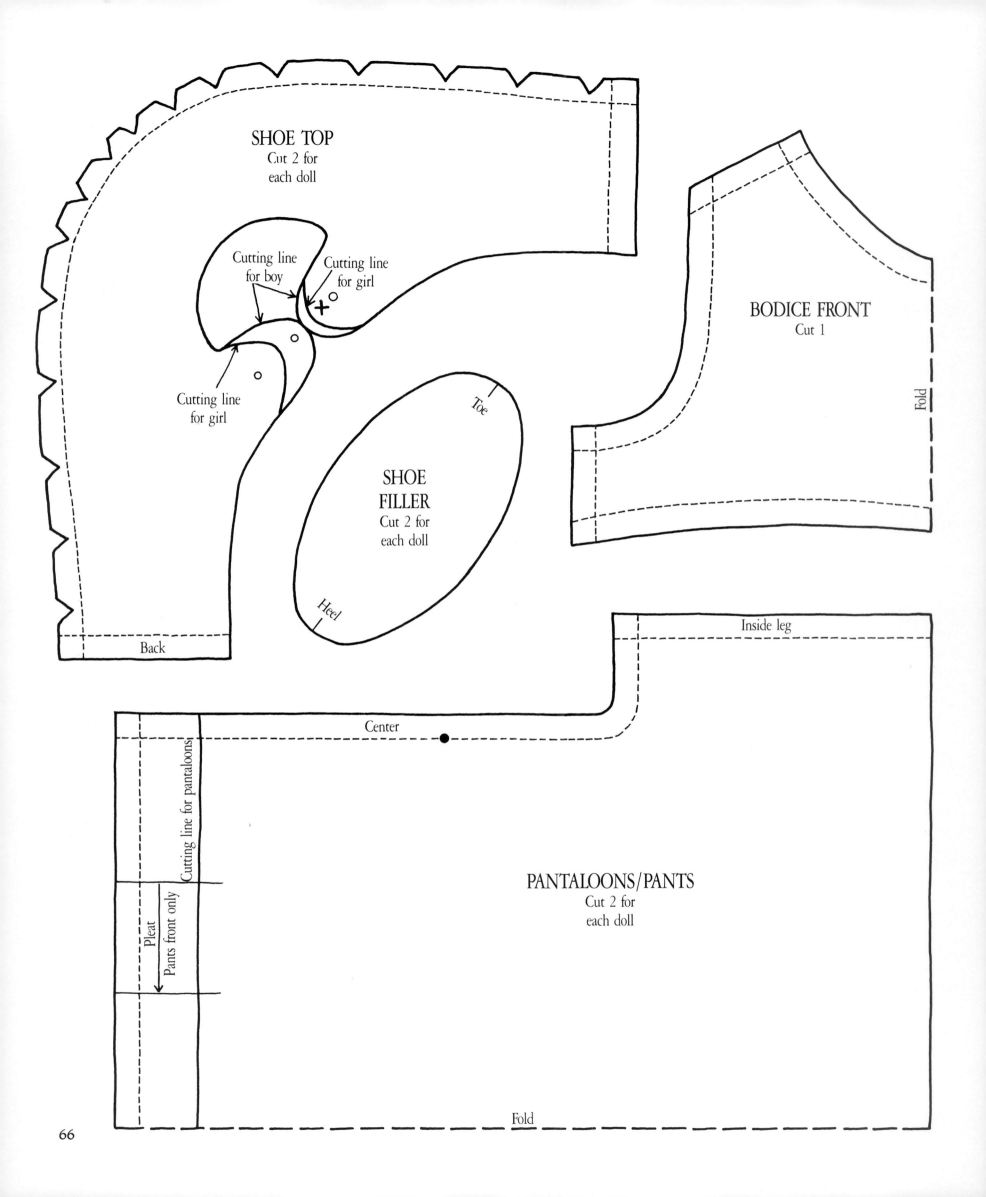

SHOE TOP
Cut 2 for
each doll

Cutting line
for boy

Cutting line
for girl

Cutting line
for girl

BODICE FRONT
Cut 1

Fold

Toe

SHOE
FILLER
Cut 2 for
each doll

Heel

Back

Inside leg

Center

Cutting line for pantaloons

Pleat

Pants front only

PANTALOONS/PANTS
Cut 2 for
each doll

Fold

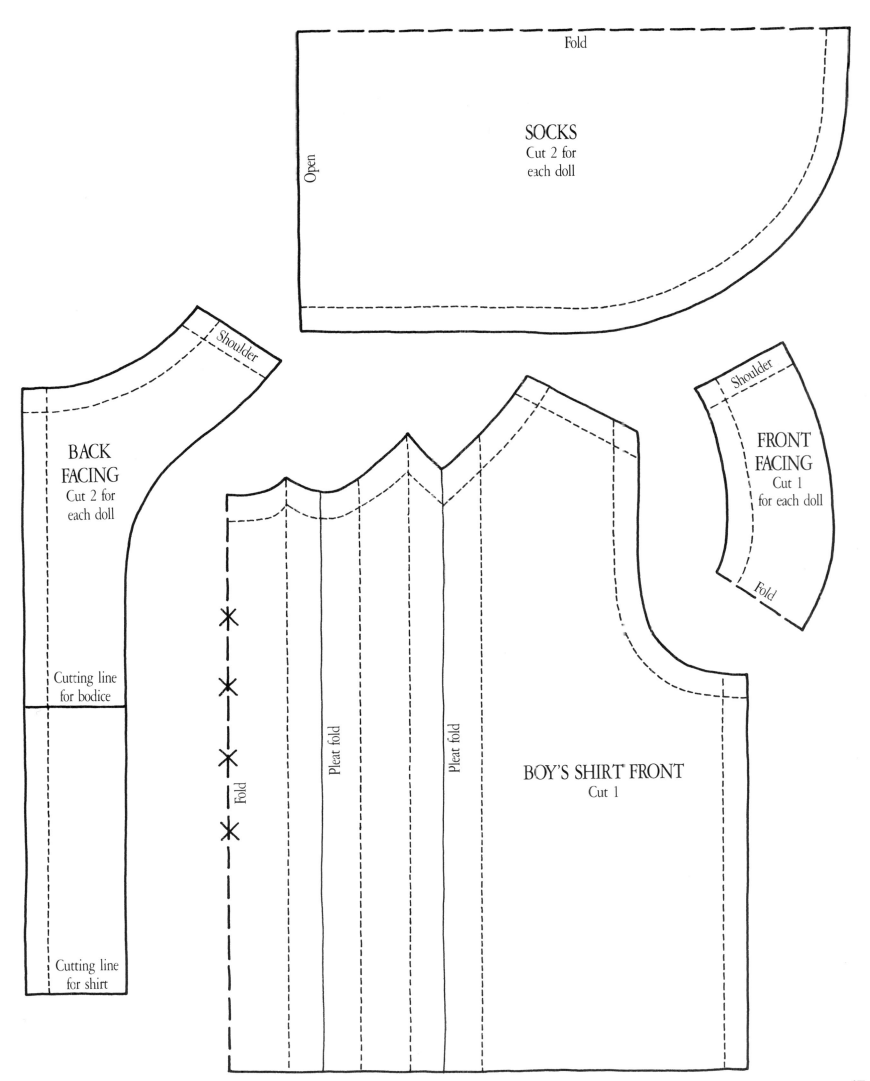

SOCKS
Cut 2 for
each doll

Fold

Open

BACK
FACING
Cut 2 for
each doll

Shoulder

Cutting line
for bodice

Cutting line
for shirt

Fold

Pleat fold

Pleat fold

BOY'S SHIRT FRONT
Cut 1

FRONT
FACING
Cut 1
for each doll

Shoulder

Fold

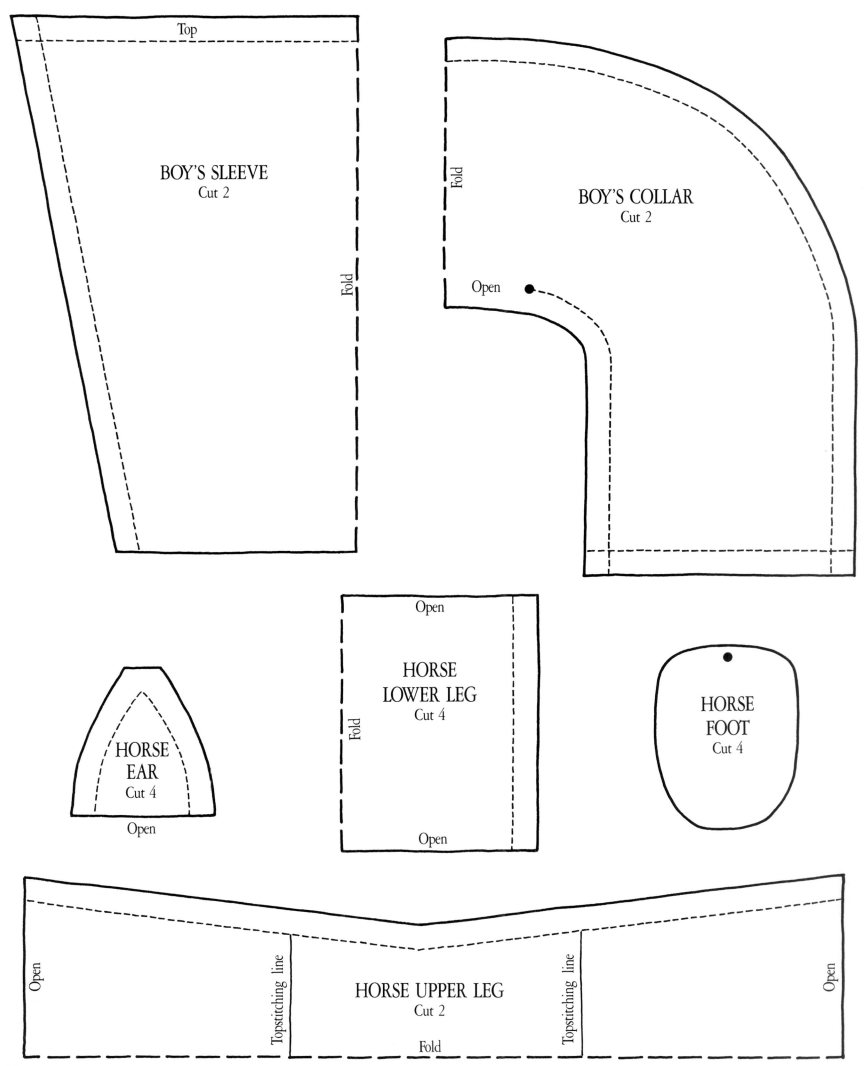

BOY'S SLEEVE
Cut 2

Top

Fold

BOY'S COLLAR
Cut 2

Fold

Open

HORSE
EAR
Cut 4

Open

Open

HORSE
LOWER LEG
Cut 4

Fold

Open

HORSE
FOOT
Cut 4

Open

Topstitching line

HORSE UPPER LEG
Cut 2

Topstitching line

Open

Fold

68

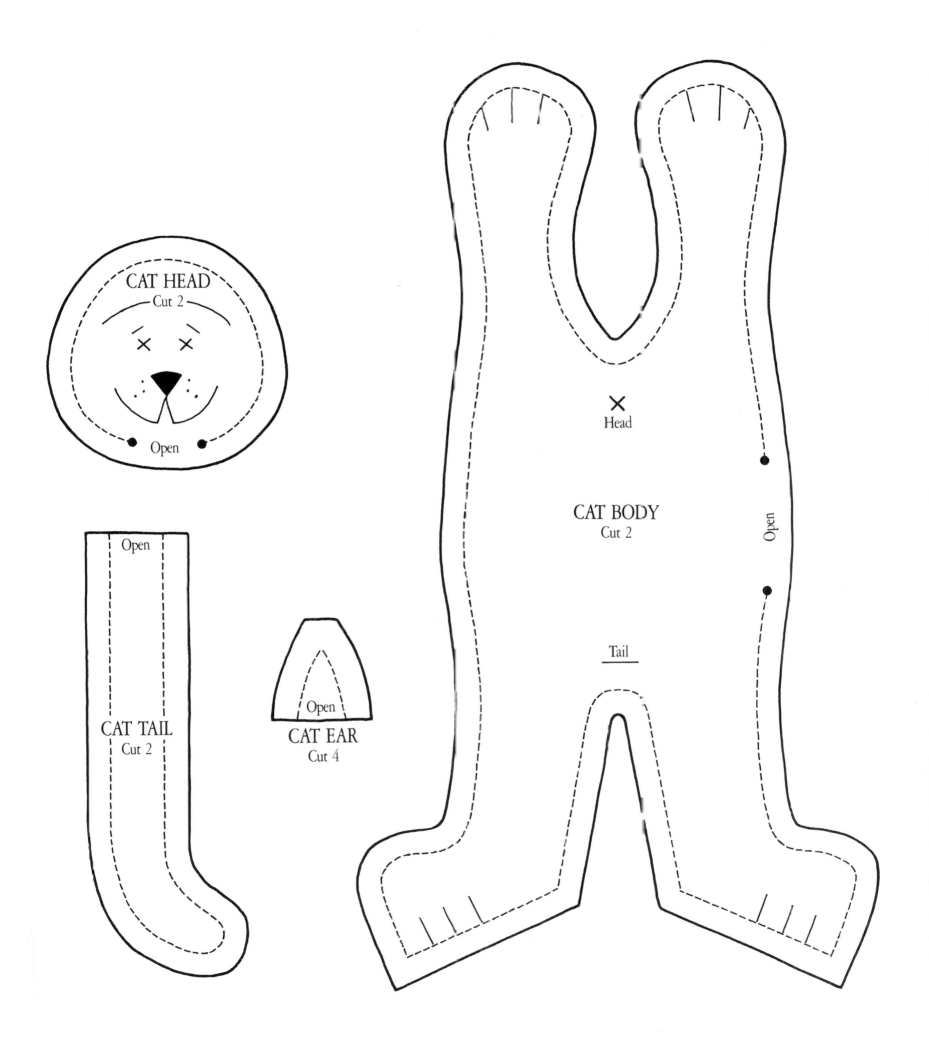

CAT HEAD
Cut 2

Open

CAT BODY
Cut 2

Head

Open

Tail

CAT TAIL
Cut 2

Open

CAT EAR
Cut 4

Open

Redheaded Twins

What's cuter than one little red-haired pixie of a doll? TWO little red-haired pixies, of course! Amy and Albert are two of a kind with impish grins, down-home clothing, and naturally curly hair. Use the same patterns to make both 13-inch-tall bodies, which you then can dress and embellish as you like. We used bouclé yarn for the hair and a fine-tip permanent fabric marker to draw the faces. These redheaded twins are great country collectibles, but they can be children's playmates, too, as they're suitable for heavy-duty loving.

GENERAL INSTRUCTIONS

The instructions are for sewing one doll body. Repeat these directions to make the second doll. The clothing instructions for each doll are given separately.

FACE AND HEAD

1. Lay a muslin face piece atop the pattern on page 72. With the black fabric marker, trace the eyes, eyebrows, and the nose. With the rust fabric marker, trace the mouth and freckles.
2. Apply blush to the cheeks.
3. Matching the dots, sew the head side pieces to the face and to the head back piece. Clip curves; turn the head right side out.

ARMS

1. Sew the arm pieces together in pairs, leaving the tops open for stuffing.
2. Clip the curves of the hands, and turn the arms right side out.
3. Firmly stuff the arms with fiberfill to the top-stitching lines. Align the seams and sew across the lines. (See the tip on page 134 for topstitching using the zipper foot.)
4. Lightly stuff the upper arms with fiberfill; baste the openings closed.

BODY

1. Sew four body pieces together in pairs along the center body seam. Leave one of the pairs open between the dots for stuffing; this seam will be the center back of the body.
2. Using ⅛-inch seams, sew the arms, with the thumbs pointing up, to one of the assembled body pieces between the upper side seam dots.
3. Sew the body front to the body back at the side seams, encasing the arms in the seams.
4. Aligning the center fronts and center backs of head and neck pieces, insert the head into the neck opening. Sew the neck seam. For added stability, sew the neck seam again, in the seam allowance, ⅛ inch from the first seam.
5. Turn the body right side out through the back opening. Firmly stuff the head and neck area; place extra fiberfill in the cheeks for shaping.
6. To help the doll sit better, pour plastic filler beads into the lower body up to the bottom of the opening. Firmly stuff the rest of the body with fiberfill; hand-sew the opening closed.

LEGS

1. Sew the leg pieces together in pairs, leaving the tops open for stuffing.
2. Clip the foot curves and turn the legs right side out. Firmly stuff the legs to the topstitching lines.
3. Pinch each leg so the back and front leg seams are aligned and centered. Sew across each top-stitching line. Each upper leg remains unstuffed.
4. Turn the top edges of the legs under ¼ inch; sew across the folded edges to close the legs.
5. Hand-sew the legs to the body atop the side seams, leaving ¼ inch between the legs at the center body seam.

HAIR

1. For the boy's hair, cut a 2½x5-inch piece of cardboard. Wind the yarn around the 2½-inch width of the cardboard until the yarn is padded and 3 inches wide.
2. Gently slide the yarn off the cardboard. Place a piece of paper under the yarn and sew through the paper and the yarn at one side of the looped ends. Pull the paper away from the yarn, and cut the yarn loops opposite the sewn end.
3. With a hot-glue gun, place a circle of glue on the top of the head. Arrange the sewn end of yarn to form a circle in the glue. Trim the yarn to fashion the hair.
4. For the girl's hair follow steps 1-3 *above,* except use a 5½-inch square of cardboard. Cut bangs and tie a ponytail with the ⅛-inch-wide ribbon on the top of her head.

GIRL'S DRESS

1. Cut one of the bodice pieces along the fold line to make two bodice back pieces.
2. Sew the bodice front to the bodice backs at the shoulder seams. Press the seams open.
3. Press under ⅛ inch along the neckline edge and ¼ inch along the center back bodice edges. Topstitch close to the folds.
4. Sew gathering stitches along one side of each sleeve square. Pull up the gathers to fit the sleeves into the armhole openings of the bodice. Pin and sew the sleeves to the bodice.
5. Press under a ¾-inch hem for each sleeve at the wrist edges. Sew the elastic ⅝ inch from the folds on the wrong fabric side, stretching the elastic as you sew.
6. Sew the underarm and side seams of the bodice.
7. Sew the 5-inch sides of the skirt together.
8. Sew gathering stitches along one unfinished edge of the skirt. Pull up the gathers, fitting the skirt to the bodice waist. Lap the bodice backs ¼ inch and sew the skirt to the bodice waist.
9. Press under ¼ inch twice for the skirt hem; machine- or hand-sew the hem in place.
10. Apply a snap to the back of the bodice, or slip-stitch the dress to the doll.

GIRL'S PANTALOONS

1. For pantaloons tips and diagrams, refer to the tip box on page 130.
2. To establish the inside leg seams, fold one of the 7½-inch squares in half to form a 3¾x7½-inch rectangle. Use a pencil to make a dot ¼ inch from the fold on both fabric layers on one 3¾-inch side.
3. Make a dot on the fold 4½ inches above the first dots. Unfold the fabric and use a ruler to connect each edge dot to the fold dot, forming a narrow V shape. Place the marked square on top

continued

of the unmarked square. Sew along the pencil lines to form inseams. Cut along the fold between the stitching to the point of the V.

4. Press under a 1-inch hem for each leg opening. Sew the elastic ⅞ inch from the fold on the wrong side, stretching the elastic as you sew.

5. Sew the two side leg seams together and turn the pantaloons right side out. Press under the waist edge ¼ inch. Sew the elastic ⅛ inch from the fold on the wrong side, stretching the elastic as you sew.

BOY'S SHIRT

1. Follow steps 1-4 and 6 for Girl's Dress on page 71 with the following exceptions: the shirt piece cut in half on the fold becomes the shirt fronts; gather each sleeve on one of the 2½-inch sides.

2. Press under ¼ inch for the shirt hem. Topstitch close to the folded edge.

3. For cuffs, roll back the sleeves ¾ inch two times. Press the cuffs in place.

4. Dress the doll; slip-stitch the shirt fronts together, or apply closures as desired.

5. Cut a triangle scarf from a fabric scrap and tie it around the doll's neck, as shown in the photo on page 70.

BOY'S OVERALLS

1. Sew the two bib pieces together along the top edge between the small dots. Clip the curves and turn the bib right side out; press.

2. Sew the two overalls pants pieces together along the center front seam. Clip the curves; press the seam open.

3. Matching the center front dots, sew the pants to the bib at the waistline seam. Press the seam allowance toward the pants, and topstitch close to the seam through all fabric thicknesses.

4. Sew the center back seam of the pants and bib. Sew the inner leg seams; clip curves and turn the overalls right side out.

5. To form the pants cuffs, roll back each leg ½ inch two times; press cuffs in place.

6. To make the overalls straps, press under ¼ inch on all raw edges of both the 1x4½-inch strips. Fold the strips in half lengthwise, wrong sides together; press. Topstitch along the center long edge of the strip to finish the straps.

7. Join one edge of each strap to the bib front by sewing buttons at Xs on the pattern, sewing through both the bib and the straps. Slip overalls onto doll; cross the straps in the back and tack them ½ inch from the center back seam, adjusting the length to fit.

BOY'S GLASSES

1. Using the pattern on page 73, bend the gold wire to form the glasses.

2. With flesh-color thread, tack the glasses to the doll's face just above the eyebrows.

72

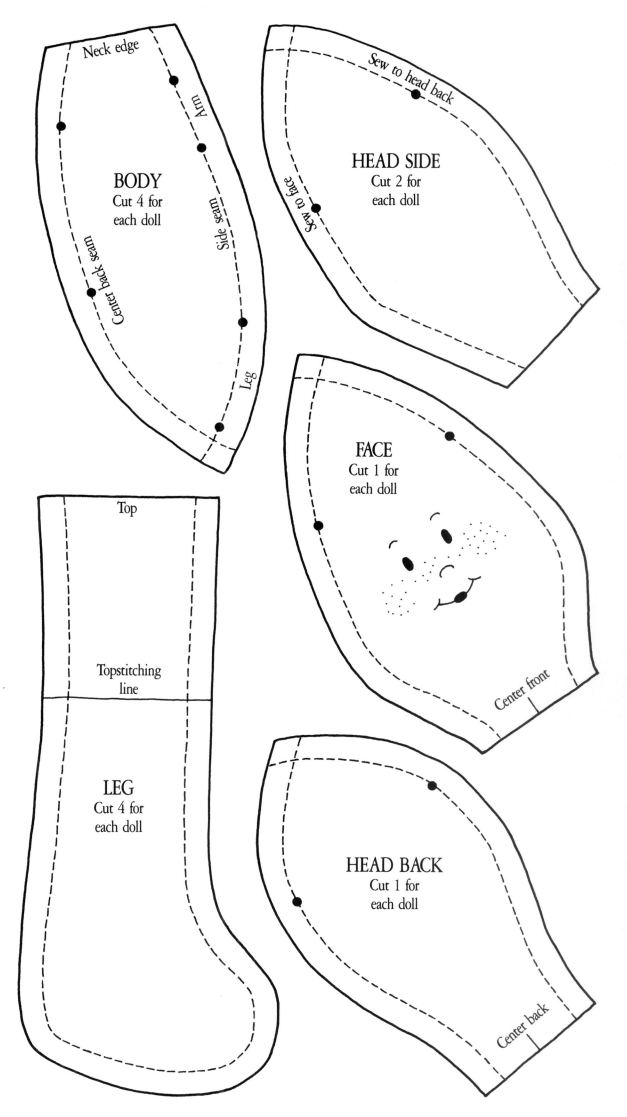

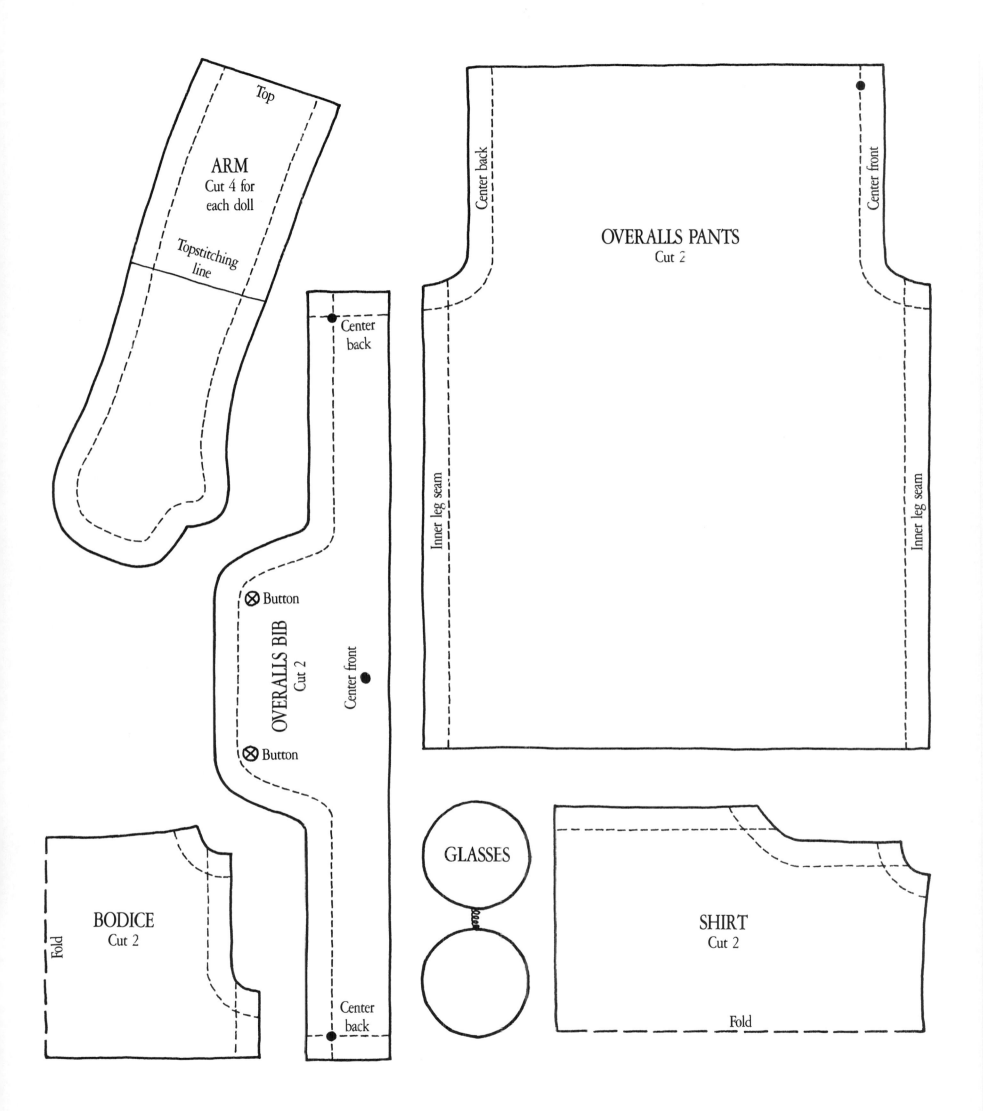

ARM
Cut 4 for
each doll

Top

Topstitching line

OVERALLS PANTS
Cut 2

Center back

Center front

Inner leg seam

Inner leg seam

Center back

⊗ Button

OVERALLS BIB
Cut 2

Center front

⊗ Button

Center back

BODICE
Cut 2

Fold

GLASSES

SHIRT
Cut 2

Fold

Sir Rupert Rabbit

This dashing gentleman rabbit could easily be second cousin to the White Rabbit in Lewis Carroll's *Alice's Adventures in Wonderland*. He's smartly dressed in a fashionable vest, silky ascot, and a pocket watch that suggests that rabbits have much to do and must be on time. This debonair fellow is made using scraps of contrasting fur for his cheeks and inner ears. Use him to welcome spring as he stands 19 inches tall next to an Easter basket of dyed eggs or peeping through a bouquet of daffodils.

MATERIALS FOR
SIR RUPERT RABBIT

½ yard of short-nap fur for body

¼ yard of a contrasting fur for
ears and cheeks

¼ yard of print fabric (A) for vest

¼ yard of a coordinating print fabric (B) for
collar, pocket flap, and vest lining

¼ yard of silky fabric for ascot

Two 1¾-inch-diameter D doll joints

Two ⅝-inch-diameter half-dome shank
buttons for eyes

One 18-mm black triangle for nose

Three fancy buttons for vest

½ yard of ⅜-inch-wide braid trim for vest

Purchased felt doll top hat

6 inches of metal chain for watch fob

⅓ yard of ⅜-inch-wide satin ribbon

Small silk flowers and leaves

Crafts glue

1½-inch-diameter snap frame with hanger

1½-inch-diameter picture of a clock face

Dollmaker's needle; fishing line

Black and tan carpet threads

◆

PREPARING THE PATTERNS

Trace the full-size patterns, *opposite* and on
pages 78–81, onto tracing paper. For the
body, join the AB line on page 78 with
the AB line on page 79 to make one
complete pattern. Cut out the patterns.

◆

CUTTING THE FABRICS

Refer to Cutting the Fabrics on page 30
for tips about cutting fur.

From body fur, cut:
- ◆ Two body
  fronts
- ◆ One body back
- ◆ Two feet
- ◆ Two soles
- ◆ Four arms
- ◆ Two heads
- ◆ Two muzzles
- ◆ Two ears
- ◆ One 5-inch-
  diameter circle
  for tail

*From contrasting fur,
cut:*
- ◆ Two ears
- ◆ Two cheeks

*From each print A and
B fabric, cut:*
- ◆ Two vest fronts
- ◆ One vest back
- ◆ Two tails
- ◆ Two collars
- ◆ One pocket flap

From silky fabric, cut:
- ◆ Two ascots

GENERAL INSTRUCTIONS

1. After cutting the fur, transfer the Xs to the pile side of the fabric using brightly colored tailor's tacks (see the tip box, page 31). The remaining construction markings can be transferred to the wrong side of the pile.

2. Before stitching fur pieces together, brush the pile away from the seam line. After sewing, use a straight pin to pull the pile from the seam. This technique blends the fur and conceals the seams. Trim the pile remaining in the seam allowance to reduce bulk.

BODY

1. Sew the body front pieces together along the center front seam.

2. Sew the body front to the body back at the sides, leaving openings at the leg openings and between the dots on both sides.

FEET

1. To shape the toes, sew the darts in each foot. Sew the center back seam of each foot.

2. With right sides facing and raw edges even, slip a foot into each leg opening, matching the ankle and leg dots. Sew around the ankles to join the feet to the legs.

3. Pull out the feet from inside the legs. Pin a sole to the bottom edge of each foot, matching the dots on each sole to the center dart seam and the center back seam of each foot. Sew the soles to the feet. Turn the body right side out.

ARMS

1. Sew arms together in pairs, leaving openings between the dots. Turn each arm right side out.

2. Determine which side of each arm will be the inner arm (the side closest to the body). Make sure both arms face forward. Snip a couple of threads at both inner arm and upper body Xs, making holes large enough for the stem of the joint to fit snugly through the arm and into the body.

3. Insert a joint into the inner arm through the opening. Push the stem through the snipped hole and into the body hole. On the inside of the body, slide the spacer disk onto the stem. Push the locking disk onto the stem as far as it will go. Repeat to joint the second arm.

4. Firmly stuff the legs and lower body with fiberfill. Hand-sew one of the side openings closed. Finish stuffing the body; hand-sew the remaining side closed. Firmly stuff the arms and hand-sew the arm openings closed.

5. Using a dollmaker's needle that is double-threaded with tan carpet thread, take a deep stitch through the foot, between the Xs. Start the sewing at one X and bring the needle out at the other

X. Take the thread around the top of the foot, and return the needle back into the first X. Pull the thread tightly to create an indentation that causes the toes to turn up. Repeat the stitch once more, then tie off the thread. Shape the toes of the second foot in the same manner.

HEAD

1. Sew the head pieces together, leaving an opening between the dots. Clip the curves and turn the head right side out. Firmly stuff the head with fiberfill; hand-sew the opening closed.

2. Sew the muzzle pieces together along the center front seam. Turn the muzzle right side out and stuff. Turn under the raw edges of the muzzle; pin it to one head piece (front) along the muzzle placement line. Hand-sew the muzzle to the head.

FACE

1. Sew a gathering stitch on the seam line of each cheek. Slightly pull up the threads to create a pouch and leave an opening. Stuff the cheeks. Pull the thread to close the opening; knot the thread. Hand-sew the cheeks to the head at each X, placing the gathered side next to the head.

2. Using a dollmaker's needle that is double-threaded with black carpet thread, sew the eyes to the head where indicated. Make one straight stitch for each eyebrow. Make a straight stitch across the muzzle for the mouth; pull the thread to form a slight indentation. Knot the thread.

3. Glue the nose triangle to the tip of the muzzle.

4. For each whisker, pull a single strand of fishing line through the muzzle between the nose and the cheeks. Cut the line, leaving a 2½- to 3-inch tail on each side of the muzzle. Tie an overhand knot in each tail as close to the muzzle as possible. Make four more whiskers in the same manner.

EARS

1. Sew the ears together in pairs, matching a body fur ear with a contrasting fur ear and leaving the bottom edges open. Turn each ear right side out.

2. Turn under the bottom edge of each ear ¼ inch and fold the ear in half lengthwise; tack the fold in place. Blindstitch the ears to the head with the contrasting fur facing forward.

3. Hand-sew the head to the top of the body.

TAIL

1. Sew a gathering stitch on the seam line of the tail circle. Slightly pull up the threads to create a pouch and leave an opening. Stuff the tail. Pull the threads to close the opening; knot the thread. Hand-sew the tail to the body at the X, placing the gathered side next to the body.

VEST FRONTS

1. Pair each fabric B vest collar piece with a fabric A lining piece. Sew the matched pieces together, leaving the neck and shoulder edges open. Clip curves and turn each collar right side out; press.

2. Pin the neck and shoulder edges of each collar to a fabric A vest front with the collar linings and the right sides of the vest fronts together. Baste the collars in place.

3. Stitch the fabric B pocket flap to the fabric A lining, leaving an opening between the dots. Trim the corners, turn the flap right side out, and press. Pin the flap to the right side of a vest front on the placement line. Topstitch the flap to the vest along the top edge. Set the vest fronts aside.

VEST BACK AND SHOULDERS

1. Sew the top edge of the fabric A tails to the fabric A vest back. Repeat with the lining tails and back.

2. Sew vest fronts to vest back at the shoulder seams. Sew lining fronts to lining back at the shoulder seams. Press shoulder seams open, and press the tail seam toward the vest back.

VEST ASSEMBLY

1. Lay the vest (fabric A) atop the vest lining (fabric B). Match all edges and pin in place.

2. Join the lining to the vest by sewing around the entire perimeter, leaving the side seams open between the dots.

3. Trim the points, and clip the curves. Turn the vest right side out by pulling the fabric through one side seam. Press the vest. Turn under the lining (fabric B) in each of the side seam openings and hand-sew the openings closed.

4. Turn under and hand-sew each of the vest (fabric A) side seam openings closed.

FINISHING

1. Glue the braided trim around the outside edges of the collars and across the bottom edge of the pocket flap.

2. Slip the vest onto the rabbit, overlapping the center front edges ⅝ inch. Sew the decorative buttons evenly spaced down the front of the vest, sewing through all layers of fabric.

3. Fold the pleat in the vest back. Hand-sew the pleat in place from the neck edge to tail seam.

4. Place the picture of the watch in the snap frame. Tack one end of the watch chain under the middle button and the other end under the pocket flap. Tack the watch to the chain.

5. Glue the ribbon around the hat for a hatband. Trim the hat with flowers and leaves. Tack the hat in the rabbit's hand.

ASCOT

1. Sew the ascot pieces together, leaving an opening between the dots. Turn ascot right side out and press. Hand-sew the opening closed.

2. Tie the ascot around the rabbit's neck and tuck the ends inside the vest.

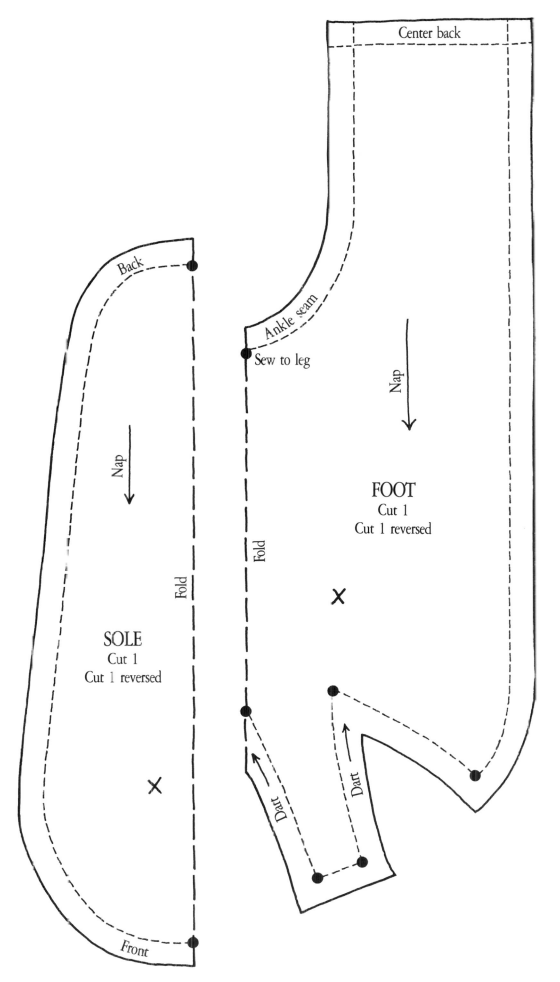

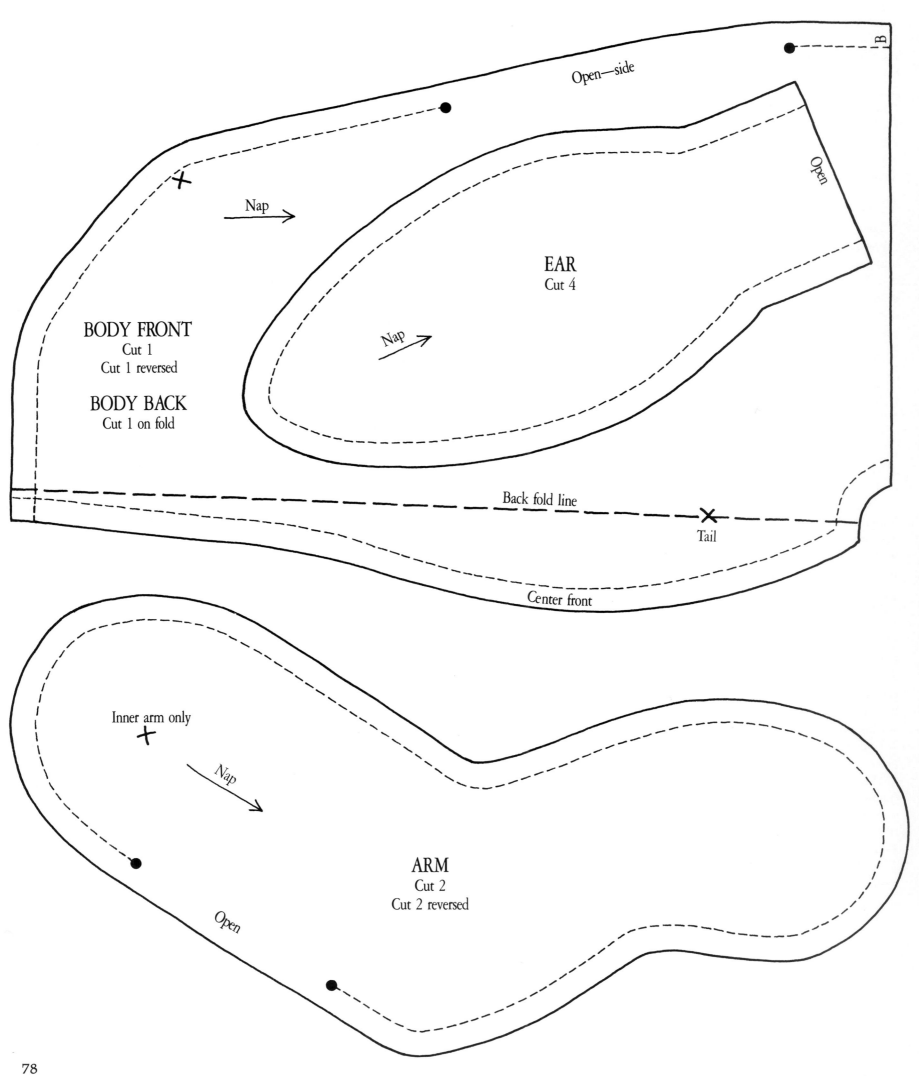

Open—side

B

Open

EAR
Cut 4

Nap →

Nap →

BODY FRONT
Cut 1
Cut 1 reversed

BODY BACK
Cut 1 on fold

Back fold line

Tail

Center front

Inner arm only

Nap →

ARM
Cut 2
Cut 2 reversed

Open

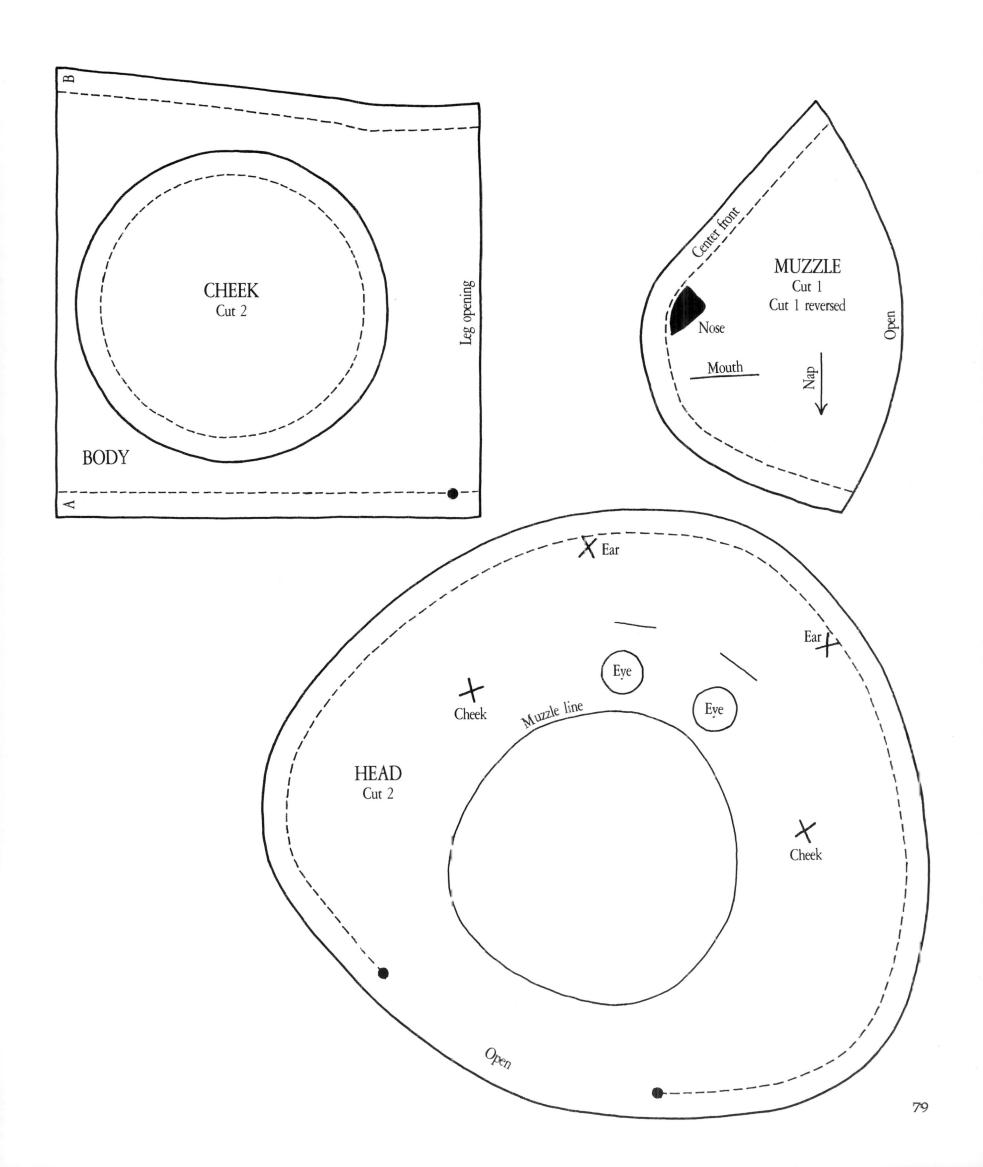

CHEEK
Cut 2

BODY

B

A

Leg opening

MUZZLE
Cut 1
Cut 1 reversed

Center front

Nose

Mouth

Nap

Open

Ear

Ear

Eye

Eye

Cheek

Muzzle line

Cheek

HEAD
Cut 2

Open

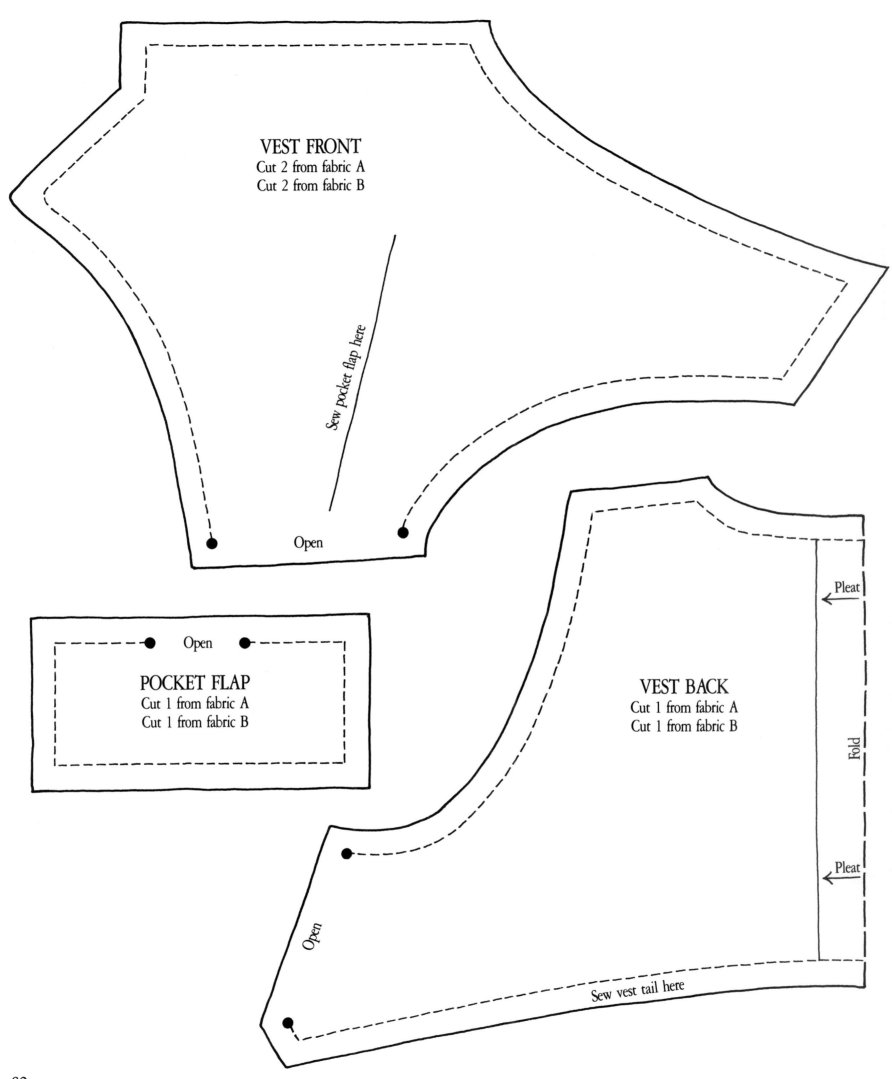

VEST FRONT
Cut 2 from fabric A
Cut 2 from fabric B

Sew pocket flap here

Open

POCKET FLAP
Cut 1 from fabric A
Cut 1 from fabric B

Open

VEST BACK
Cut 1 from fabric A
Cut 1 from fabric B

Pleat

Fold

Pleat

Open

Sew vest tail here

80

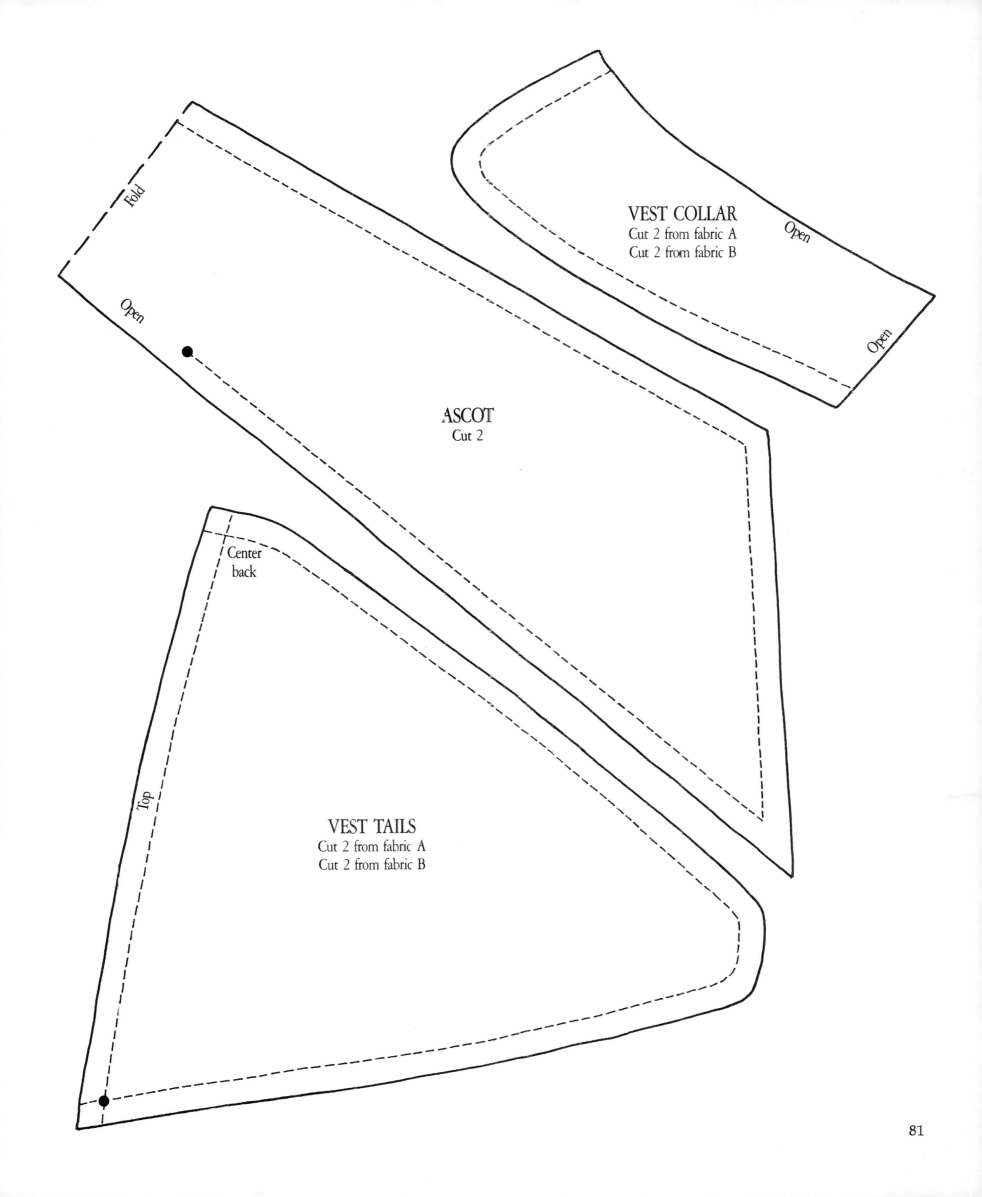

Fold

Open

ASCOT
Cut 2

VEST COLLAR
Cut 2 from fabric A
Cut 2 from fabric B

Open

Open

Center
back

Top

VEST TAILS
Cut 2 from fabric A
Cut 2 from fabric B

Florence & Phoebe

Give thanks for the homespun goodness of these long-legged angels with patchwork wings! All angels are sisters in heaven, but Florence and Phoebe are true kindred spirits. They dress alike in simple skirts with lace-trimmed bodices. They walk alike on spindly legs that bend at the knee and end in high-top boots "laced" with cross-stitches of buttonhole twist. And both are 26 inches tall. So you can tell them apart, give your angels unique hairdos and one-of-a-kind faces drawn with fine-tip permanent markers.

GENERAL INSTRUCTIONS

The instructions are for sewing one doll. Repeat these directions to make the second doll.

ARMS AND HANDS

1. Sew the short end of one arm to a hand that has the thumb pointing to the left. Make another arm/hand unit in the same manner. Make the two remaining arm/hand units with the thumbs pointing to the right. Sew the units together in pairs, leaving the tops open. Clip curves and turn each arm right side out.
2. Lightly stuff each hand with fiberfill. Topstitch the fingers along the placement lines.
3. Firmly stuff each arm to about 1 inch below the opening. Pin the top of each arm together, with the seams at the sides.

LEGS

1. Sew a short end of one leg to the top of one shoe that has the toe pointing to the left. Make another leg/shoe unit in the same manner. Then make two leg/shoe units with the toes pointing to the right. Sew the units together in pairs; leave the tops open. Clip curves; turn legs right side out.
2. Firmly stuff each shoe. Insert one 5-inch dowel into each leg; stuff 1 inch more. Insert another 5-inch dowel. Pin the top of each leg together so the seams run up the center front and center back.

HEAD AND BODY

1. Trace the facial features onto a head piece, using the brown permanent marker. Sew the head to one body piece for the front. Stitch the second head to the second body piece for the back.
2. Pin the arms to the body front between the dots with the thumbs pointing toward the center of the body and the raw edges even. Pin the body back to the body front. Sew the body sections together, leaving openings between the small dots at one side and the bottom.
3. Clip curves and turn the body right side out.
4. Turn under the bottom openings ¼ inch. Insert the legs into the openings with the toes pointing forward; topstitch or hand-sew in place.
5. Firmly stuff the head and body. Hand-sew the side opening closed.

SKIRT

1. Fold the waistband in half lengthwise. Machine-sew across each short end. Turn the waistband right side out and press; set aside.
2. Press under one long edge of the skirt rectangle ¼ inch. Press under the same edge ½ inch and sew in place for hem.
3. Pin the short edges of the rectangle together. Sew the edges together from the hem to 3 inches below the top of the skirt. This seam will become the center back seam.

4. Gather the unfinished edge of the skirt to fit the waistband. Sew the waistband to the skirt.

5. Place the skirt on the doll, tacking the waistband closed.

WINGS

1. Refer to the tip on pages 86 and 87 to make two 12x18-inch pieces of crazy patchwork. Cut out the wings from the pieces.

2. Sew the wings together along the straight edges, leaving an opening between the dots. Sew the muslin wings together along the straight edges. Do not leave an opening in the muslin. Press seams open on both pieces.

3. Sew the outside edges of the two wing pieces together. Clip the curves and turn the wings right side out. Hand-sew the opening closed. Tack the wings to the center of the angel's back.

FLORENCE'S HAIR

1. For the bangs, cut two ¾-inch pieces of the flax. Tack or glue the flax pieces to the forehead ½ inch above the facial features. Trim the ends of the flax in a straight line just above the eyebrows.

2. For the wig, locate the center of the remaining strand of flax and spread it to a width of 2½ inches. Machine-stitch across the center to form a part. Center the wig's part on the doll's head, covering the top edges of the bangs with the front edge of the wig. Glue the wig in place.

3. Comb the wig and fashion it into braids at the sides of the head, tying the braid ends with package twine. Add additional glue around the face and neck edges to hold the hair in place.

PHOEBE'S HAIR

1. For the bangs, cut five ¾-inch pieces of curly wool. Tack or glue the pieces to the head, side by side, ½ inch above the facial features. Trim the ends in a straight line just above the eyebrows.

2. For the remainder of the hair, glue eight to ten 2½-inch-long tufts of wool along the head seam.

FINISHING THE DOLL

1. Brush the cheeks with blush.

2. To lace the shoes, thread a needle with a single strand of buttonhole twist. Referring to the drawing, *above,* leave a 4-inch tail, and sew half Xs from the top edge of the shoe to the dot; then complete the second half of the Xs from the dot to the top of the shoe. Leaving a 4-inch-long tail, cut the thread. Tie the tails in a bow.

3. Tack lace around each wrist over the seam.

4. For Florence, drape the handkerchief around her neck with the handkerchief corner at the center front. Glue or tack the ends of the handkerchief in place at the back of the body.

5. For Phoebe, tack lace around the neckline over the seam. Tack a V-shape neckline from the shoulders to the center front of her dress. Sew the buttons to the center front of the dress inside the V shape.

6. For Florence's halo, shape the artificial greenery into a circle and glue it to the top of her head.

7. Tack the fingers of Florence's hands together as shown in the photo on pages 82 and 83.

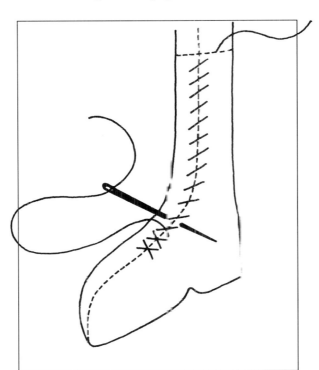

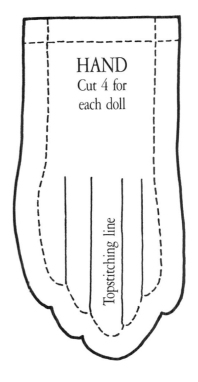

HAND
Cut 4 for
each doll

Topstitching line

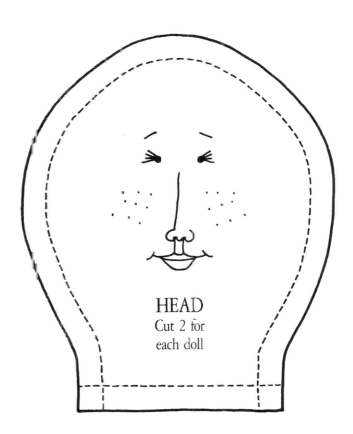

HEAD
Cut 2 for
each doll

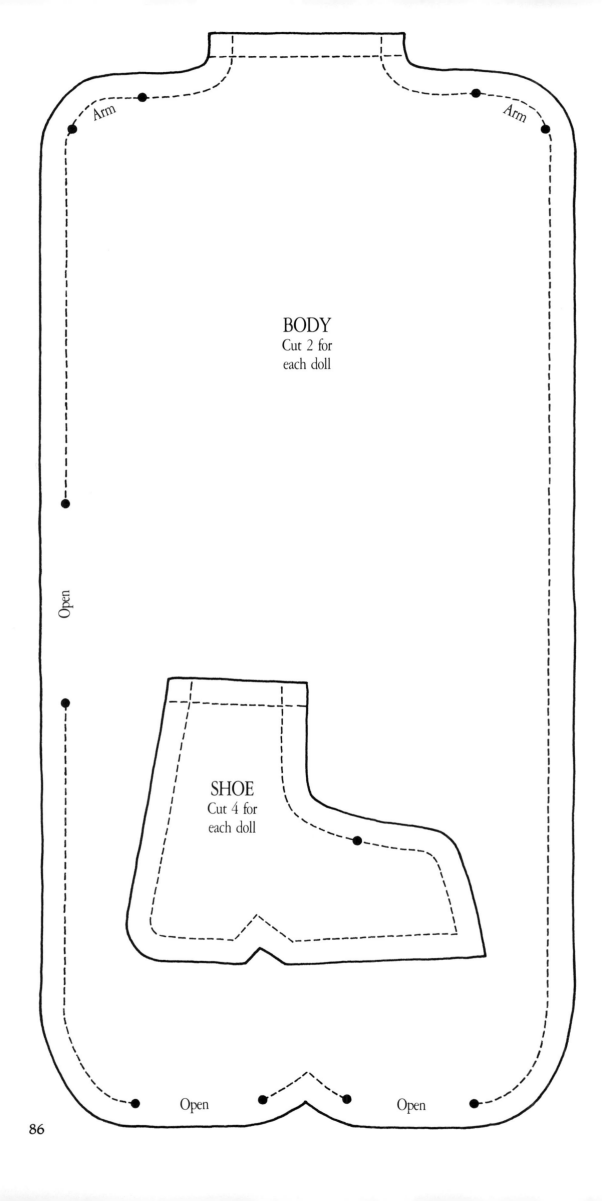

BODY
Cut 2 for
each doll

Arm

Arm

Open

SHOE
Cut 4 for
each doll

Open

Open

SCRAP FABRIC WINGS

Use this technique to make crazy patchwork wings for the angels if you do not have a cutter's quilt (an old tattered quilt that is beyond use but has usable patches that can be cut from the quilt and used for creative sewing) or any suitable pre-quilted fabric.

Begin with a 14x20-inch piece of muslin for the foundation for *each* wing. Use scraps of other fabrics for the patchwork to sew onto the foundation piece in the following manner.

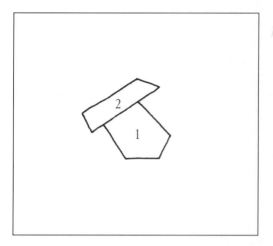

1. Sew a scrap that has five or six sides to the center of the foundation muslin. With right sides facing, sew the next fabric piece onto any side of the first piece using a ¼-inch seam allowance. Flip the second piece right side up and press it flat.

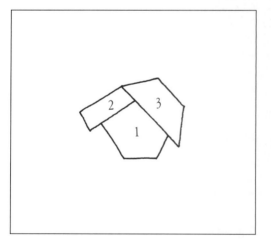

2. Sew a third piece, with right sides facing, onto the next side of the center piece, making sure it completely covers the edges of the first two pieces. Trim the excess fabric from the seam allowance. Flip this piece right side up and press.

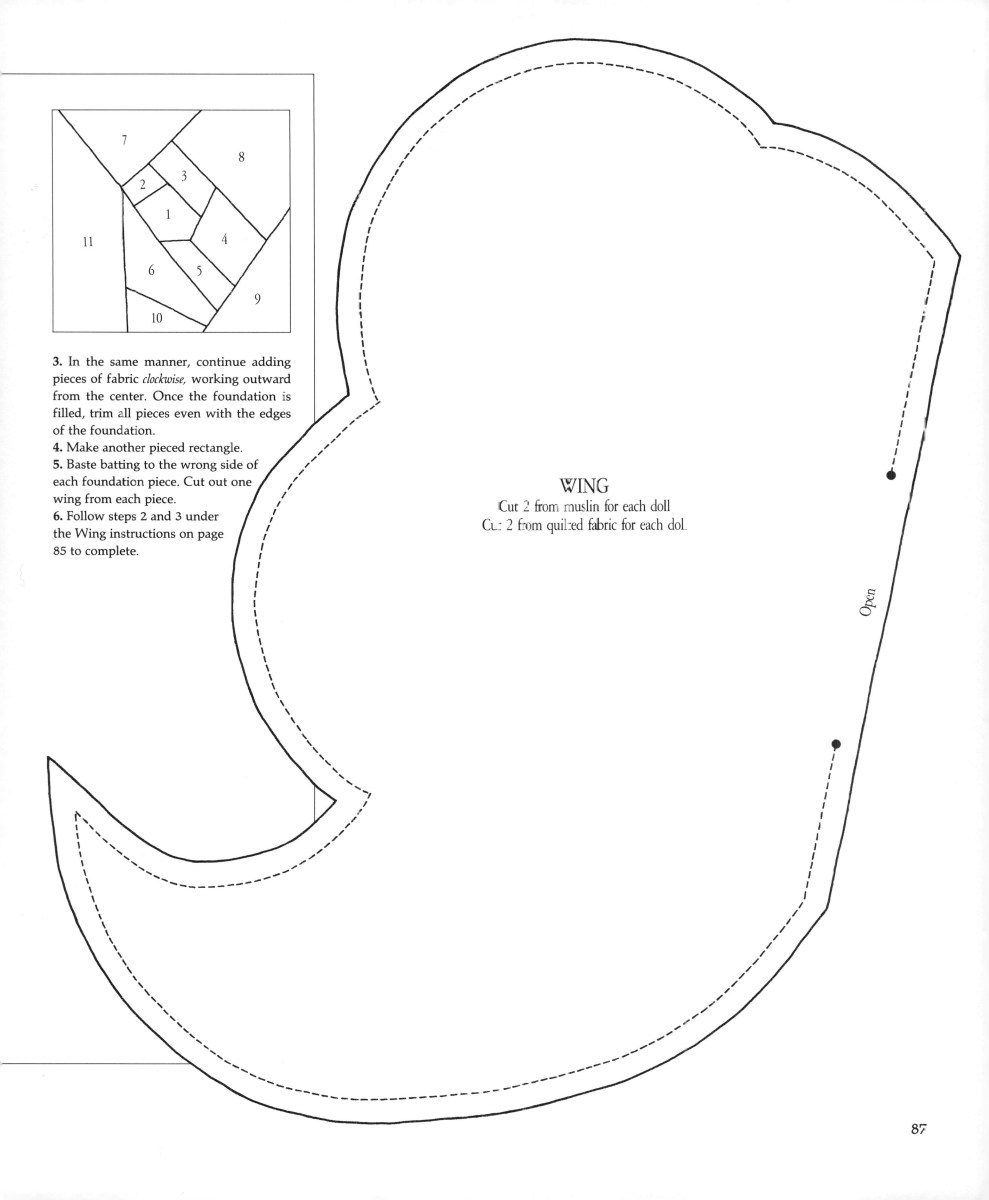

3. In the same manner, continue adding pieces of fabric *clockwise,* working outward from the center. Once the foundation is filled, trim all pieces even with the edges of the foundation.

4. Make another pieced rectangle.

5. Baste batting to the wrong side of each foundation piece. Cut out one wing from each piece.

6. Follow steps 2 and 3 under the Wing instructions on page 85 to complete.

WING
Cut 2 from muslin for each doll
Cut 2 from quilted fabric for each doll

Open

Pauline

Every antique lover knows the refined
dolls of a century ago, those with perfect
ringlets and elegant clothing. But the rough,
homemade dolls of rural folk were loved
to the last fiber of their stuffing, used up, and
worn out. Our renditions of these primitive
dolls are ideal collectibles for today's lover of
country crafts.

Pauline and Paulette are 13 inches tall. Their
bodies are made of a coarse fabric, hand-sewn
with running stitches of embroidery floss. The
seam allowances remain outside of the doll.

Paulette

Paulette is fashioned just like Pauline.
Both winsome critters are loosely
stuffed so they sit easily on a shelf
or a pint-size chair. Their bloomers
and dresses are simple shapes, easy to cut
and sew, that are gathered at the neck and
sleeves. Plaids, checks, and calico fabrics
enhance the homespun look of the outfits.

These are just two of the possibilities that
you can make from these basic body patterns.
With a little alteration, you can create puppies,
pigs, or a whole clan of creature cousins.

MATERIALS FOR PAULETTE THE BUNNY

¼ yard of osnaburg, or any ecru even-weave fabric

¼ yard of muslin

¼ yard of blue print fabric

Two ¼-inch-diameter buttons

One skein *each* of navy and red embroidery floss

Scraps of pink embroidery floss

9 inches of ¹⁄₁₆-inch-wide ribbon

Scrap of iron-on interfacing

Scrap of pink fabric

Polyester fiberfill; crafts glue

Powder blush

◆

PREPARING THE PATTERNS

Trace the full-size patterns for Paulette on pages 92, 93, and 95 onto tracing paper. Cut out the patterns.

◆

CUTTING THE FABRICS

The cutting instructions for pieces that have no patterns include ¼-inch seams.

From osnaburg or even-weave fabric, cut:
◆ One head gusset
◆ Two head sides
◆ Two body fronts
◆ Two body backs
◆ Four ears
◆ Four arms
◆ Four legs

From muslin, cut:
◆ Two pantaloons
◆ Two hearts for the necklace

From blue print, tear:
◆ One 10x6-inch dress front
◆ One 6-inch square for dress back
◆ Two 7x4½-inch dress sleeves
◆ Two 8x1¼-inch strips for dress ties

GENERAL INSTRUCTIONS

1. All body pieces are hand-sewn together with running stitches using six strands of navy embroidery floss. Stitches should be ¼ inch in length, ¼ inch from the raw edges, and a scant ¼ inch apart.
2. Hand-sew all the pieces together with *wrong sides facing.*

PAULETTE'S HEAD

1. Sew the ear pieces together in pairs, leaving the tops open. Do not stuff the ears.

2. Sew the center front seam of the head side pieces from the small dot to the neck edge. Matching the nose dots, pin the head gusset to the head side pieces.
3. Flop one ear to mirror the other ear. Fold the ears in half on the fold line. With the folded edge facing the back of the head, pin the ears where indicated on the head sides. Sew the gusset to the head sides, catching the ears in the seam.

PAULETTE'S LEGS AND ARMS

1. Sew the legs and arms together in pairs, leaving the tops open.
2. Lightly stuff the paws with fiberfill to the gathering line.
3. With a double strand of thread that matches the fabric, hand-sew running stitches through both layers of fabric, crossing the gathering lines at the ankles and wrists. Pull the threads to gather the fabric. Knot the threads to secure the gathers.

PAULETTE'S BODY

1. Sew the center back seam of the body back pieces together.
2. Beginning at the neck edge, sew the center front seam of the body front pieces together to the dot.
3. Pin the front and back body pieces together at the side seams. Insert the arms and legs in the body between the matching pair of dots. Sew the body pieces together, catching the arms and legs in the seams, leaving the neck open.
4. Firmly stuff the head and the body with fiberfill. Sew the head to the body at the neck opening, adding fiberfill as necessary.

PAULETTE'S DRESS

1. To form the shoulder seams and the neck opening, match the 6-inch sides of the dress front with the dress back. With right sides together, machine-sew a 1-inch seam on the opposite edges of each of the 6-inch sides (see the drawing, *below*).

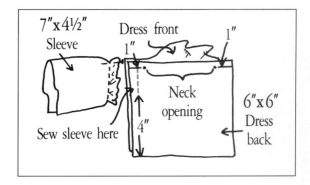

2. With red floss, hand-sew running stitches around the neck opening, ½ inch from edge. Begin and end the sewing at the center of the dress back. Leave enough floss to gather the neckline and tie a bow.
3. Machine-sew a gathering stitch along one 7-inch side of each sleeve. Use a pin to mark the center of the gathering stitches. Pull up the gathers until the sleeve edges measure 4 inches.
4. With right sides facing, center the marked gathered sleeve edges on the shoulder seams. Machine-sew the sleeves to the dress.
5. Fold a small pleat in one of the 1¼-inch sides of each tie. Pin the pleated end of each tie ½ inch below each sleeve seam. With right sides facing, machine-sew the arm and side seams, catching the ties in the seam. Turn the dress right side out.
6. With red floss, sew decorative running stitches ¼ inch from the sleeve and hem edges. To gather the fabric at the wrists, sew running stitches 1 inch from the raw edges. Begin and end the sewing opposite the underarm seams. Leave enough floss to gather and tie a bow.
7. Slip dress onto doll, pull up gathers at the neckline and wrist, and tie floss into bows. Tie the dress ties into a bow at the back of the doll.

PAULETTE'S PANTALOONS

1. With right sides facing, machine-sew the front and back pantaloon pieces together at the inner leg and side seams. Clip the inner leg seam as marked; turn the pantaloons right side out.
2. With floss, sew decorative running stitches ¼ inch from the raw edge of each leg opening.
3. To fit the pantaloons to Paulette's body, sew floss running stitches ¼ inch from the waist edge, and 1 inch from the leg edges. Begin and end the sewing at the center front of each leg and the waist. Leave enough floss so it can be tied into bows at the ankles and waist. Slip the pantaloons onto the doll, pull up gathers, and tie bows.

FINISHING PAULETTE

1. For eyes, sew buttons to front of head at Xs. Begin sewing at the back of the neck, and bring the needle out at one of the eye placements. Thread the button onto the needle, and return the needle through the eye placement and to the back of the neck. Pull the threads to indent and shape the eye. Knot the thread to secure the shaping. Sew the other button eye in the same manner.

2. To make the nose, fuse interfacing to the back of the pink fabric scrap. Trace around the heart pattern on the pink fabric; cut out the heart. Using three strands of pink floss, outline the heart with 1/8-inch-long running stitches. Glue the heart to the face, placing the tip of the heart at the intersection of the head sides and gusset.

3. Apply blush to the cheeks.

4. Place a little wad of fiberfill between the two muslin hearts. Sew the hearts together with red floss running stitches 1/8 inch from the raw edge.

5. Loop the 1/16-inch-wide ribbon around Paulette's neck. Glue the ribbon ends to the heart.

MATERIALS FOR PAULINE THE KITTY

1/4 yard of osnaburg, or any even-weave fabric

1/4 yard of muslin

1/4 yard of blue print fabric

Two 6-mm black beads

Two skeins of navy blue embroidery floss

One skein of pink embroidery floss

Scrap of iron-on interfacing

Scrap of pink fabric

One wooden heart 1 inch in diameter

Polyester fiberfill; crafts glue

Powder blush

◆

PREPARING THE PATTERNS

Trace the full-size patterns on pages 93–95 onto tracing paper. Cut out the patterns.

◆

CUTTING THE FABRICS

From osnaburg or even-weave fabric, cut:
- ◆ One head front
- ◆ Two head sides
- ◆ Two head backs
- ◆ Two bodies
- ◆ Four ears
- ◆ Four legs

From muslin, cut:
- ◆ Two pantaloons

From blue print, cut:
- ◆ Two dress pieces

GENERAL INSTRUCTIONS

1. All body pieces are hand-sewn together with running stitches using six strands of embroidery floss. Stitches should be 1/4 inch in length, 1/4 inch from the raw edges, and a scant 1/4 inch apart.

2. Unless otherwise specified, stitch all pieces with *wrong sides facing.*

PAULINE'S EARS

1. Sew the ear pieces together in pairs along the side seams only.

2. Fold the small dots to the large dot to form a pleat in each ear; tack pleats to secure.

PAULINE'S HEAD

1. Sew the head side pieces together along the center front seam from the dot to the neck.

2. Using thread that matches the fabric, machine- or hand-sew two rows of gathering stitches between the dots on the head sides.

3. Match the large dots of the head front and head side pieces, and pin the pieces in place. Adjust cheek gathers to fit between the dots. Sew the front and side pieces together with the floss. Do not remove the gathering stitches.

4. Sew the head back pieces together along the center back seam.

5. Pin the front and back head pieces together. Insert the pleated edge of the ears between the head pieces at the markings. Sew the head pieces together, catching the ears in the seam and leaving the neck open.

PAULINE'S LEGS

1. Sew the leg pieces together in pairs, leaving the tops open for stuffing.

2. Lightly stuff the paws with the fiberfill to the gathering line.

3. Pinch the legs so the back and front seams are aligned and centered. With a double strand of thread that matches the fabric, hand-sew running stitches through both layers of fabric, crossing the gathering line. Pull the threads to gather the ankles; knot the threads to secure the gathers. Do not stuff the upper legs.

PAULINE'S BODY

1. Pin the two body pieces together. Insert the top edge of the legs between the dots on the body. Hand-sew the body pieces together, catching the legs in the seam and leaving the neck open.

2. Stuff and gather the paws following steps 2 and 3 of the Leg instructions, *above.* Do not stuff the arms.

---

3. Stuff the head and body with fiberfill. With floss, sew the head to the body at the neck opening, stuffing the neck as necessary.

PAULINE'S PANTALOONS

1. Machine-sew the pantaloon pieces together at the inner leg and side seams. Clip the inner leg seam as marked on the pattern; turn the pantaloons right side out.

2. Use floss to sew decorative running stitches 1/4 inch from the raw edge of the leg openings.

3. To fit the pantaloons to Paulette's body, use floss to sew running stitches 1/4 inch from the waist edge and 1 inch from the leg edges. Begin and end the sewing at the center front of each leg and the waist. Allow enough floss so it can be tied into bows at the ankles and waist. Slip the pantaloons onto the doll, pull up gathers, and tie floss into bows.

PAULINE'S DRESS

1. With right sides facing, machine-sew the side, underarm, and shoulder seams. Turn the dress right side out.

2. Sew decorative running stitches 1/4 inch from the edge of each sleeve, using the navy floss.

3. To trim the dress, sew running stitches 1/2 inch from the neck edge, 1 inch from the sleeve edge, and 1/4 inch from the hem edge. Begin and end the sewing at the center fronts for the hem and neck edges, and at the upper arm seam in the sleeve. Leave enough floss to gather and tie bows.

4. Slip dress onto the doll, pull up gathers, and tie floss into bows.

FINISHING PAULINE

1. For eyes, sew buttons to front of head. Begin sewing at the back of the neck, and bring the needle out at one of the eye placements. Thread a button onto the needle, and return the needle through the eye placement to the back of the neck. Pull the threads to indent and shape the eye. Knot the thread to secure the shaping. Sew the other button eye to the doll in the same manner.

2. To make the nose, fuse interfacing to the back of the pink fabric scrap. Trace around the heart pattern on the pink fabric; cut out the heart. Using three strands of pink floss, outline the heart with 1/8-inch-long running stitches. Glue the heart to the face, placing the tip of the heart at the intersection of the head sides and gusset.

3. Apply blush to the cheeks.

4. To make the necklace, drill two holes through the center top of the wooden heart. Thread six strands of navy floss through the holes, and tie the floss into a bow at the front of the heart.

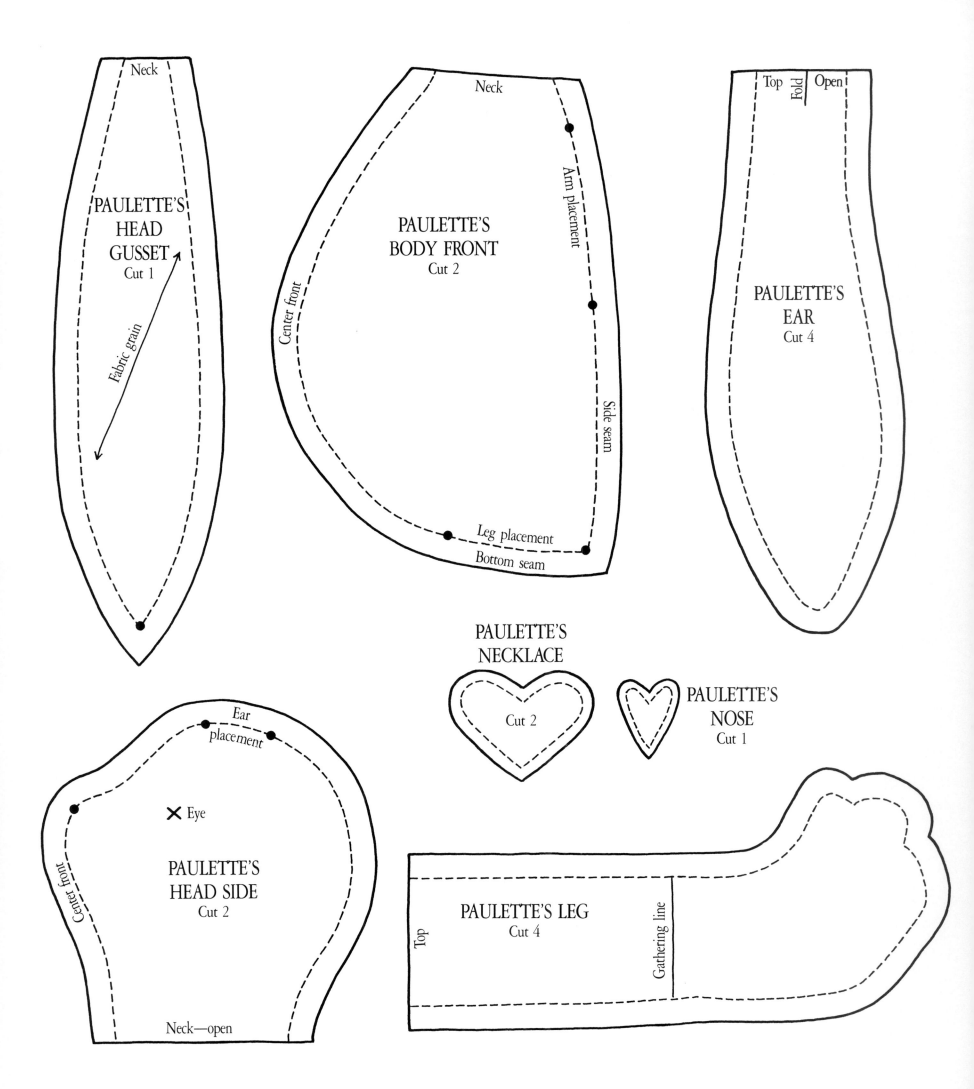

PAULETTE'S
HEAD
GUSSET
Cut 1

Neck

Fabric grain

PAULETTE'S
BODY FRONT
Cut 2

Neck

Center front

Arm placement

Side seam

Leg placement

Bottom seam

Top Fold Open

PAULETTE'S
EAR
Cut 4

PAULETTE'S
NECKLACE

Cut 2

PAULETTE'S
NOSE
Cut 1

Ear
placement

✕ Eye

Center front

PAULETTE'S
HEAD SIDE
Cut 2

Neck—open

Top

PAULETTE'S LEG
Cut 4

Gathering line

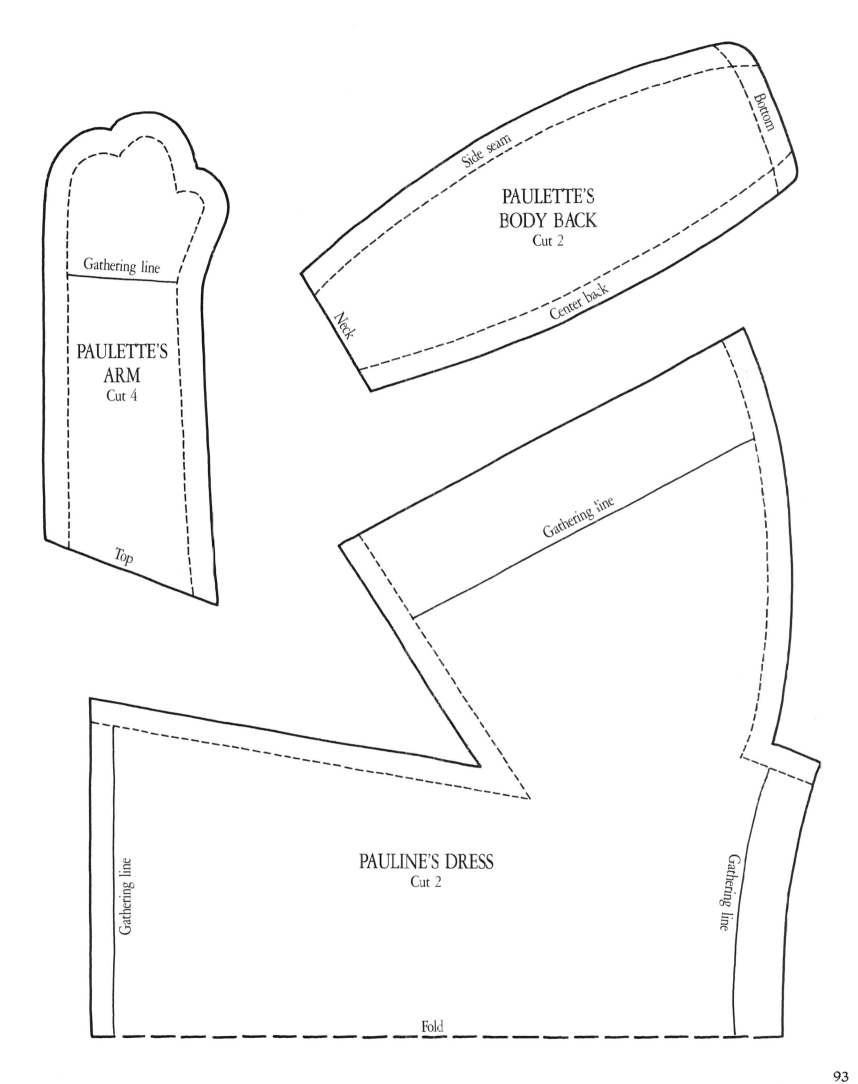

PAULETTE'S
ARM
Cut 4

Gathering line

Top

PAULETTE'S
BODY BACK
Cut 2

Side seam

Bottom

Neck

Center back

Gathering line

PAULINE'S DRESS
Cut 2

Gathering line

Gathering line

Fold

93

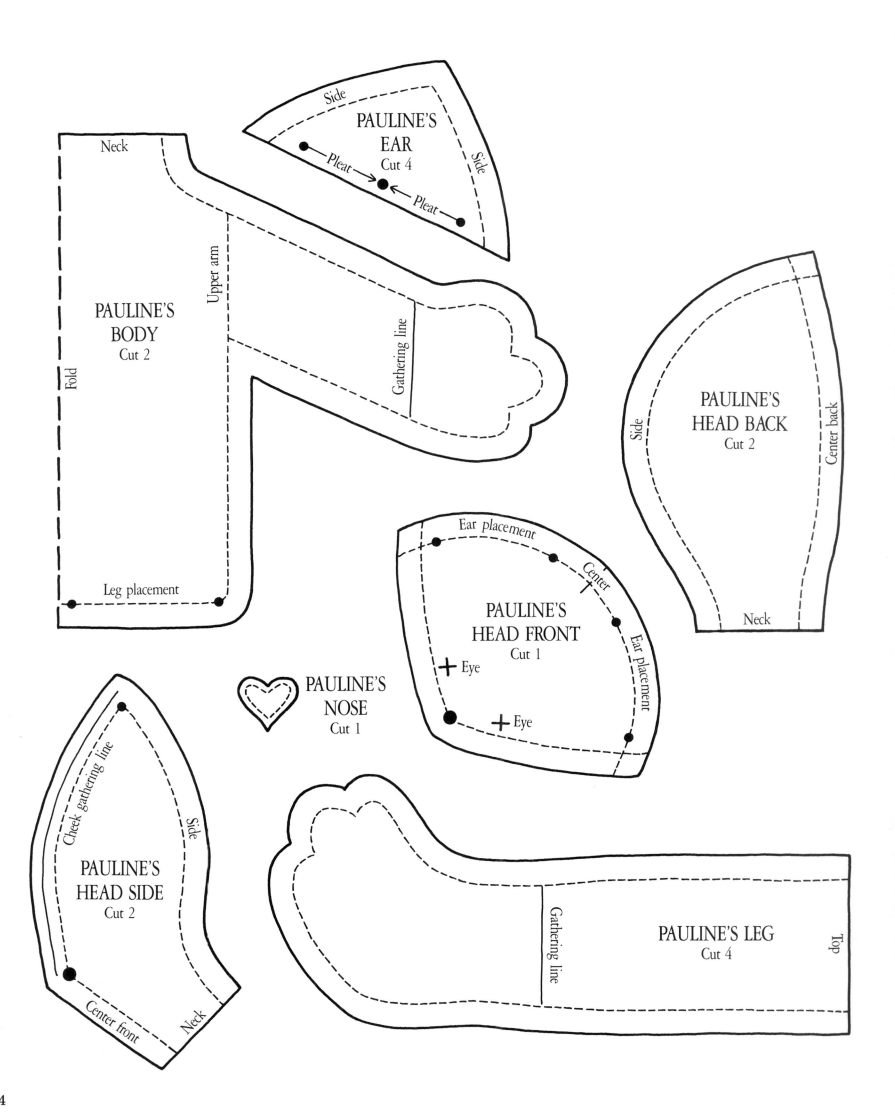

PAULINE'S
EAR
Cut 4

Side
Side
Pleat
Pleat

Neck

PAULINE'S
BODY
Cut 2

Fold

Upper arm

Gathering line

Leg placement

PAULINE'S
HEAD BACK
Cut 2

Side

Center back

Neck

Ear placement

Center

PAULINE'S
HEAD FRONT
Cut 1

Ear placement

Eye

Eye

PAULINE'S
NOSE
Cut 1

Cheek gathering line

Side

PAULINE'S
HEAD SIDE
Cut 2

Center front

Neck

Gathering line

PAULINE'S LEG
Cut 4

Top

94

PAULINE'S PANTALOONS

Front   Back

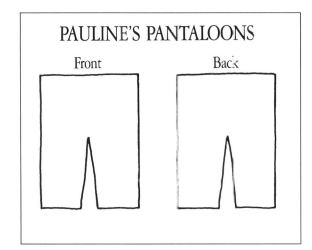

PAULETTE'S PANTALOONS

Front   Back

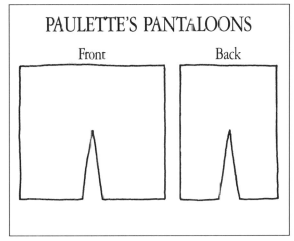

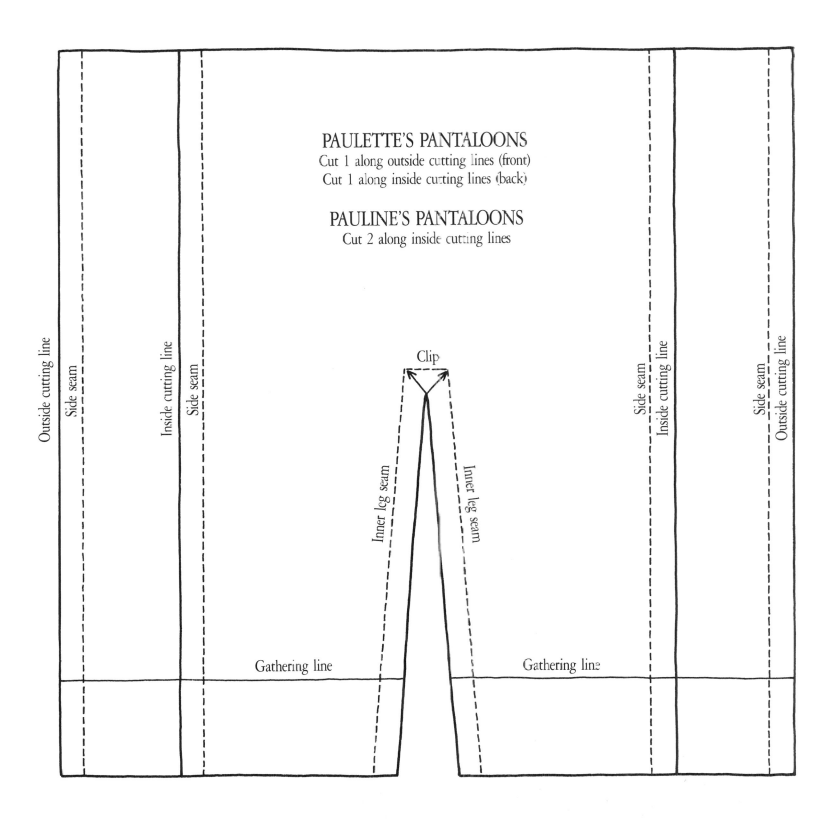

PAULETTE'S PANTALOONS
Cut 1 along outside cutting lines (front)
Cut 1 along inside cutting lines (back)

PAULINE'S PANTALOONS
Cut 2 along inside cutting lines

Outside cutting line

Side seam

Inside cutting line

Side seam

Clip

Inner leg seam

Inner leg seam

Side seam

Inside cutting line

Side seam

Outside cutting line

Gathering line

Gathering line

MR. FROG

No run-of-the-mill amphibian is this 20-inch-tall frog, an eyeful of green elegance in a fabric-covered boater hat. With popping eyes made of wooden beads, his glance is absolutely "ribbett"-ing. Wooden beads also pinpoint his fingers and toes, while his snappy bow tie makes him a dandy dresser wherever he goes. Use the same patterns to make a Ms. Frog version, adding ribbons and a straw hat.

MATERIALS FOR MR. FROG

½ yard of green broadcloth for body

⅛ yard of green and black striped fabric for legs

Scrap of peach cotton for mouth

Scrap of muslin for throat

Scrap of calico for stomach

¼ yard of green silky fabric for hat

Eight 15-mm brown wooden beads

Ten 10-mm brown wooden beads

Two 20-mm natural wooden beads

One 7x11-inch piece of cardboard

Two ¾-inch-diameter backer buttons for eyes

Tapestry needle; masking tape

Rubber band; fabric glue

Polyester fiberfill

Plastic filler beads

⅓ yard of ⅝-inch-wide ivory ribbon

One 2-inch-diameter ivory ribbon rose

◆

PREPARING THE PATTERNS

Trace the full-size patterns on pages 98 and 99 onto tracing paper. Cut out the patterns.

◆

CUTTING THE FABRICS

The cutting instructions for pieces that have no patterns include ¼-inch seams.

From green broadcloth, cut:
- One body back
- Two arm fronts
- Four feet

From green and black stripe, cut:
- Two legs

From calico, cut:
- One stomach

From peach cotton, cut:
- One mouth

From muslin, cut:
- One throat

From green silky fabric, cut:
- One 10½-inch-diameter circle
- One 3½x7½-inch bow tie
- One 1⅜x2-inch bowknot

From cardboard, cut:
- One 5½-inch-diameter circle
- One 1×10¼-inch rectangle

BODY FRONT

1. Matching the dots, sew the darts in the mouth piece. Trim the dart seams to ¼ inch; press.
2. Pin the top edge of the throat to the bottom half of the mouth, matching the dart seams with the top throat dots and easing to fit. Sew the edges together between the top dots; clip curves. Press under the bottom throat edge ¼ inch.
3. Sew the top of each arm front to the throat side, matching the small dots. Press the seams open.
4. Sew the inside seam of each arm front to the top sides of the stomach between the dots; press.

BODY BACK

1. Sew the four darts on the body back piece. Trim the dart seams to ¼ inch; press the seams open.
2. To attach each eye, thread a tapestry needle with three strands of thread. Hold the backer button against the wrong side of the body back fabric at the X. Insert the needle through the backer button and fabric, through the opening in one 20-mm bead, through the opening in one 10-mm bead, then back through the large bead, the fabric, and the backer button. Knot the thread.

ASSEMBLING THE BODY

1. Sew the assembled body front to the body back, easing the fit across the head and arms; leave openings between the dots on the bottom of the body and between the throat and stomach.
2. Clip the curves; turn the body right side out. Press under the raw edges ¼ inch.

LEGS AND FEET

1. Sew each leg together at the sides, leaving openings at top and bottom edges. Turn legs right side out.
2. Press under the top edge of each foot ¼ inch. Sew the feet together in pairs, leaving the tops open. Clip curves; turn feet right side out. Fill feet with plastic filler beads.
3. Insert the bottom of each leg into the top of each foot ¼ inch, matching the leg seam with one of the foot seams. Topstitch the feet to the legs.
4. Stuff the legs with fiberfill. Baste the top edges of the legs together.
5. Pin the legs into the body, placing each leg seam at the center of the body and spacing the legs 1 inch apart. Topstitch across the opening, encasing the legs in the seam.
6. Stuff the arms with fiberfill through the throat opening. Fill the bottom two inches of the body with plastic beads. Stuff the top part of the body and head with fiberfill. Use your fingers to push the center of the mouth inward so the bottom edge of the mouth rolls outward to form a lip. Hand-sew the opening closed.

FINISHING THE FROG

1. Use the tapestry needle and matching thread to shape the mouth. Start sewing at the X between the mouth darts, pushing the needle through the lower lip and out at the center of the throat/stomach seam. Pull the thread to roll the lip; knot.
2. To shape the nose, insert the tapestry needle behind one eye, push it out at one nose X, sew running stitches across the mouth to the other nose X, and return the needle back through the opposite eye. Pull the thread; knot to secure.
3. Sew one 15-mm bead to the end of each toe. Sew one 10-mm bead to each fingertip.

HAT

1. Center and draw a 3½-inch-diameter circle inside the 5½-inch-diameter cardboard circle for the hat brim. Cut out the drawn circle and save it for the hat top.
2. Overlap and staple the short ends of the cardboard rectangle so it fits into the brim opening.
3. Tape the top, the rim, and the brim circle together with masking tape to assemble the hat.
4. Run a bead of glue around the crown. Center the 10½-inch fabric circle over the hat. Drape the fabric over the crown. Place a rubber band around the hat sides to hold the fabric in place; evenly space the fabric fullness.
5. Take the fabric across the brim to the underside, and glue the raw edges inside the hat.
6. Let the glue dry. Remove the rubber band. Tack the ivory ribbon around the crown for the hatband. Glue the ribbon rose over the band seam.
7. Tack the hat to the back of the frog's head.

FROG'S BOW TIE

1. Sew the 7½-inch edges of the bow tie and the 2-inch edges of the bowknot strip together; turn them right side out. Press and center the seams between the side folds.
2. With the seam up, tack the bow tie ends together to form a loop. Crease folds at the sides, keeping the tacked ends in the center.

3. Wrap the knot strip around the center of the bow tie, keeping the seam to the inside; tack the ends together. Tack the tie at the frog's throat.

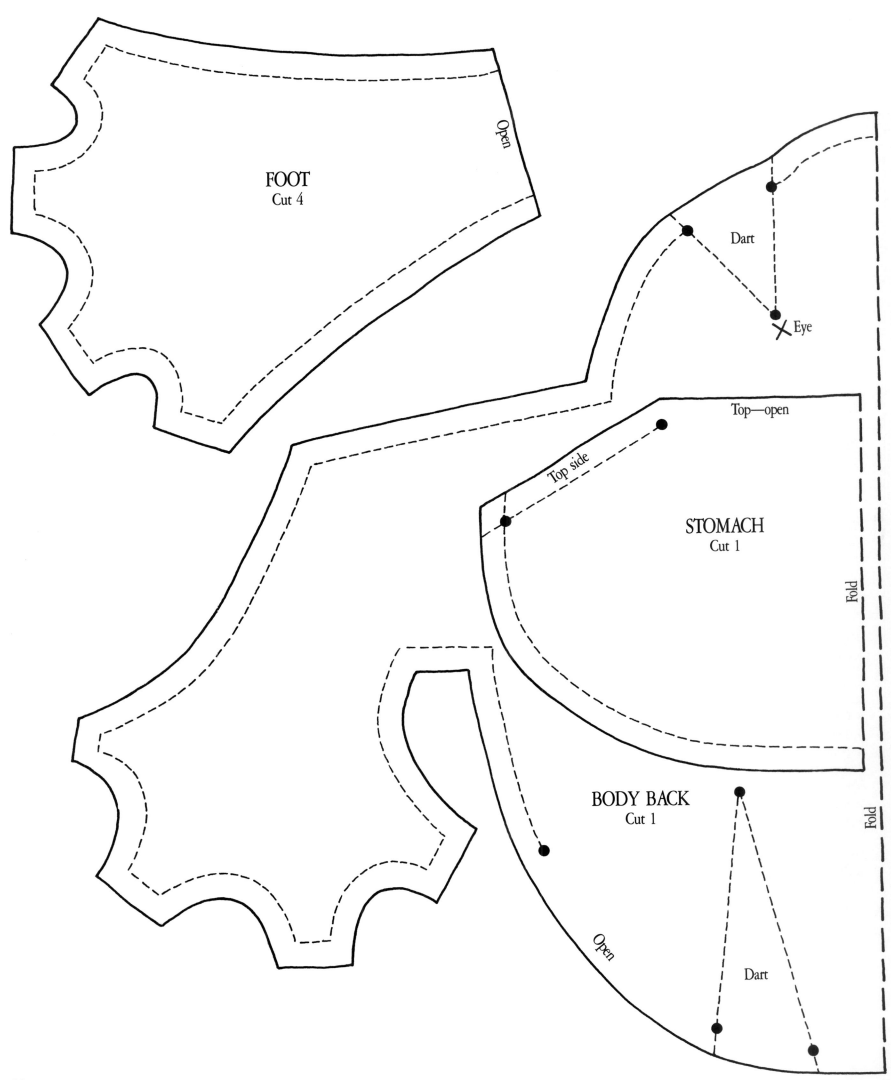

FOOT
Cut 4

Open

Dart

Eye

Top—open

Top side

STOMACH
Cut 1

Fold

Fold

BODY BACK
Cut 1

Open

Dart

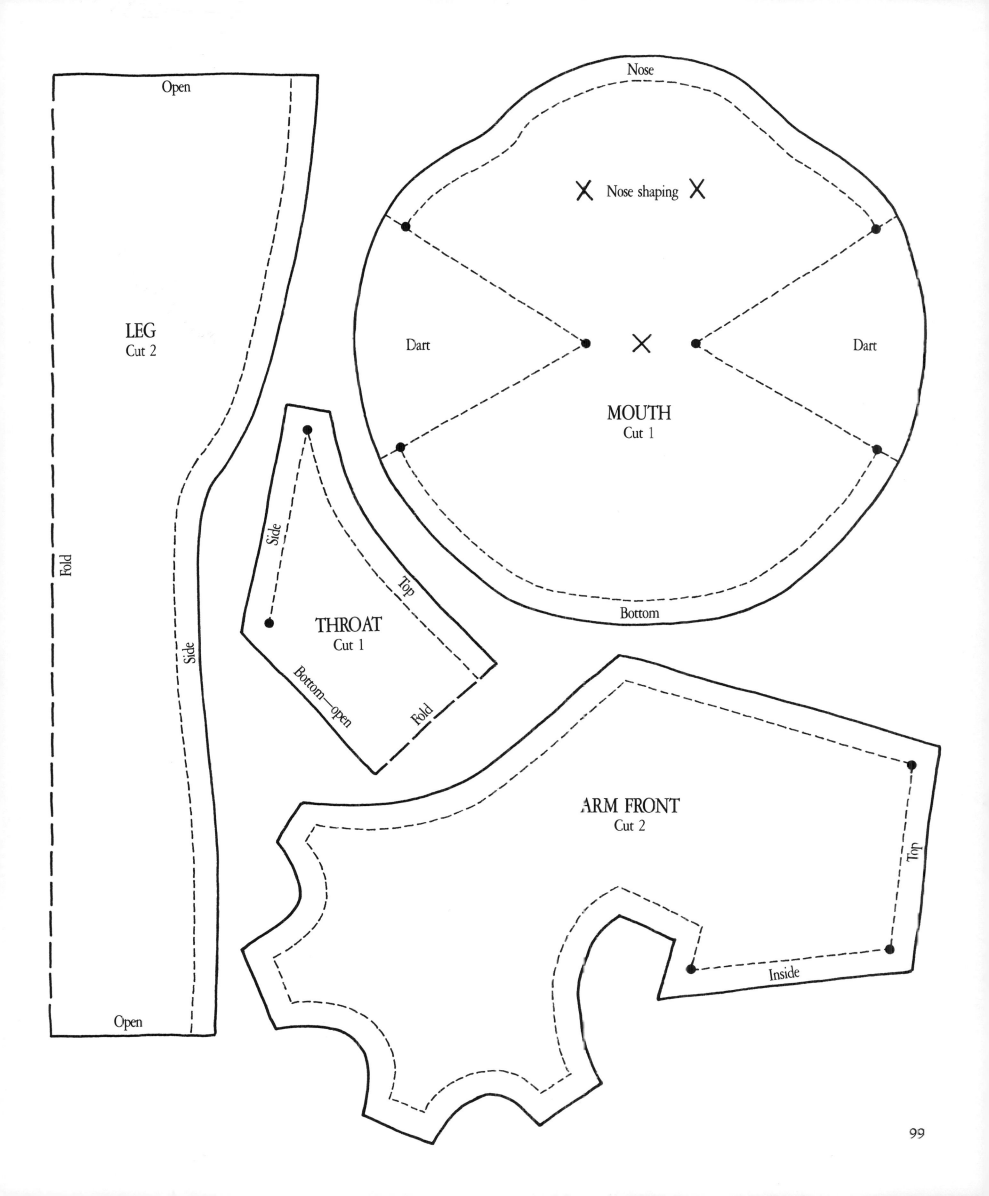

LEG
Cut 2

Open

Fold

Side

Open

Nose

✗ Nose shaping ✗

Dart

✗

Dart

MOUTH
Cut 1

Bottom

Side

THROAT
Cut 1

Top

Bottom—open

Fold

ARM FRONT
Cut 2

Top

Inside

99

NOAH'S ARK

The biblical narrative of Noah building his ark and gathering the animals, the flooding of the earth, and the sign of the rainbow continues to be among the favorite Scripture stories. Over the years, many toys have been crafted that captivated children's imaginations to re-create this wonderful story through play. Here, Noah and his wife assemble rabbits, elephants, rhinoceroses, zebras, giraffes, and turtles two by two. A tiny dove sits on a perch to await his flight. The box-shape hull opens and serves as a place to store the pieces when not in play.

MATERIALS FOR NOAH'S ARK

7 feet of 1x6-inch clear pine

2 feet of 1x8-inch clear pine

10½ inches of ¼-inch dowel

4 inches of ⅜-inch dowel

4½ inches of ³⁄₁₆-inch dowel

4 inches of ⅛-inch dowel

Wood glue

Four No. 6x1-inch wood screws

1½x3½-inch scrap of leather or two small brass hinges

1 yard of ⅛-inch-diameter cotton string

Dark walnut or other warm brown stain

Table saw; scroll saw; and band saw

Drill with ¹⁄₁₆-, ⅛-, ³⁄₁₆-, ¼-, ⅜-, and ¾-inch bits

Screwdriver

Wood clamps

Small carving knife

Electric belt sander

Coarse- and fine-grit sandpaper

Wood plane

Black permanent marker

◆

CUTTING INSTRUCTIONS

Use the table saw to cut all pieces for the ark as square with the grain as possible. Mark the name of each piece directly on the wood with a pencil.

From the 1x6-inch pine, cut:
- Two 5x12-inch hull sides (A)
- Two 5x8½-inch hull ends (B and C)
- Two 4x8-inch house sides (F)
- Two 4½x5-inch house ends (G)
- One 3½x10½-inch roof (H)

From the ³⁄₁₆-inch dowel, cut:
- Three 1-inch cleat shafts
- One 1½-inch bird perch

From the ⅛-inch dowel, cut:
- Three ½-inch cleat handles
- Two 1-inch pegs

From the 1x8-inch pine, cut:
- One 7x12-inch hull bottom (E)
- One 7x12-inch deck (K)

PREPARING THE PIECES

1. For deck supports and house mounts, cut four 1½x1¼-inch rectangles from the wood scraps; cut each piece diagonally to make eight triangles. Set four triangles aside for deck supports. The remaining four triangles will be house mounts. Referring to the drawing, *below,* use the drill to countersink a ⅜-inch hole about ¼ inch deep in the center of each house mount triangle; then drill a ⅛-inch hole through the center. Set house mounts aside.

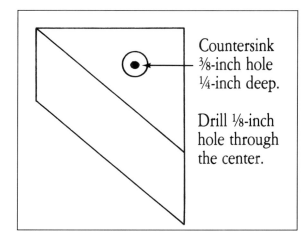

Countersink ⅜-inch hole ¼-inch deep.

Drill ⅛-inch hole through the center.

2. Referring to the drawing, *below,* use the scroll saw to cut the ramp door (D) in one hull end (C). Mark the bottom edge of the door so the grain will match when assembled.

3. In one of the house sides (F), cut a centered door opening 3 inches high and 3 inches wide. Use the band saw to split the 3x3-inch piece so one piece is about ¼ inch thick. Cut the ¼-inch-thick piece in half to make two 1½x3x¼-inch doors (I). On the remaining piece, trace the door latch and the anchor (see patterns on page 105). Drill ³⁄₁₆-inch holes as marked in each. Cut out both pieces.

4. Referring to the drawing, *opposite, top,* cut the roof angles in the house ends (G). Drill a ¾-inch hole in each piece as shown in the drawing.

5. Use a band saw to split the ¾-inch thickness of the roof (H) to make two 3½x10½x⅜-inch pieces.

6. Sand smooth all pieces.

HULL

1. Draw a line parallel to and 1¼ inches from one 12-inch edge (top) of *each* hull side (A). Referring to the drawing, *opposite, bottom,* align the top edge of the 1½-inch side of each deck support at the line. Glue in position. Allow to dry for at least 4 hours.

2. Put a thin coat of glue evenly along the ¾x12-inch surfaces of the hull bottom (E). Position the bottom of the hull sides against the glue; press in place. Spread a thin layer of glue along both ¾x12-inch surfaces of the deck (K) and place the deck between the hull sides, resting it on the deck supports. Clamp the sides with wood clamps at the top and bottom corners, making sure all pieces are lined up carefully on the ends. Let dry 8 hours.

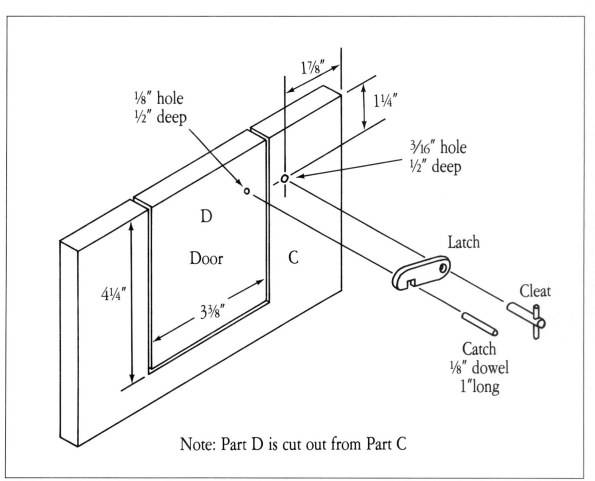

⅛" hole ½" deep

1⅞"

1¼"

³⁄₁₆" hole ½" deep

D

4¼"

Door   C

3⅜"

Latch

Cleat

Catch ⅛" dowel 1"long

Note: Part D is cut out from Part C

3. Meanwhile, plane about ⅛ inch off the bottom edge of the ramp door (D). Glue the leather strip on the bottom edge of the ramp door with an excess ¾ inch sticking out on the outside of the door. Fold the excess leather against the glued portion and place the door in a vise or in clamps to secure the glue and crease the leather for proper door function.

4. After 2 hours, glue the remainder of the leather strip to the ramp door opening on the hull end (C). Line it up carefully and evenly with the outside and press it firmly in place. Let it dry for several hours.

5. When the glue is dry on the hull pieces, sand the ends to ensure perfectly flat surfaces before gluing on the hull ends (B and C). Stain the inside of the hull ends; guard against getting stain on the ends and edges where you need a good glue bond. Apply wood glue to both ends of the hull. Line up each end, making sure the ramp door is at the top. Clamp the pieces at each corner and let dry 8 hours. Sand all joints again to make sure they are even and no excess glue is on the outside. (Glue will prevent the wood from taking the stain.)

6. For the ladder, from scrap pieces, cut two ³⁄₁₆×⅜×4¾-inch strips and five ³⁄₁₆×⅜×1⅞-inch strips. Sand all pieces. Glue the five short strips onto the two long strips, keeping them square and evenly spaced. Set a weight on the ladder rungs until they are dry (at least 4 hours). Stain the front and sides of the ladder; leave the back unstained. Line up the ladder on the side of the hull and make a pencil line down each side. Place a narrow strip of clear plastic or masking tape where the ladder will be glued.

continued

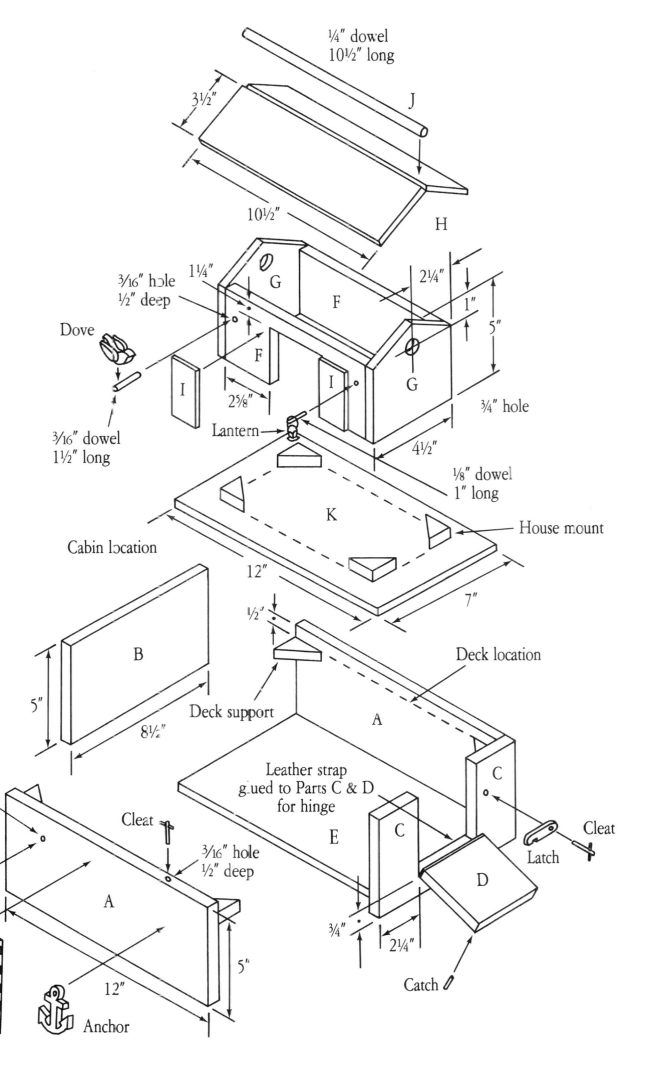

7. Stain the remainder of the hull.

8. Lay the hull on its side and remove the strips of tape marking the ladder position. Apply glue to the markings and place the ladder in position. Set a weight on the ladder until the glue is dry.

HOUSE

(Refer to the drawings on page 103 as you work through these steps.)

1. Apply wood glue to the ¾×4-inch surfaces of each house side (F). Referring to the top drawing on page 103, position the house ends (G) against the glue, carefully lining up the corners; press into place. Clamp the top and bottom of all corners. Apply glue to the short edges of the four house mounts and press them firmly into the bottom of each corner with the countersunk hole on top. Set the house aside to dry overnight. (Be careful when clamping the side where the door is cut out in order to protect the thin strip remaining over the door.)

2. Sand all joints of the house until they are even and smooth. Glue the doors (I) on either side of the door opening and clamp in place until dry. Stain the house inside and outside, except the top edges where the roof will be glued in place.

3. Position the house on the center of the deck. Attach the house to the deck by screwing the four wood screws through the house mounts and into the deck.

4. Squeeze wood glue along the top edges of one side of the house. Center one roof section with the top edge even at the peak of the roof. Hold the roof in place until the glue begins to set; then repeat with the second roof piece. When the roof is dry, glue the 10½-inch piece of ¼-inch dowel (J) in the groove at the peak of the roof. Allow the glue to dry 4 hours. Stain the outside and underside of the roof.

CLEATS AND PEGS

1. Referring to the drawings on pages 102, 103, and *above right,* make three cleats from the shaft and handle dowels. Drill a ⅛-inch hole about ³⁄₁₆ inch from one end of each cleat shaft. Sand the end nearest the hole until it's slightly rounded. Insert a cleat handle into the hole; center and glue in place. Stain all pieces except the last ½ inch of the shaft, which will be glued. At the same time, stain the door latch, the bird perch, the two ⅛-inch dowel pegs, and the string.

2. Mark and drill ³⁄₁₆×½-inch holes for the rope cleat, the anchor cleat, the bird perch, and the door latch cleat on the hull. *Do not* drill for the door catch yet. Slip the door latch onto one cleat and glue the cleat into the hole in the hull end. Glue the remaining cleats into the appropriate holes. Glue the bird perch into the hole in the house.

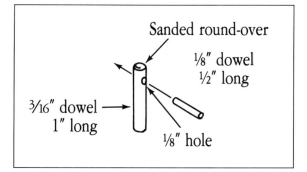

Sanded round-over
⅛" dowel ½" long
³⁄₁₆" dowel 1" long
⅛" hole

3. Mark and drill a ⅛×½-inch hole for the door catch. Drill a ⅛-inch hole for the lantern. Glue a ⅛-inch dowel peg into each hole.

4. Cut the string in half. Make three or four loose loops and knot them together. Glue the string to the cleat at the left of the ladder.

ANCHOR

1. Use the carving knife to round the edges on the front of the anchor. Sand it to the desired shape with coarse sandpaper. Sand until smooth with fine sandpaper. Stain the anchor.

2. Knot the remaining string in the hole at the top of the anchor and glue the anchor in place on the hull. Wrap the other end of the string around the peg above the anchor. Add a dot of glue to secure the end of the string.

LANTERN

1. Refer to the drawing, *below,* to make the lantern. For the base, rotate the tip of the ⅜-inch dowel against the belt sander until the edges are rounded. Use the scroll saw to cut off ³⁄₁₆ inch from the rounded tip; set aside.

2. For the lamp, round the end of the dowel again. Cut off ½ inch from the rounded tip. Referring to the drawing, *below,* shape the other end of the ½-inch piece with a gradual slope.

3. Drill a ¹⁄₁₆-inch hole through the top of the lantern about ³⁄₁₆ inch down from the top.

4. Glue the base to the lantern with wood glue.

5. Color the base, top, and stripes with the black marker.

6. Bend a 1½-inch piece of black wire to form a handle. Insert the ends into the holes in the sides of the lantern. Hang the lantern on the dowel to the left of the door.

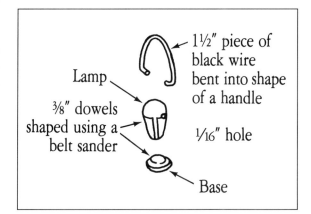

1½" piece of black wire bent into shape of a handle
Lamp
⅜" dowels shaped using a belt sander
¹⁄₁₆" hole
Base

MATERIALS FOR NOAH AND HIS ANIMALS

18 inches of 1x6-inch poplar or pine

Brown, gray, black, dark red, blue, light green, dark green, pink, and white acrylic paints

Scroll saw and band saw

No. 0 round and No. 8 flat paintbrushes

Drill with ⅛-inch bit

Electric belt sander (optional)

Coarse- and fine-grit sandpaper

Woodburning pen with fine tip

Graphite paper

Clear polyurethane varnish

Small carving knife

Dark walnut or other warm brown stain

Wood glue

◆

CUTTING INSTRUCTIONS

Trace Noah, his wife, and animals onto 1x6-inch wood, aligning the arrows on the patterns with the grain of the wood. Cut out shapes with scroll saw. With band saw, split one scrap of the wood to ½-inch thickness for the bird; split another scrap to a ¼-inch thickness for the wings. Trace and cut out the bird and wings with the scroll saw.

From the 1x6-inch wood, cut:
- ◆ One Noah
- ◆ One wife
- ◆ Two of *each* animal

From ½-inch-thick poplar scrap, cut:
- ◆ One bird body

From ¼-inch-thick poplar scrap, cut:
- ◆ Two bird wings

NOAH AND THE ANIMALS

1. Use fine sandpaper to sand all surfaces of each figure until smooth. Using graphite paper, trace the details of the figures onto the wood pieces. Use the woodburning pen to burn the detail lines onto the figures.

2. Referring to the photo on pages 100 and 101, paint each figure. Paint Noah's garment dark red; paint his hair and beard gray. Leave his hands and face natural.

3. Paint Noah's wife's garment blue; paint her hair black and her veil white with a blue band. Leave her hands and face natural.

4. Paint the elephants light gray, except the eyes. Paint a black pupil in each eye and add a white highlight.

5. Paint the giraffes' manes, feet, and spots brown, leaving the faces, lower legs, and areas between spots natural. Paint a black pupil in each eye and add a white highlight.

6. Paint the rabbits' eyes pink with white highlights. Leave the remainder of the rabbits natural.

7. Paint the rhinoceroses gray, except the eyes. Paint a black pupil in each eye and add a white highlight.

8. Paint the turtles' heads and feet light green and the shells dark green. Paint markings on the shells with light green. Paint a black pupil in each yellow eye.

9. Paint the zebras' manes, noses, tails, feet; and stripes black, leaving the natural wood color as the light-color stripes. Paint a black pupil in each eye and add a white highlight.

10. When the paint is dry, apply a coat of varnish.

DOVE

1. With a small carving knife, round the edges of the bird's body and wings, leaving the areas flat where the wings attach to the body. Sand smooth the bird's body and wings.

2. Glue the wings to the body. Allow the glue to dry. Stain the bird. Add a dot of black paint for the eye.

3. Glue the dove on the dowel on the ark.

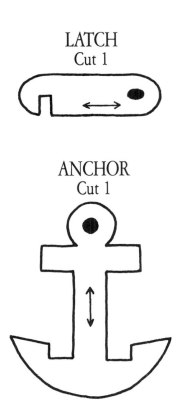

Angelina

If bears had wings, they couldn't possibly be more adorable than this "bearly" 8-inch-tall heavenly angel at *left*. Patchwork wings, made from scraps of an old quilt, are glued to the back of the jointed body. The braid trim across her chest suggests she wears the wings like a parachute. A halo of star garland encircles her head. See the photo on page 3 for a more earthly version of this same bear.

MATERIALS FOR ANGELINA

¼ yard of distressed mohair fur

Scrap of coordinating felt for paws

8x12-inch piece *each* of muslin and cutter's quilt or other prequilted fabric (See box on pages 86 and 87 for tips to make quilted fabric for wings, if desired)

⅓ yard of ¼-inch-wide gold braid

Star garland, greenery, or twigs for halo

Two shanked 6-mm black glass eyes

Ten ¾-inch hardboard joint disks

Five ⁶⁄₃₂x½-inch roundhead screws

Five ⁶⁄₃₂ locknuts

Brown embroidery floss

5-inch-long dollmaker's needle

Button thread

Hot-glue gun

Polyester fiberfill

◆

PREPARING THE PATTERNS

Trace the full-size patterns on pages 108 and 109 onto tracing paper. Cut out the patterns.

◆

CUTTING THE FABRICS

When working with fur, trace the pattern pieces onto the wrong side of the fur. Cut *each* pattern piece individually from one layer of fabric. Reverse the patterns, trace, and cut the remaining pieces. Notice the nap arrows for placing the patterns on fur. When cutting fur, work from the wrong side of the fabric. Snip along the cutting lines and cut only through the backing fabric.

From mohair, cut:
- ◆ Two heads
- ◆ One gusset
- ◆ Two bodies
- ◆ Two inner arms
- ◆ Two outer arms
- ◆ Four legs
- ◆ Four ears

From felt, cut:
- ◆ Two footpads
- ◆ Two paws

From muslin, cut:
- ◆ Two wings

From quilt, cut:
- ◆ Two wings

GENERAL INSTRUCTIONS

1. Transfer the muzzle lines and X markings to the pile side of the fabric using brightly colored tailor's tacks. (See the tip on page 31.) Transfer all other markings to the wrong side of the fur.
2. Before sewing the fur pieces together, brush the pile away from the seam line. After sewing, use a straight pin to pull the pile from the seams to blend the fur. To reduce bulk in the seams, trim the pile in the seam allowances.

HEAD

1. Sew the head pieces together along the center front seam from the tip of the nose (large dot) to the neck. Referring to drawing, *below*, baste the gusset to the head pieces, matching the large dots. Machine-sew the gusset to the head pieces, leaving an opening between the small dots as shown on the gusset piece. Turn the head right side out.

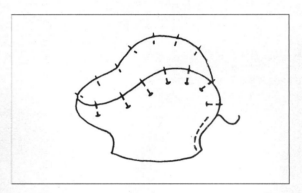

2. Hand-sew small running stitches around the neck edge using a double strand of button thread. Tightly pull the threads to close the neck, leaving an opening large enough to insert one screw for jointing the body. Securely knot the threads of the gathered neck.

BODY

1. Sew the body pieces together, leaving openings at the neck and between the small dots at the center back.
2. Snip one or two threads of the fur backing at each of the Xs to create small holes for the joints. Turn the body right side out.
3. Close the neck opening in the same manner as the Head (Step 2, *above*). Set the body aside.

ARMS AND LEGS

1. Sew a felt paw to each inner arm along the straight edges. Sew inner and outer arms together in pairs, leaving openings between the small dots. Snip one or two threads of the fur backing at each of the Xs to create small holes for the joints. Turn each arm right side out and set them aside.

continued

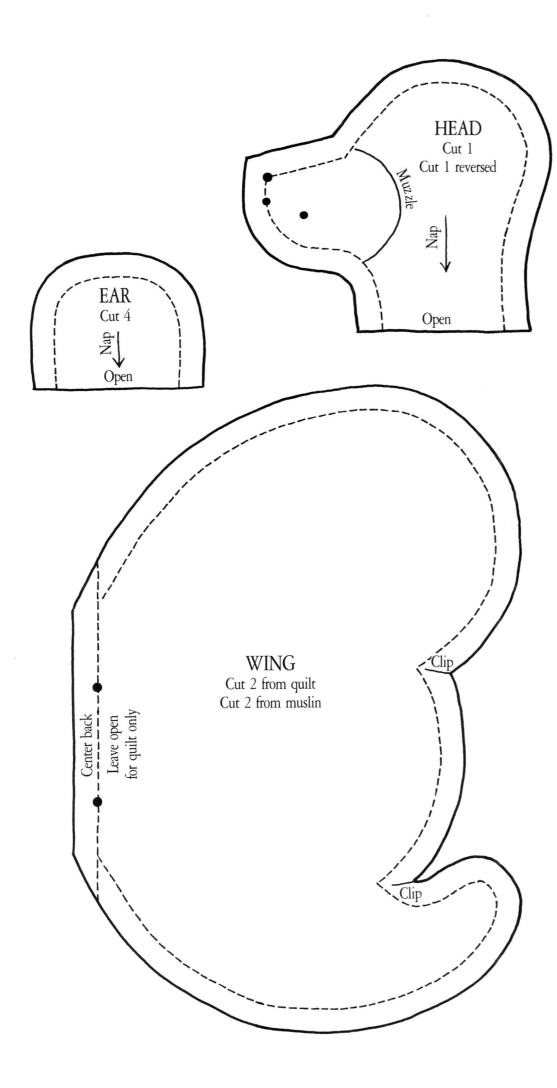

EAR
Cut 4

Nap

Open

HEAD
Cut 1
Cut 1 reversed

Muzzle

Nap

Open

WING
Cut 2 from quilt
Cut 2 from muslin

Center back

Leave open
for quilt only

Clip

Clip

2. Sew the legs together in pairs, leaving openings at the bottom edges and between the small dots.

3. Referring to drawing, *below,* baste a footpad to the bottom of each leg opening. Machine-sew the footpads to the legs. Snip one or two threads of the fur backing at each of the Xs on only one side of each leg to create small holes for the joints. *Note:* The sides with the holes will face the body when the legs are jointed. Turn each leg right side out.

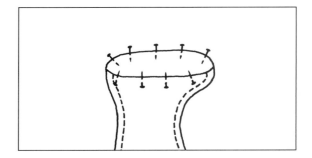

JOINTING THE BEAR

1. To joint the body, insert each roundhead screw through a hardboard disk. Place one assembly inside the head and one in each arm and leg with the stem of the screw poking through the small holes. Push the stem of each screw into the corresponding hole on the body. Place a second hardboard disk onto the stems of the screws. Secure each screw inside the body with a locknut. Use a locknut driver and a screwdriver to tighten the joints. Attach the arms, legs, and head to the body in this manner, threading each joint so the locknut is inside the body.

2. Firmly stuff the head, body, arms, and legs with fiberfill. Hand-sew each opening closed.

FACE

1. Use a small pair of scissors to trim the mohair pile to ⅛ inch from the muzzle line to the tip of the nose.

2. Sew the button eyes to the front of the head using a double strand of button thread in the dollmaker's needle. Begin sewing at the back of the head near the base of the neck. Bring the needle out at one of the X eye placements on the gusset. Thread the button onto the needle and return the needle through the eye placement to the back of the neck. Pull the threads to indent the eye socket, and knot securely to hold the shaping in place. Sew the second button to the head in the same way.

3. Using four plies of embroidery floss, satin-stitch the area shaded on the gusset for the nose. Without breaking the thread, sew a straight stitch from the bottom of the nose to the small dot on the head seam. Connect each remaining small dot in the muzzle to the seam dot with straight stitches, forming an inverted V-shaped mouth. (See the stitch diagrams on page 7.)

4. Sew the ears together in pairs, leaving the bottom edges open. Clip the curves and turn each ear right side out. Slip-stitch the ears closed.

5. To shape each ear, use a double-threaded needle to pull the two bottom corners together; knot to secure. Position the ears on the head and hand-sew them in place.

FINISHING

1. Center the gold braid at the back of the bear's neck. Bring the ends of the braid to the front, crossing them over the chest, and tying them in a knot at the bear's back waist.

2. Form a halo from a star garland, twigs, or greenery. Hot-glue or hand-sew the halo to the back of the bear's head.

3. Sew the muslin wings together along the center back seam. Press the seam open. Sew the quilt wings together along the center back seam, leaving an opening between the small dots.

4. Sew the muslin wings to the quilt wings along the curved edges. Grade the seams and clip the curves. Turn wings right side out and hand-sew the opening closed.

5. Hot-glue or tack the wings to the center of the bear's back.

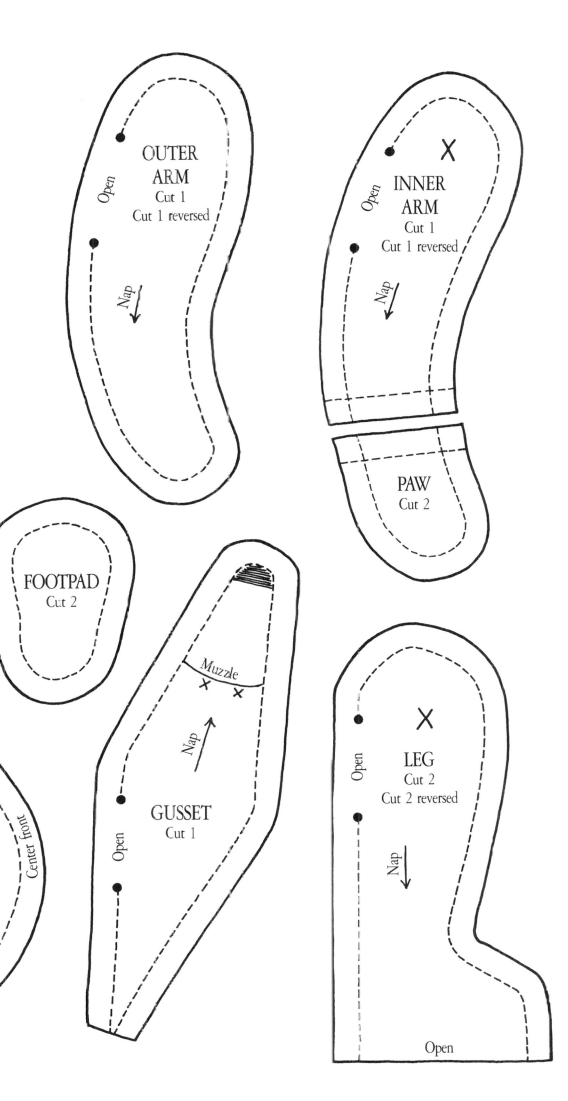

TOPSY-TURVY TWOSOME

This old-fashioned version of the topsy-turvy doll is an extraordinary cat-and-mouse game. On one side of the skirt is a prim and proper city mouse; on the opposite side is a rather authoritative country cat. Both dames are dressed in sweet and charming clothing that is becoming to their domestic habitats. This topsy-turvy duo stands 17½ inches tall.

MATERIALS FOR TOPSY-TURVY CAT AND MOUSE BODY

¼ yard of short-nap fur for cat's body

¼ yard of velour for mouse's body

Scrap of suede, synthetic suede, or felt for mouse's ears

Two 12-mm cat eyes with metal washers

Two ¼-inch-diameter ball buttons for mouse's eyes

One ¼-inch-diameter pink pom-pom for mouse's nose

Black pearl cotton and embroidery floss

Black carpet thread

Medium-weight fishing line

Hot-glue gun

Stiff-bristle brush

Powder rouge

Polyester fiberfill

◆

PREPARING THE PATTERNS

Trace the full-size body patterns on pages 114 and 115 onto tracing paper. Cut out the patterns.

◆

CUTTING THE FABRICS

When working with fur, *each* fabric piece should be *individually* cut from a single layer of fabric. First trace the pattern pieces onto the wrong side of the fur. Then flop the patterns and trace the mirror image. (Note the nap arrows for placing the patterns on the fur.) When cutting out the fur pieces, cut on the wrong side of the fabric, take small snips along the cutting lines, and cut only the backing fabric.

For cat, from fur, cut:
◆ Two bodies
◆ Two cat head fronts
◆ One head back
◆ Four cat ears
◆ Four cat paws

For mouse, from velour, cut:
◆ Two bodies
◆ Two mouse head fronts
◆ One head back
◆ Four mouse paws

From suede, cut:
◆ Two mouse ears

GENERAL INSTRUCTIONS

1. After cutting the fabrics, transfer the Xs and the ear placements to the pile side of the fur, using brightly colored tailor's tacks (see tip on page 31). The remaining construction markings can be transferred to the wrong side of the pile.

2. Before stitching fur pieces together, brush the pile away from the seam line. After sewing, use a straight pin to pull the pile from the seam. This technique blends the fur and conceals the seams. Trim the pile in the seam allowance.

CAT'S AND MOUSE'S PAWS

1. Sew the cat's paws together in pairs, leaving the tops open. Trim the seam allowances to ⅛ inch; turn each paw right side out.

2. With wrong sides facing, sew the mouse's paws together in pairs, leaving the tops open. Trim the seams to 1/16 inch; do *not* turn.

3. Lightly stuff each paw with fiberfill; sew across the opening. Set the paws aside; they will be attached to the sleeves when making the dress.

CAT'S HEAD AND BODY

1. Sew the two head front pieces together along the center seam. Trim the seams to ⅛ inch.

2. Sew one body piece to the assembled head front piece at neck edge; sew one body piece to head back at neck edge.

3. Sew the head/body pieces together, leaving an opening below the body dots and across the bottom edge.

4. Turn the body right side out. Attach the cat eyes to the head, following the package instructions. Turn the body so the wrong side is facing out. Set the body aside.

MOUSE'S HEAD AND BODY

Repeat steps 1 through 3 for the Cat's Head and Body, *above.*

CONNECTING THE BODIES

1. Sew the bottom front of the cat body to the bottom front of the mouse body. Then sew the bottom back of the cat body to the bottom back of the mouse body. Sew the opening of *one* side body seam together. Turn the doll right side out through the other side opening.

2. Firmly stuff the doll with fiberfill. Hand-sew the remaining side opening closed. Refer to the drawing, *right,* to note how the doll will look at this point in the assembly.

3. Brush all the cat seams to blend the fur.

FINISHING

1. Sew the cat's ears together in pairs, leaving the bottom edges open. Trim the seams and turn each ear right side out. Turn under the bottom edges of each ear ¼ inch. Hand-sew the ears to the head at the markings.

2. Fold a pleat in each mouse ear as marked on the pattern. Glue the pleat in place with hot glue. Glue the ears to the head at the markings.

3. For the cat's face, use one strand of pearl cotton to satin-stitch the nose indicated by the shaded area on the pattern. For a mouth, make one straight stitch, ⅝ inch long, from the bottom of the nose. Sew two more straight stitches, each about ⅜ inch long, at right angles to the first. For whiskers, pull four lengths of carpet thread through the muzzle just below the nose. Tie overhand knots in both ends of the thread close to the muzzle to hold them in place. Trim the whiskers evenly.

4. For the mouse's face, sew the pom-pom to the tip of the nose. Sew the ball button eyes to the head at the Xs. For eyebrows, use one ply of embroidery floss to make one straight stitch, about ⅜ inch long, above each eye. Use fishing line to make the whiskers as directed in Step 3, *above.* Brush powder rouge on the cheeks.

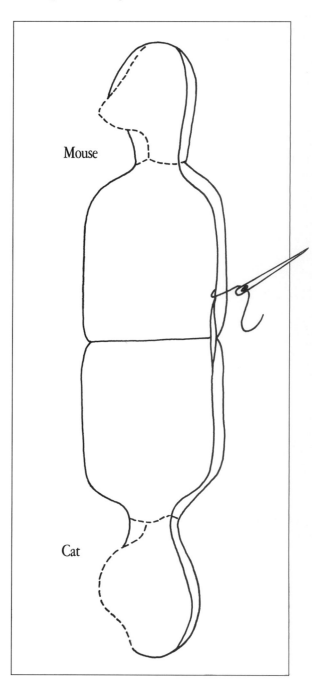

Mouse

Cat

MATERIALS FOR TOPSY-TURVY CAT AND MOUSE CLOTHING

⅜ yard of cotton print (A) for cat's dress

¼ yard of a coordinating print (B) for cat's apron

½ yard of 1½-inch-wide flat lace for cat's apron trim

¼ yard of ¼-inch-wide flat lace for cat's sleeve trim

One 6-inch square of lace fabric for cat's collar

One 1-inch-diameter fancy button for cat's brooch

⅜ yard of cotton print (C) for mouse's skirt and sleeves

¼ yard of a coordinating print (D) for mouse's bodice

One 2x4¼-inch piece of lace fabric for mouse's bodice inset

Eight ¼-inch-diameter gold beads for mouse's bodice

One 7-inch piece of pregathered ribbon for mouse's collar

1 yard of narrow black cord for mouse's bodice lacing

◆

PREPARING THE PATTERNS

Trace the full-size clothing patterns on page 115 onto tracing paper. Cut out the patterns.

◆

CUTTING THE FABRICS

The cutting instructions for pieces that have no patterns include ¼-inch seams.

From fabric A, cut:
◆ One bodice front
◆ Two bodice backs
◆ Four bodice sleeves
◆ One 13½x30-inch skirt

From fabric C, cut:
◆ One 13½x30-inch skirt
◆ Four bodice sleeves

From fabric B, cut:
◆ One 9x15-inch apron skirt
◆ One 6½x2-inch apron waistband
◆ Two 16x2¼-inch apron ties

From fabric D, cut:
◆ Two bodice fronts
◆ Two bodice backs
◆ Two peplums
◆ Two 1x4-inch cuffs

CAT'S BODICE

1. Sew the bodice front to the bodice backs along the shoulder/side seams. Stay-stitch along the neck opening. Press under the neck edge along the stay stitching, clipping as necessary to make the edge lie flat; topstitch in place.

2. Press under ¼-inch seam allowance on the center back bodice pieces. Slip the bodice onto the cat side of the doll; slip-stitch the center back edges together.

MOUSE'S BODICE

1. Sew one of the 4¼-inch sides of the lace inset to one bodice front edge. Sew the opposite side of the lace to the other bodice front edge. (Bodice front now should be one piece.) Press seams away from the inset.

2. Repeat steps 1 and 2 for the Cat's Bodice, *above,* to make the bodice on the mouse side of the doll.

SKIRT

1. Sew the 13½-inch edges of each skirt rectangle together. Press the seams open.

2. Place one skirt inside the other, matching the seams. Sew the skirts together along one long edge to make the hem. Press the seam open.

3. Press under ¼ inch on both remaining raw edges for the waist. Turn the skirt so both right sides are facing out and wrong sides are facing. Press the skirt, keeping all edges even.

4. Align the folded edges at the waist. Sew gathering stitches around the waist, close to the edge, through both skirt fabrics. With the mouse's skirt fabric facing out, slip the skirt over the mouse's head; adjust the gathers to fit at the waist. Blind-stitch the skirt to the doll's waist, sewing through the bodice and body.

PEPLUM

1. Sew the peplum pieces together, leaving an opening between the dots. Clip the curves, turn the peplum right side out, and press. Hand-sew the opening closed.

2. Fold the pleats in the direction of the arrows; pin pleats in place. Fit the peplum to the mouse's waist, matching the center fronts at the bodice center front. Adjust the pleats to make the peplum fit. Hand-sew the peplum to the bodice, covering the waist edge of the skirt.

SLEEVES

1. Sew the ¼-inch-wide lace to the right side of the bottom of each fabric A cat sleeve.

2. Sew each sleeve piece together to make a pair from the A fabric for the cat and a pair from the B fabric for the mouse. Clip the curves; turn each sleeve right side out and press.

3. Lightly stuff each sleeve with fiberfill. Insert the appropriate paw into each sleeve, aligning the edge of the lace or fabric with the placement line marked on the paw pattern. Hand-sew the sleeves to each paw.

4. Press under ¼ inch on all edges of the cuffs (fabric D). Press the cuffs in half lengthwise. Hand-sew the edges together. Glue each cuff over the sleeve and paw of each arm of the mouse doll.

5. To attach the arms, insert a double-threaded dollmaker's needle through the bodice and body at one shoulder X and out at the opposite shoulder X. Thread a sleeve onto the needle at the X; return the needle back through the body to the first X. Thread the other sleeve onto the needle. Pull the threads to slightly gather the sleeves; knot the ends. Conceal the thread ends inside the body.

CAT'S APRON

1. Press under one 15-inch edge of the apron skirt ¼ inch. With the right side facing out, topstitch the 1½-inch-wide lace over the folded edge. Press under the 9-inch sides of the apron skirt and raw edge of lace ⅛ inch twice; topstitch. Sew a gathering thread close to the remaining raw edge.

2. Press under one 6½-inch edge and both 2-inch edges of the apron waistband ¼ inch. Adjust the apron gathers to fit the raw edges of the waistband. Sew the apron to the waistband. Press the waistband in half so the folded edge covers the seam allowance on the wrong side.

3. Press under the 16-inch edges and one 2¼-inch edge of each apron tie ⅛ inch twice; topstitch. Make a tuck in the raw edge of each tie so the edges fit into the side edges of the waistband; pin in place. Topstitch the waistband to the apron and along the short edges to secure the ties. Tie the apron around the cat's waist.

FINISHING

1. Fold the 6-inch lace square in half diagonally, forming a triangle. Drape the lace around the cat's neck with the point at the center front. Tack the ends together at the back of the head. Sew the decorative button at the neck for a brooch.

2. Sew the gold buttons to the mouse's bodice at the Xs. Beginning at the top of the bodice and at the center of the lacing cord, wrap the cord around the top pair of buttons and tack in place. Cross the cord and attach it to the next pair of buttons. Repeat the lacing two more times. Tie the ends of the cord into a bow.

3. Hand-sew the pregathered ribbon around the neckline of the mouse's dress.

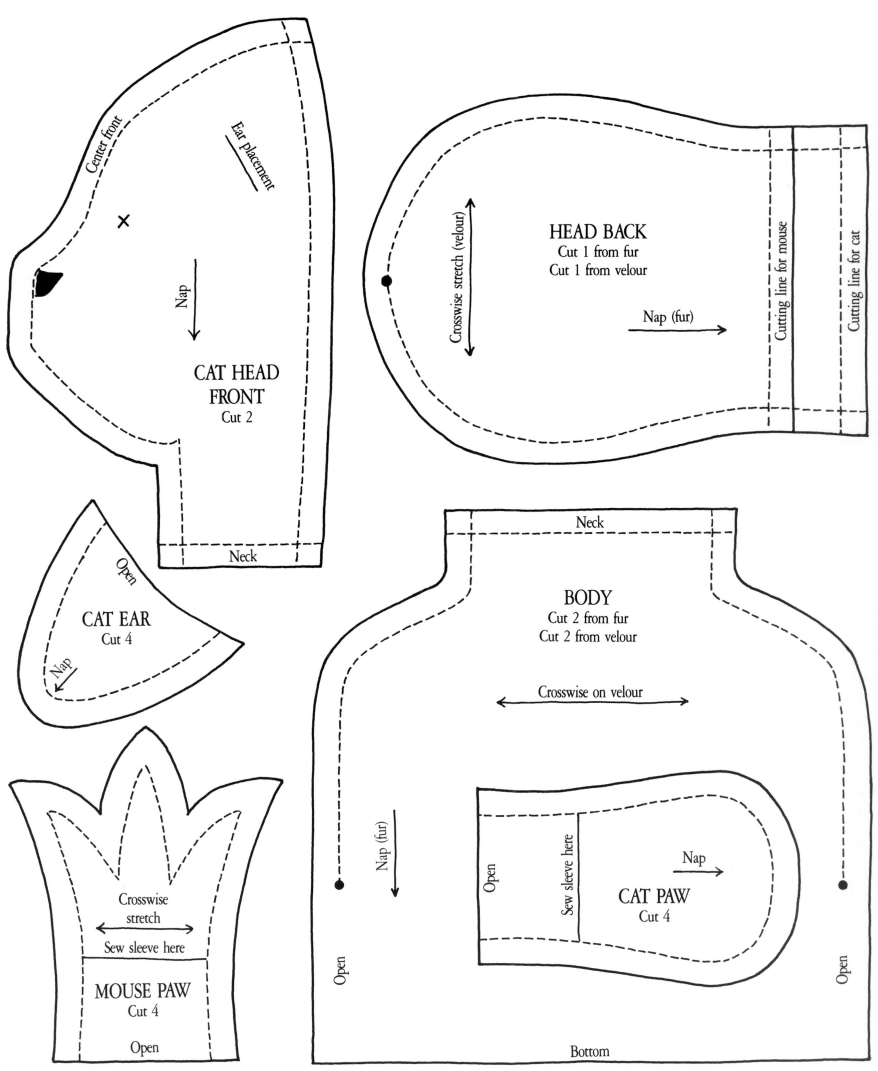

CAT HEAD
FRONT
Cut 2

Center front

Ear placement

Nap

Neck

HEAD BACK
Cut 1 from fur
Cut 1 from velour

Crosswise stretch (velour)

Nap (fur)

Cutting line for mouse

Cutting line for cat

CAT EAR
Cut 4

Open

Nap

Neck

BODY
Cut 2 from fur
Cut 2 from velour

Crosswise on velour

Nap (fur)

Open

Open

MOUSE PAW
Cut 4

Crosswise
stretch

Sew sleeve here

Open

CAT PAW
Cut 4

Open

Sew sleeve here

Nap

Open

Bottom

114

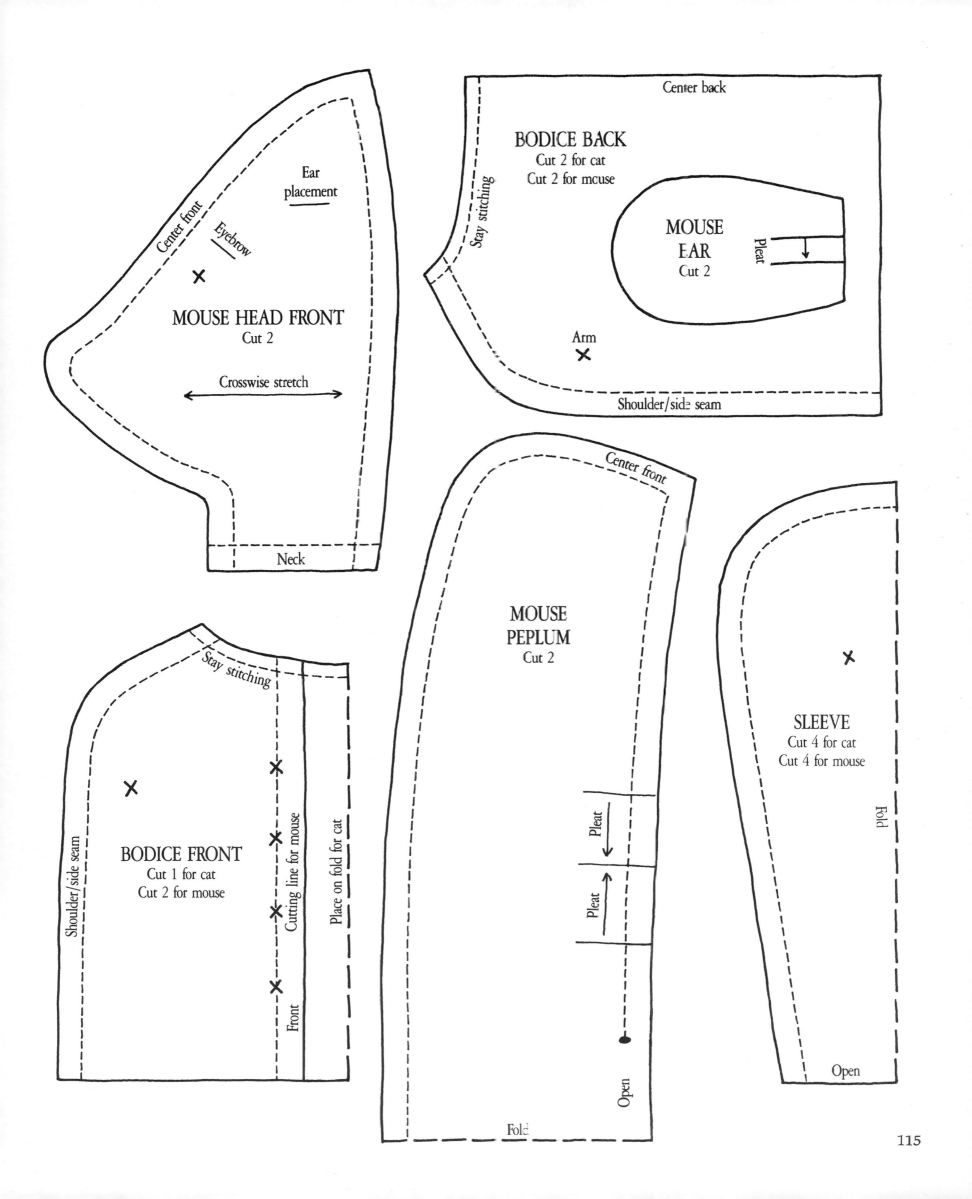

MOUSE HEAD FRONT
Cut 2

Center front

Eyebrow

Ear placement

Crosswise stretch

Neck

BODICE BACK
Cut 2 for cat
Cut 2 for mouse

Center back

Stay stitching

Arm

Shoulder/side seam

MOUSE EAR
Cut 2

Pleat

MOUSE PEPLUM
Cut 2

Center front

Pleat

Pleat

Open

Fold

BODICE FRONT
Cut 1 for cat
Cut 2 for mouse

Stay stitching

Shoulder/side seam

Cutting line for mouse

Place on fold for cat

Front

SLEEVE
Cut 4 for cat
Cut 4 for mouse

Fold

Open

115

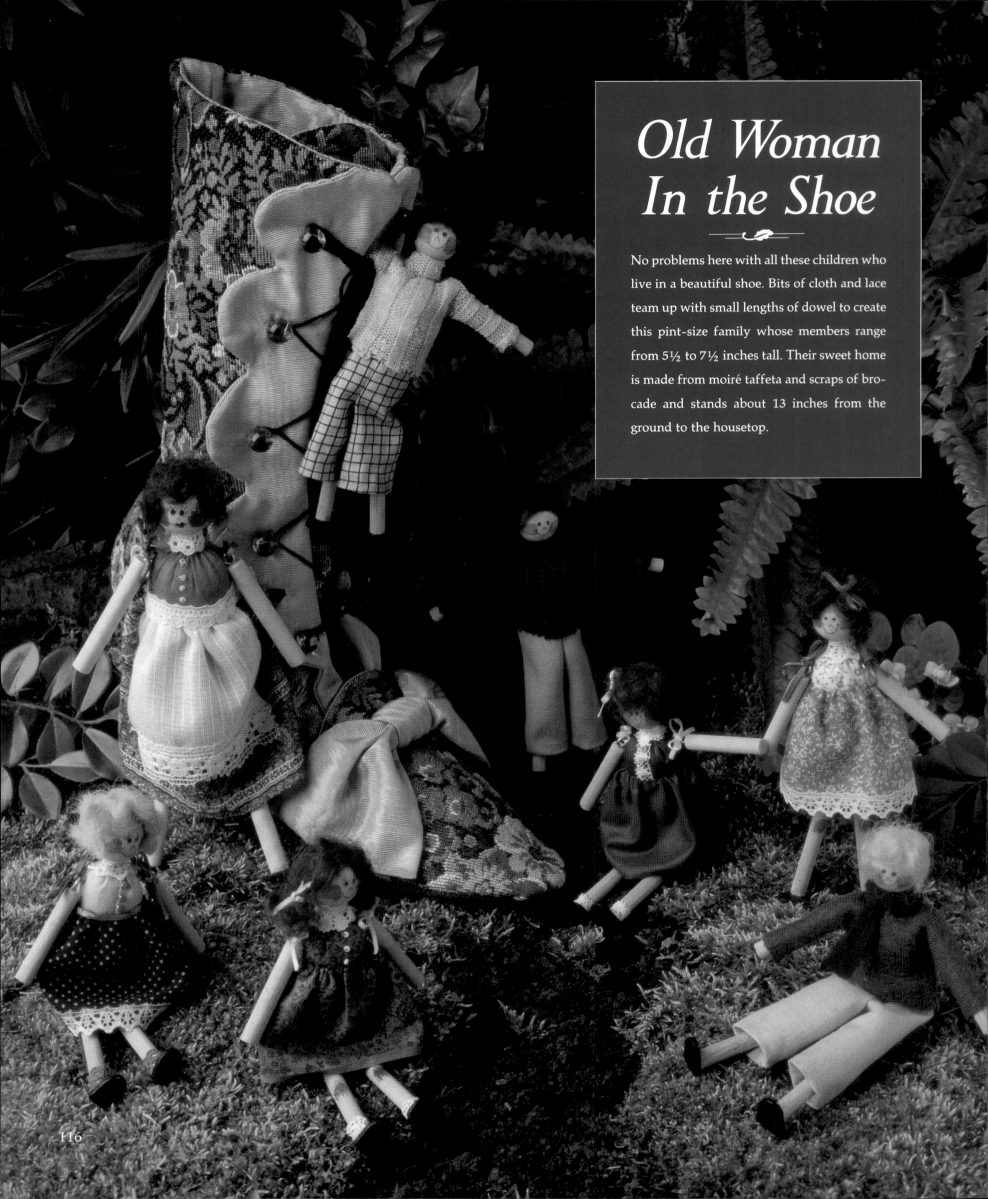

Old Woman In the Shoe

No problems here with all these children who live in a beautiful shoe. Bits of cloth and lace team up with small lengths of dowel to create this pint-size family whose members range from 5½ to 7½ inches tall. Their sweet home is made from moiré taffeta and scraps of brocade and stands about 13 inches from the ground to the housetop.

MATERIALS FOR THE SHOE

⅓ yard of tapestry fabric

⅓ yard of coordinating moiré fabric

10 ball-shape buttons

1 yard of narrow black cording

12-inch square of black felt

Size 3 black pearl cotton

3x2½x2½-inch block of plastic foam

8x12-inch piece of poster board

4-inch square of mat board

Small serrated knife

Hot-glue gun

———◆———

PREPARING THE PATTERNS

Trace the shoe patterns on pages 119–121 onto tracing paper. Cut out the patterns.

———◆———

CUTTING THE FABRICS

From tapestry fabric, cut:
- ◆ Two shoe bodies
- ◆ One shoe toe
- ◆ One tongue

From moiré fabric, cut:
- ◆ Two shoe bodies
- ◆ One shoe toe
- ◆ One tongue
- ◆ Four scallop trims
- ◆ 6-inch square for bow
- ◆ 1½x3-inch bow center

From black felt, cut:
- ◆ One complete sole
- ◆ One outer heel cover
- ◆ One front heel cover
- ◆ ⅝x⅞-inch bottom heel cover

From poster board, cut:
- ◆ One complete sole
- ◆ One middle sole
- ◆ One innersole

From mat board, cut:
- ◆ One toe sole

SHOE TOE

1. Sew the tapestry and moiré shoe toe pieces together along the stitching line. Clip curve, turn toe right side out, and press. Baste the raw edges of the toe together.

SHOE BODY

1. Sew two moiré scallop trim pieces together, leaving the top, bottom, and center front edges open. Trim away the excess fabric between the scallops and clip the curves. Turn the piece right side out. Repeat to complete the second scallop trim piece. Press both pieces.

2. Baste the center front seam of each scallop trim to the center fronts of each body tapestry piece.

3. Sew the tapestry shoe body pieces together along the center back seam; press seam open. Repeat with the moiré shoe body pieces. Sew the tapestry and moiré bodies together along the center front and top edges, encasing the scallop trim. Trim corners; clip curves. Turn the piece right side out and press. Baste the matching bottom raw edges together.

4. Pin the finished edge of the shoe toe along the toe placement line on *one* side of the shoe body, aligning the dot on the body with the corresponding dot on the shoe toe. Topstitch in place. Repeat on the other side of the toe. *Note:* The space between the dots on the toe will not be topstitched to the body.

SHOE TONGUE

1. Sew the tapestry tongue to the moiré tongue, leaving the bottom edge open. Clip the curves and turn the tongue right side out. Baste the bottom edges together.

2. Position the bottom edge of the tongue, with the tapestry side faceup, under the top of the shoe toe. Hand-stitch in place.

SHOE SOLE

1. Glue the mat-board toe to one side of the complete poster-board sole. Glue the middle sole to the opposite side of the poster-board sole. To create an arch, fold the complete sole upward where the toe sole and middle sole meet. Then fold the heel area down.

2. Position the sole along the bottom edges of the shoe, leaving ¼-inch seams along the fabric edge. Fold the seams of the shoe over the bottom of the sole and glue the edges in place. Insert the poster-board innersole inside the shoe; glue it in place.

3. Glue the felt sole over the bottom of the sole.

SHOE HEEL

1. Use straight pins to attach patterns A and B, which are inside the box on page 121, to the plastic foam block; align the front and top edges of the side view pattern with a corner of the block. Use the serrated knife to shape the block into a heel as shown in drawings 1 and 2, *right.*

2. Glue the outer heel cover to the sides of the heel, lapping the edges on the top, bottom, and front about ¼ inch on each of the foam sides; trim to fit. Glue the front heel cover to the front of the heel; trim to fit. Glue the bottom heel cover to the bottom of the heel; trim to fit. Glue the heel to the back of the sole.

3. Glue the cording around the edge of the sole.

FINISHING

1. Sew a button at each X on the scallop pieces.

2. Fold the bow square in half and stitch across the ends and side, leaving an opening for turning. Turn the bow right side out and press. Turn under the long edges of the bow center rectangle ¼ inch and press. Wrap it around the center of the bow and tack in place at the back. Tack the bow to the center of the toe 1 inch below the top seam.

3. Cut one 2-yard piece of pearl cotton for the lacing cord. Cut six 6-inch pieces of pearl cotton to make one tassel and bundle them together. Tie one end of the lacing cord around the center of the bundle. Fold the bundle in half. Wrap a short piece of pearl cotton around the bundle three or four times ¼ inch from the fold. Tie the ends into a knot. Trim the ends of the tassel. Make another tassel on the other end of the cord.

4. Beginning at the center of the cord, lace the shoe from the bottom to the top around the matching buttons on the scallop trims. As you lace the shoe, maintain an opening between the front edges that equals the width of the tongue. Tie the ends of the cord into a bow.

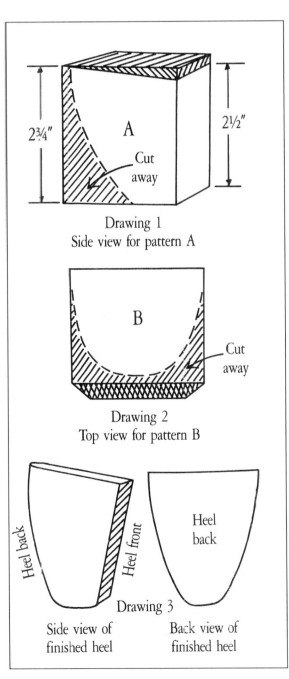

2¾"   2½"

A

Cut away

Drawing 1
Side view for pattern A

B

Cut away

Drawing 2
Top view for pattern B

Heel back   Heel front   Heel back

Drawing 3

Side view of finished heel   Back view of finished heel

GENERAL INSTRUCTIONS

The following instructions are for making either the mother, girl, or boy doll. Repeat the instructions for additional dolls.

HEAD

1. Cut a 4-inch length of dowel for the mother's body or a 2-inch length for the girl's or boy's body. Glue one dowel end into a bead head hole.
2. With the felt pen, draw a face on the bead. Thin the red acrylic paint with water. Paint red circles on the bead for cheeks.

BODY

1. For the mother, sew the 4-inch sides of the body piece together. For a child, sew the 2½-inch sides of the body piece together. Turn the body right side out.
2. Double-thread a needle and sew small running stitches close to one body edge. Slip the sewn edge onto the body dowel. Position the body ½ inch below the head. Pull up the threads so the fabric fits snugly around the dowel; securely knot the threads. Glue the fabric gathers to the dowel.
3. Firmly stuff the body with fiberfill. Turn the bottom edge of the body under ¼ inch. Sew running stitches through both layers of folded fabric. Gather the threads to close the opening; knot to secure the threads.
4. For the mother or girl, glue a piece of lace at the neck to cover the raw edge of the body.

LEGS

1. Cut two 3-inch pieces of dowel for the mother's and boy's legs. Cut two 2-inch pieces of dowel for the girl's legs.
2. Cut a ⅝-inch piece from each end of a Popsicle stick for the mother's shoes. Cut a ½-inch piece from each end of a Popsicle stick for each child's shoes. Paint both sides of each shoe black. Glue one shoe to the flat side of each dowel leg, aligning the cut edge of the stick with the edge of the dowel. For the girl, thin red paint with water and paint red circles for knees on the dowels.
3. Insert a screw eye into the top of each leg.
4. Use carpet thread to sew the screw eyes to the bottom of the body.

ARMS

1. Cut two 2-inch pieces of dowel for the mother's arms. Cut two 1½-inch pieces of dowel for each child's arms. Insert a screw eye into one end of each arm dowel.
2. To attach the arms on the mother and girl dolls, refer to the drawing in the box on page 119. First, double-thread a tapestry needle with 12 inches of ⅛-inch-wide ribbon. Insert the needle through the body, ½ inch below the neck. Pull the ribbon so equal lengths are on both sides of the body.

Cut the ribbon at the needle. Slip the screw eye of one arm onto one piece of ribbon. Tie the ends of the ribbons into a bow close to the body. Dot the bowknot with glue. Attach the other arm in the same manner.
3. For the boy, use carpet thread to sew the arms ½ inch below the neck on each side of the body.

MOTHER'S CLOTHING

1. Sew the 4¼-inch sides of the skirt piece together. Turn under the raw edges at the top and bottom of the skirt ¼ inch. Topstitch one of the edges for the hem. Sew running stitches along the opposite edge. Slip the skirt onto the doll, positioning the skirt 1 inch below her neck. Pull up the threads, adjusting the waist to fit, and knot the threads; tack the skirt to the body.
2. Turn under the 2½-inch sides of the apron skirt ¼ inch; topstitch folds in place. Sew lace atop the right side of one 4½-inch edge. Gather the remaining edge to a width of 2 inches. Center the apron on a 12-inch length of narrow lace or ribbon for apron ties and waistband; hand-sew the ribbon atop the gathers on the right side of the apron. Tie the apron around the waist.
3. Sew seed beads to the dress bodice for buttons.

GIRL'S CLOTHING

1. Sew the 2¼-inch sides of the skirt as directed for the Mother's Clothing, Step 1, *above*, except tack the skirt to the body ¾ inch below her neck.
2. See the photo on page 116 for trim ideas.

BOY'S CLOTHING

1. Sew the pants pieces together at the center and inner leg seams. Turn under the bottom edge of each leg ½ inch; hand-sew in place for hems. Turn the pants right side out; slip onto doll. Turn under the waist edge ¼ inch; tack pants to body ¾ inch below the neck.
2. Sew the underarm and side seams of the sweater. Turn the sweater right side out. Make a slit at the neckline marking; slip the sweater onto the doll. Fold under ⅛ inch on the 2-inch sides of the collar. Tack or glue the collar around the neck.

FINISHING DOLLS

1. Glue a small amount of crepe wool or fleece to the top of each head for hair. Add ribbons and bows to the girl's hair, if desired.
2. For the girl's anklets, glue narrow lace at the top of each shoe.
3. For the boy's socks, use black acrylic to paint a ½-inch-wide band at the top of each shoe.
4. For the boy's muffler, tie a ½x5-inch strip of fabric around his neck.

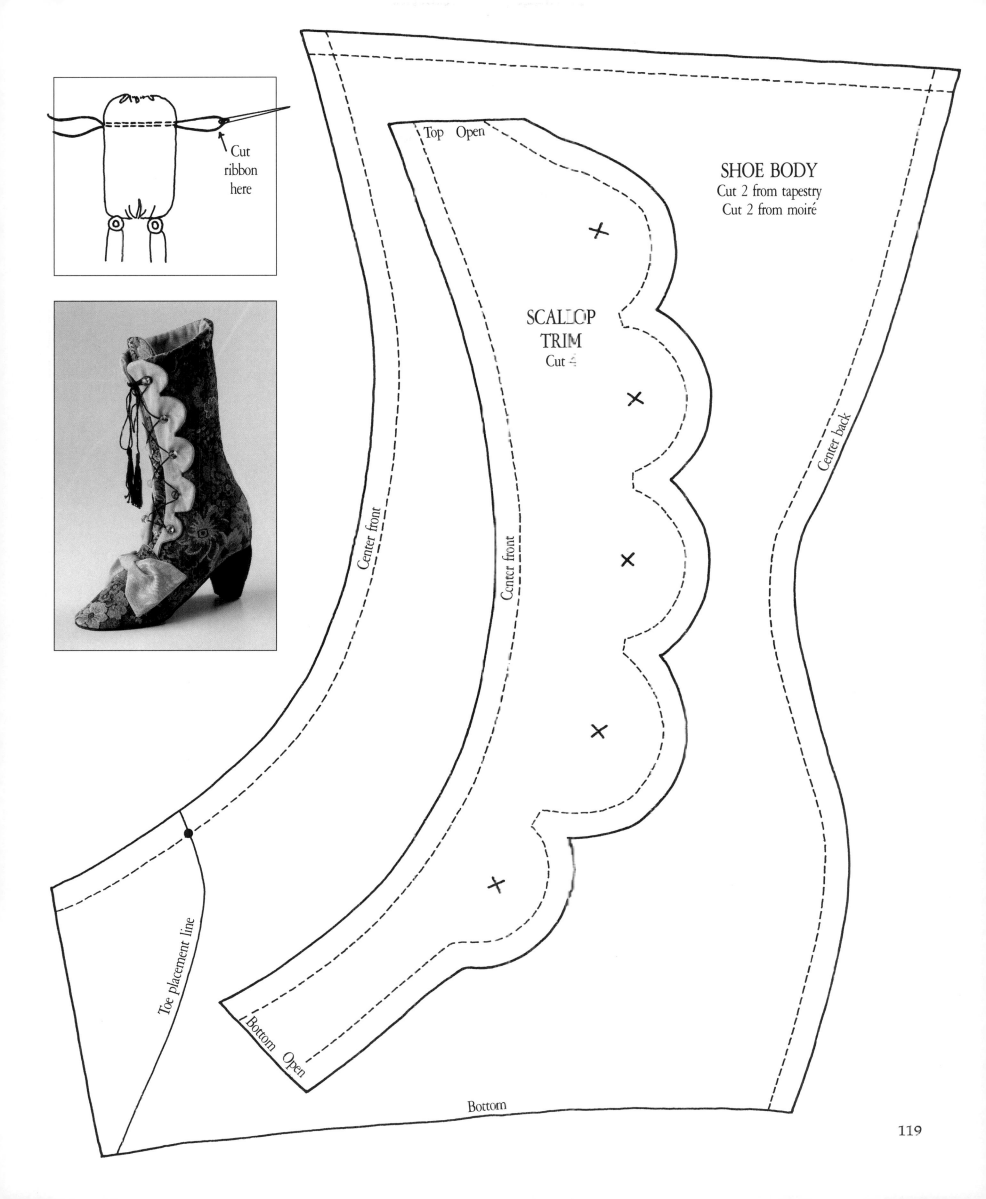

Cut ribbon here

SHOE BODY
Cut 2 from tapestry
Cut 2 from moiré

SCALLOP TRIM
Cut 4

Top Open

Center front

Center front

Center back

Toe placement line

Bottom Open

Bottom

119

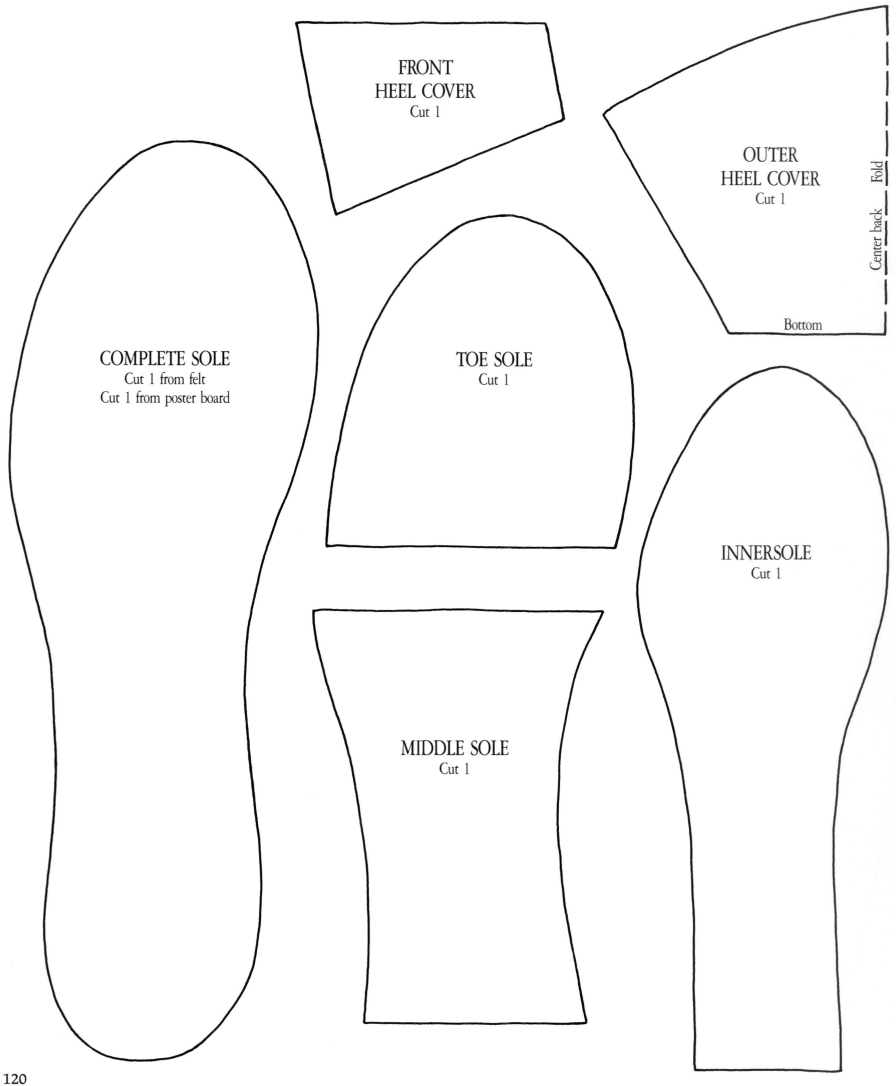

FRONT
HEEL COVER
Cut 1

OUTER
HEEL COVER
Cut 1

Center back   Fold

Bottom

COMPLETE SOLE
Cut 1 from felt
Cut 1 from poster board

TOE SOLE
Cut 1

INNERSOLE
Cut 1

MIDDLE SOLE
Cut 1

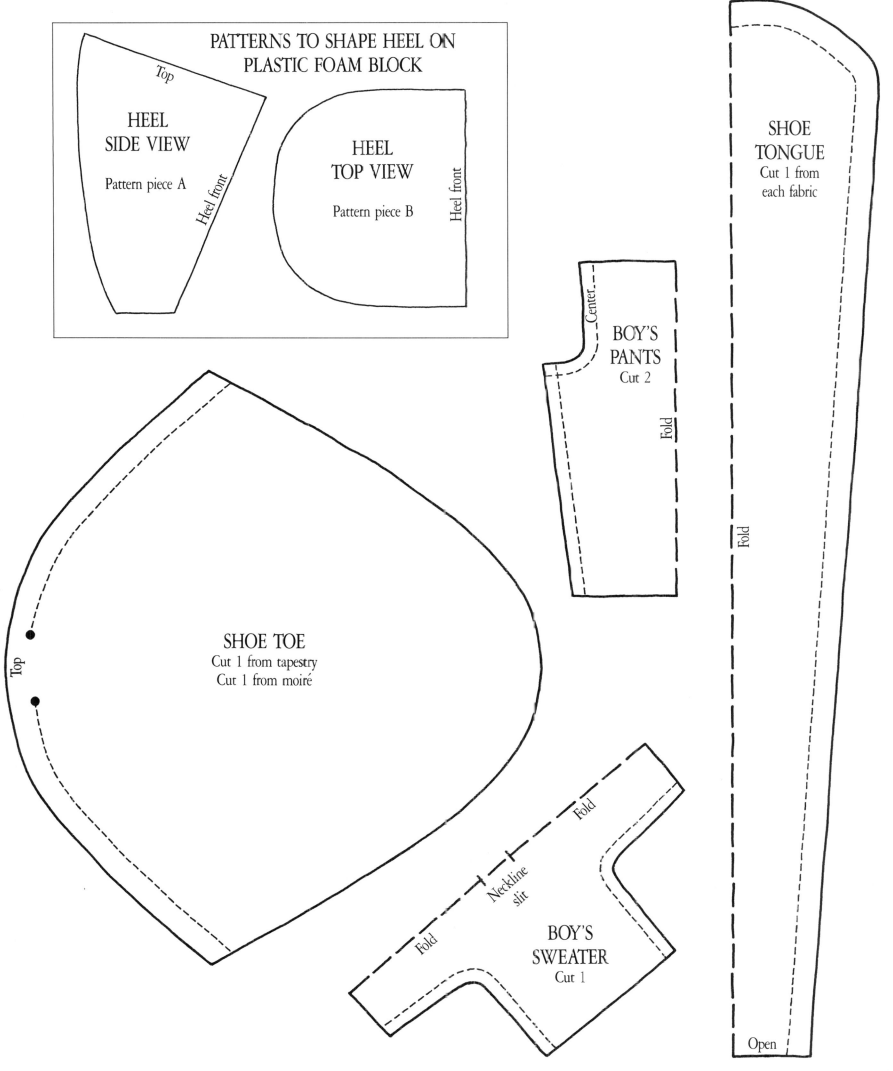

PATTERNS TO SHAPE HEEL ON
PLASTIC FOAM BLOCK

HEEL
SIDE VIEW

Pattern piece A

Top

Heel front

HEEL
TOP VIEW

Pattern piece B

Heel front

SHOE
TONGUE
Cut 1 from
each fabric

Fold

Open

Center

BOY'S
PANTS
Cut 2

Fold

SHOE TOE
Cut 1 from tapestry
Cut 1 from moiré

Top

Fold

Neckline
slit

Fold

BOY'S
SWEATER
Cut 1

Gordon
AND
Gertrude

Would you like a pair of dolls that will make heads turn? Long-necked Gordon and Gertrude are creatures of a very different sort, indeed. Rooted in old-time tradition, their heads reach the starry heights of today's whimsical collectibles. Painted spots enhance hides of tea-dyed muslin. Tea-dye their clothing, too, for that favored antique look. Both dolls are 17 inches tall.

PREPARING THE PATTERNS

Trace the full-size patterns, *opposite* and on pages 126 and 127, onto tracing paper. Cut out the patterns.

CUTTING THE FABRICS

Before cutting out the pattern pieces, tea-dye the broadcloth, plaid, checked, and osnaburg fabrics. See the box, *opposite*, for tips on dyeing fabrics.

From muslin, cut:
- Four bodies
- Eight legs
- Eight arms
- Eight ears
- Four heads

From osnaburg, cut:
- Two shirts

From broadcloth, cut:
- Two bloomers

From the plaid fabric, cut:
- One 9x19-inch skirt
- One bow tie
- Two bodice pieces

From the checked fabric, cut:
- Two pants
- Two collars

GENERAL INSTRUCTIONS

The instructions are for sewing one giraffe. Repeat instructions for second giraffe. Clothing directions for each giraffe are given separately.

BODY

1. Sew two body pieces together at the side seams. Leave the top and bottom edges open. Clip the curves; turn the body right side out.
2. Turn under the bottom edge ¼ inch; press.

LEGS

1. Sew the leg pieces together in pairs, leaving the tops open. Clip the curves; turn each leg right side out. Firmly stuff with fiberfill to within ½ inch of the top. Pinch each leg so that the seams are aligned and centered; pin to secure. Baste across the top of each leg.
2. Insert the top of each leg into the bottom of the body, easing to fit between the dots. Topstitch or hand-sew across the bottom of the body to secure the legs and close the opening.
3. Firmly stuff the body up to the top opening.

HEAD

1. Sew the two head pieces together, leaving the bottom edge open. Clip the curves; turn the head right side out. Baste under the bottom edge ¼ inch. Firmly stuff head with fiberfill.
2. Sew the ears together in pairs, leaving the bottoms open. Trim the seam allowances to ⅛ inch; clip the curves and turn the ears right side out.
3. Turn ⅛ inch of the raw edges at the base of each ear to the inside; press. Gather the bottom of each ear to measure ⅜ inch. Position the ears at the X markings on the head and stitch in place.
4. Blindstitch the giraffe's neck to the body, adding fiberfill as necessary.

ARMS

1. Sew the arm pieces together in pairs, leaving the tops open. Clip the hand curves; turn the arms right side out. Press under ¼ inch on the top opening of each arm. Firmly stuff each arm with fiberfill to within ½ inch of the top.
2. With a double-threaded needle, hand-sew a gathering thread around the top opening. Pull the thread tightly to close the opening; knot to secure the thread. Hand-sew each arm at the X markings on the body.

FINISHING

1. Paint the entire doll with antique white. Allow the paint to dry.
2. With burnt umber, paint the bottoms of the legs, the spots on the giraffe's head and neck, the eyes, and the nostrils as shown in the photo on pages 122 and 123.
3. Brush pine-colored stain over the painted surfaces. Wipe away excess stain with a cloth. Allow the remaining stain to dry.

GERTRUDE'S BLOOMERS

1. Sew the bloomers together along the side and inner leg seams. Clip curves; turn right side out.
2. Turn under the leg and waist edges ¼ inch; press. With matching sewing thread, sew running stitches close to the folded edges. Slip the bloomers onto the giraffe. Pull the threads to gather so the bloomers fit around the waist and legs. Knot the threads to secure the gathers.

GERTRUDE'S DRESS

1. Sew the shoulder seams of the bodice from the small dot to the end of each sleeve. Leave the remaining edge unstitched for the neck opening.
2. Sew the underarm and side seams.
3. Sew the 9-inch edges of the skirt together. Press under ¼ inch on one 19-inch edge for the hem. Topstitch close to the folded edge.
4. Gather and pin the unfinished edge of the skirt to fit the bodice waist, placing the skirt seam at the center of one bodice piece and adjusting the gathers evenly. Sew the skirt to the bodice.
5. Turn under the wrist and neckline edges of the bodice ¼ inch; press. With a matching thread, sew running stitches close to the folded edges. Slip the dress onto the doll with the seam at the back. Pull the threads to gather so the wrists and neckline fit around the doll. Knot the threads to secure the gathers.

GERTRUDE'S COLLAR

1. Sew the two collar pieces together, leaving an opening between the dots. Trim the seam allowance to ⅛ inch. Clip curves, turn, and press.
2. Place the collar around the doll's neck and tack the front edges at the X markings. Sew the ½-inch-diameter button over the tacked edge.

GORDON'S SHIRT

1. Sew the shoulder seams of the shirt from the small dot to the end of each sleeve. Leave the remaining edge unstitched for the neck opening.
2. Sew the underarm and side seams.
3. Press under a ¼-inch hem on the bottom of the shirt. Topstitch close to the folded edge.
4. Turn under the wrist and neckline edges of the shirt ¼ inch; press. With a matching thread, sew running stitches close to the folded edges. Slip the shirt onto the doll. Pull the threads to gather so the wrists and neckline fit around the doll. Knot the threads to secure the gathers.

GORDON'S PANTS

1. Sew the two pants pieces together at the center seams. Sew the inner leg seams. Turn the pants right side out.
2. Press under ¼ inch on the waist and leg edges. Topstitch close to the folded edge.
3. Slip the pants onto the doll. Fold the front and back waist pleats, folding the pleats toward the center seams; tack in place. Blindstitch the pants to the doll.

GORDON'S BOW TIE

1. With the bow tie folded along one long edge, sew the side and bottom edges together, leaving an opening between the dots. Trim the seam allowance to ⅛ inch and turn the tie right side out.
2. Gather the center of the bow tie and tack in place at the shirt neckline.

DYEING FABRICS

A variety of products are used by experienced dollmakers to transform everyday fabrics into timeworn- and antique-looking conversation pieces. Have fun experimenting with the dyes and the methods described *below;* they'll add character and a professional touch to your dolls.

Perhaps the most common method of "aging" fabrics is tea-dyeing. To tea-dye fabric, simply boil 8 tea bags in 4 cups of water. Remove the bags. Soak the fabric in the tea until it reaches the desired color. Remove the fabric from the tea and rinse it thoroughly in cold water. Once the fabric is dry, press it.

Additional interesting effects can be achieved by placing the strong tea solution in a spray bottle. Strategically spray the fabric, creating a marbleized effect, and allow the fabric to dry.

To create a crinkled effect, crush the fabric into a bundle after it has soaked in the tea and place it in the freezer. Once it is frozen, remove, defrost, and let dry.

Rolling the fabric into a ball and tying strings or rubber bands around it also will create an uneven effect.

You also can use fabric dyes to "age" new fabrics. Use a tan dye or other neutral colors. Mix dyes at half strength following the manufacturer's instructions. These dyes color the fabric evenly, which often is better for faces.

Acrylic paints are used on many of the projects throughout this book. The paint will harden fabric, giving it an added crispness. When using paint, have a variety of brushes available. Fine brushes work well for features, toothpicks dipped in paint will make tiny dots, and larger brushes and small pieces of sponge will cover big areas and create mottled effects.

Acrylic paints are easily thinned with water for a washed effect. They also can be blended to achieve a wide range of colors. Before you begin painting on your doll, sketch or diagram your design with pencil on a scrap of fabric and experiment until you are satisfied with the results.

Wood stains, which are widely available in a variety of shades, can be used in combination with acrylic paints or by themselves. Like paint, they will harden the fabric, and create wonderful textures.

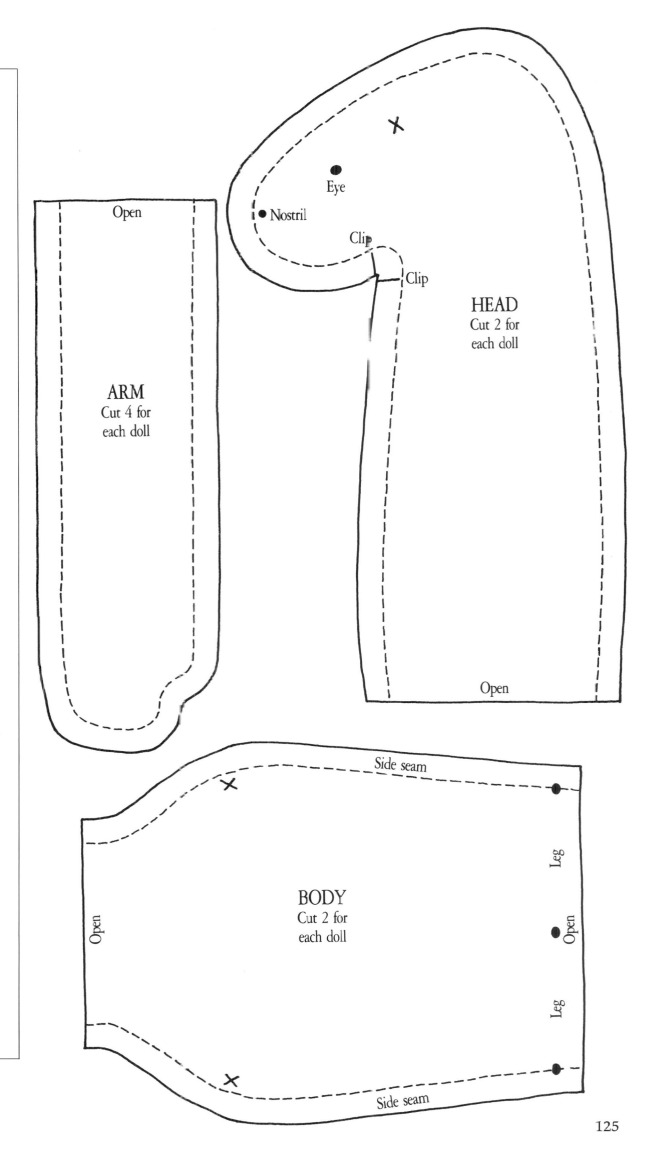

ARM
Cut 4 for
each doll

HEAD
Cut 2 for
each doll

Eye
Nostril
Clip
Clip
Open
Open

BODY
Cut 2 for
each doll

Side seam
Leg
Open
Open
Leg
Side seam

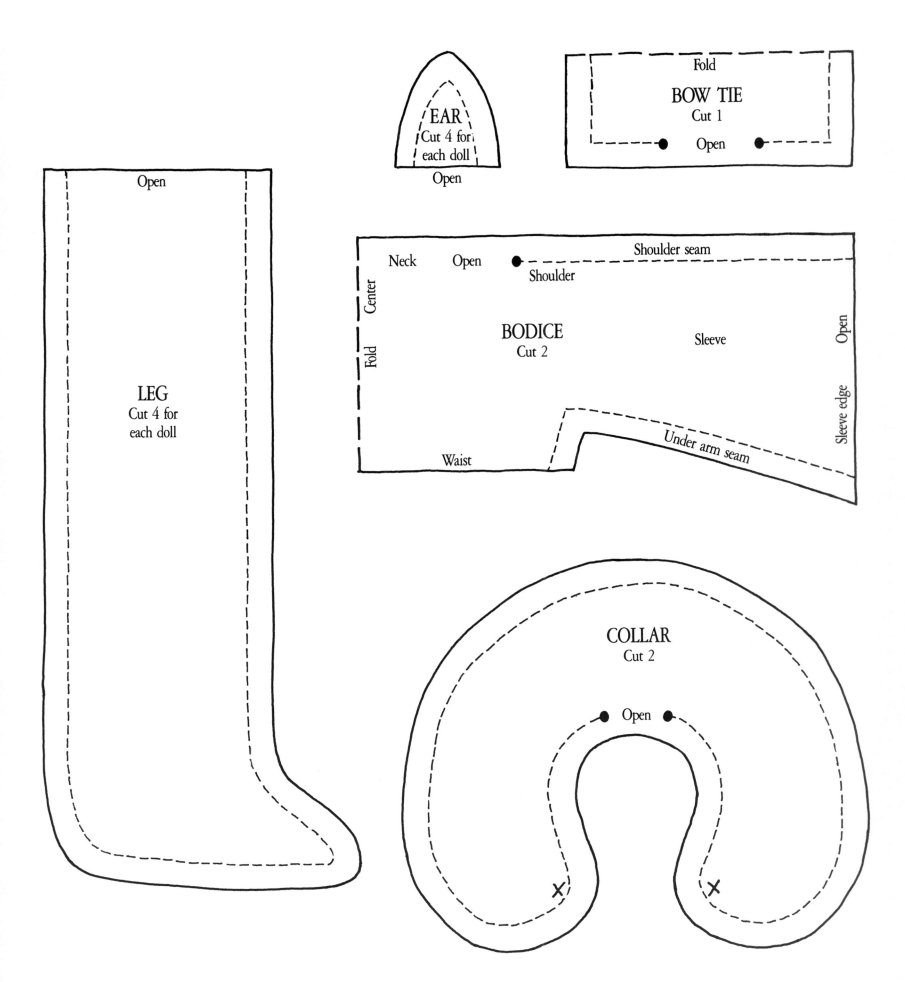

EAR
Cut 4 for
each doll
Open

Fold
BOW TIE
Cut 1
Open

Open

LEG
Cut 4 for
each doll

Neck   Open   Shoulder seam
Shoulder

Fold   Center

BODICE
Cut 2   Sleeve

Open

Sleeve edge

Waist   Under arm seam

COLLAR
Cut 2

Open

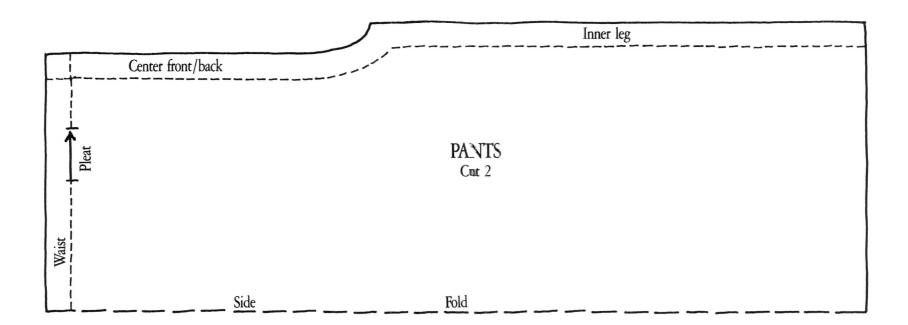

PANTS
Cut 2

Inner leg

Center front/back

Pleat

Waist

Side

Fold

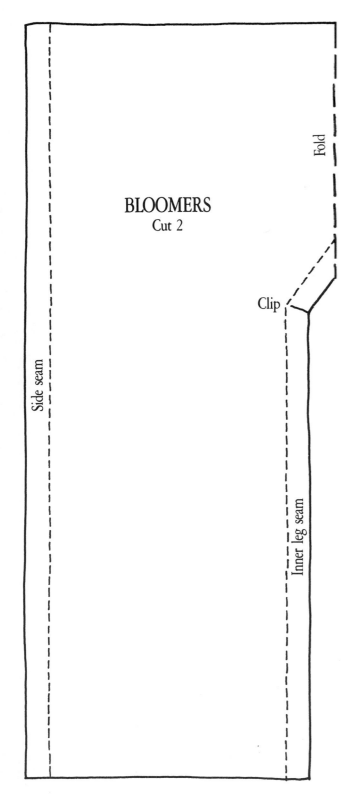

BLOOMERS
Cut 2

Fold

Clip

Side seam

Inner leg seam

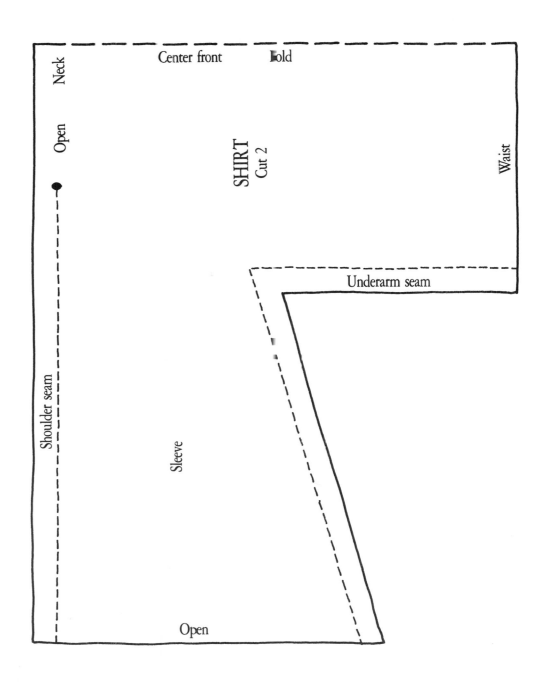

SHIRT
Cut 2

Center front

Fold

Neck

Open

Waist

Shoulder seam

Sleeve

Underarm seam

Open

SUZANNE AND REBECCA

Friends forever are these plain and fancy playmates and Suzanne's pet dog Nellie. Their easy-to-make bodies and clothing are constructed from homespun materials that express their unaffected simplicity. Suzanne's knotted hair buns are cleverly made with one skein of black embroidery floss and Rebecca's tresses are knotted strands of acrylic yarn. Both dolls stand 14 inches tall.

GENERAL INSTRUCTIONS

The instructions are for sewing one doll. Repeat these directions to make the second doll. The clothing is the same for both dolls, except when noted otherwise in the instructions.

FACES

1. Transfer the facial features to one body piece. Use light-colored dressmaker's carbon paper to transfer the features to the black fabric.
2. For Rebecca, use the fine-tip brush and burnt umber to paint the eyes and nose. Paint red lips.
3. For Suzanne, use three plies of ecru floss to embroider straight stitches for eyes. Use a single ply of ecru floss to embroider straight-stitch eyelashes and to backstitch the nose. Use a single ply of maroon floss to backstitch the mouth. (See page 7 for stitch diagrams.)

LEGS

1. Sew the legs together in pairs, leaving the tops open. Clip the curves; turn each leg right side out.
2. Firmly stuff the legs with fiberfill to within 1 inch of the top edges.
3. Pinch the top of each leg so that the front and back seams are aligned and centered. Pin, then baste the raw edges together.
4. Paint Rebecca's shoes with burnt umber, using the shaded area on the shoe pattern as a guide.

BODY

1. Sew body pieces together, leaving the bottom edge open. Clip curves; turn body right side out.
2. Turn under the bottom edge of the body ¼ inch; press. Firmly stuff the body with fiberfill.
3. Insert the legs into the bottom of the body between the dots. Pin the legs in place. Sew the bottom edges of the body close to the fold, encasing the tops of the legs inside the body.

ARMS

1. Sew the arms together in pairs, leaving the tops open. Trim the seams around the hand to ⅛ inch and clip the curves. Turn each arm right side out.
2. For Rebecca, lightly stuff the finger area with fiberfill. Topstitch the placement lines. Finish stuffing the arms to within 1 inch of the top.
3. For Suzanne, stuff the hands and arms to within 1 inch of the top.
4. For both dolls, turn under the top edge of each arm ¼ inch. With a double-threaded needle, sew running stitches along the folded edge and pull tightly to close the opening. Without breaking the thread, slip-stitch the arms, with the thumbs facing forward, to the body at the Xs.

HAIR

1. For Rebecca's hair, cut six 10-inch strands of yarn. Bundle the strands, fold the bundle in half, and use matching thread to tack the fold of the

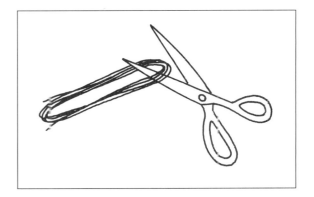

bundle to the top of the head at the dot. Tack the sides of each bundle to the sides of the head at the dots. Holding two strands together, make overhand knots at the ends of the yarn; trim the ends.
2. For Suzanne's hair, refer to the drawing, *above*, and cut the skein of floss at one of the looped ends to make a 13-inch-long bundle. Tack the floss to the head following the directions for Rebecca's hair in Step 1. Braid the ends of the floss on each side of the head. Roll each braid into a knot and sew them in place to the sides of the head just below the side tackings.

PANTALOONS

1. Mark and sew a 6-inch inseam for the pantaloons as directed in the tip box on page 130.
2. Press under ¼ inch along the bottom of each leg. Sew the side seams; press under the waist edge ¼ inch. Turn the pantaloons right side out.
3. Sew running stitches close to the folded waist edge. Slip the pantaloons onto the doll. Pull up the thread to fit the pantaloons to the doll's waist; adjust the gathers and knot the ends of the threads together.
4. Sew running stitches around the bottom of each leg. Pull up the threads to fit the pantaloons to the doll's ankles; adjust the gathers and knot the ends of the threads together.

DRESSES

1. Sew the shoulder seams of the bodice together from the dot to the sleeve opening. Press the seams open; turn under the neck opening ¼ inch. Press the wrist edges of the sleeves under ¼ inch.
2. Sew the underarm and side seams of the bodice together. Clip the underarm curve and press the seams open.
3. Sew the 8¾-inch edges of the skirt rectangle together for the center back seam. Turn under one raw edge ¼ inch two times; topstitch or sew in place for the hem. Gather the remaining raw edge of the skirt to fit the waist of the bodice. Sew the skirt to the bodice, placing the skirt seam at the center back of the bodice. Turn dress right side out.
4. Slip the dress onto the doll. Sew running stitches around each wrist. Pull up the threads to fit. Adjust the gathers; knot the thread ends together.

continued

5. To make the neckline fit the doll, fold a ¼-inch pleat at the neck edge of each shoulder seam; tack the pleats in place.

6. Tie a ribbon belt around the waist. For Rebecca's dress only, make a small ribbon bow; tack it to the center front of her dress.

JACKET

1. Cut one jacket piece along the fold line to make two front pieces. Sew the fronts to the back at the shoulder seams, sewing from the dot to the wrist; press the seams open. Sew the underarm and side seams. Clip the curves and press the seams open.

2. Press under the neck, center front, bottom, and sleeve edges ¼ inch. Topstitch all pressed edges in place. Slip the jacket onto the doll.

GLOVES

1. Sew gloves following the instructions for the Arms (see Step 1 on page 129).

2. Topstitch the finger lines.

3. Fold the gloves over Rebecca's belt; tack them in place.

DOG

1. Sew the two dog pieces together, leaving an opening between the dots. Clip the curves and turn the dog right side out.

2. Lightly stuff the legs with fiberfill. Topstitch on the placement lines to define the legs. Stuff the remainder of the dog; sew the opening closed.

3. Using six plies of floss, make a French-knot eye at the Xs on each side of the dog's head.

4. Cut a 16-inch piece of twine. Tie one end into a bow around the dog's neck; tie the other end into a knot around Suzanne's wrist.

MAKING PANTALOONS WITHOUT A PATTERN

These tips will help you make pantaloons for your doll from simple rectangles.

1. Referring to drawing 1, *below,* fold *one* bloomer rectangle in half with the long edges together. Use a pencil to make a small dot on both layers of fabric ¼ inch from the fold (see A marking on drawing). Make another dot on the fold using the measurement given in the directions for the doll you are making or make the dot about two-thirds of the way up from the bottom edge (see B marking on drawing).

2. Referring to drawing 2, unfold the rectangle. Use a ruler to connect the A dots with the B dot. Place the marked rectangle on top of the unmarked rectangle, keeping all edges even. Sew the rectangles together along drawn lines.

3. Referring to drawing 3, cut between the stitching lines up to the B dot.

4. Finish the waist, side seams, and leg openings following the instructions for the doll.

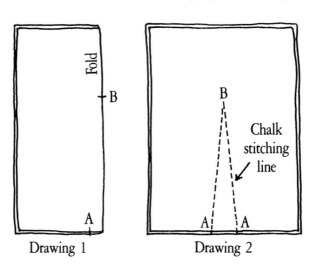

Drawing 1   Drawing 2   Drawing 3

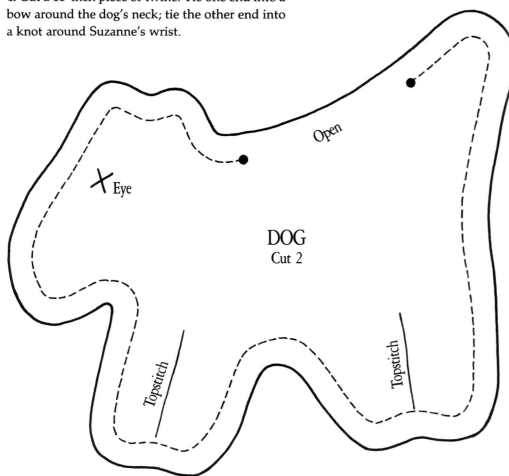

DOG
Cut 2

X Eye

Open

Topstitch

Topstitch

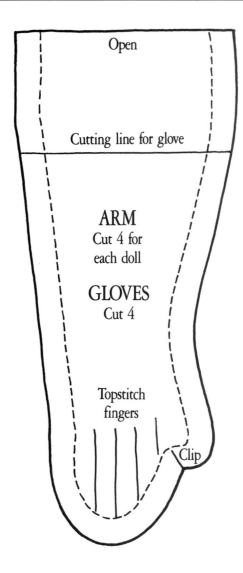

Open

Cutting line for glove

ARM
Cut 4 for
each doll

GLOVES
Cut 4

Topstitch
fingers

Clip

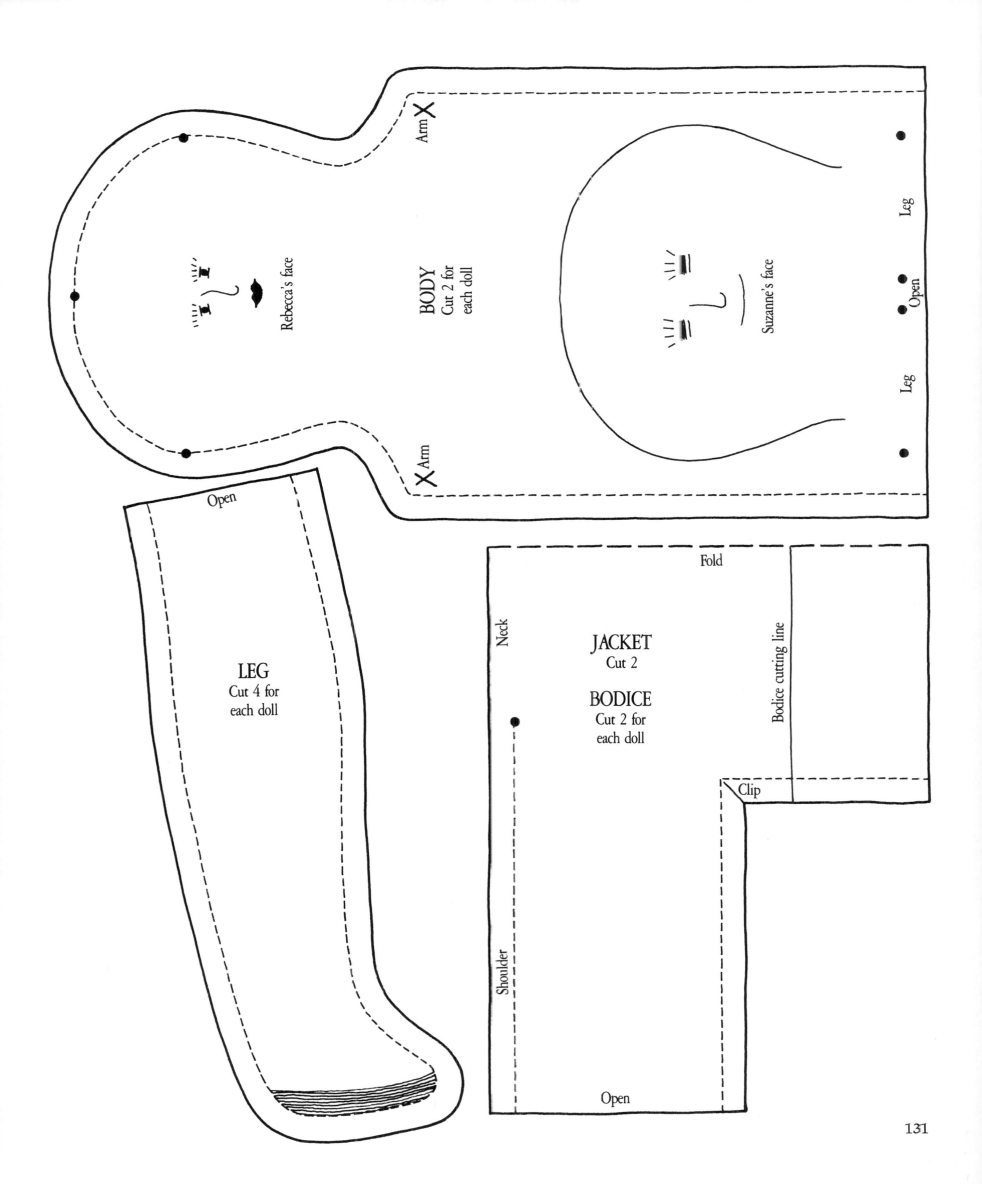

Arm X

Rebecca's face

BODY
Cut 2 for
each doll

Suzanne's face

Leg

Open

Leg

X Arm

Open

LEG
Cut 4 for
each doll

Fold

Neck

JACKET
Cut 2

BODICE
Cut 2 for
each doll

Bodice cutting line

Clip

Shoulder

Open

131

FERDINAND

Who would ever guess that a bull could look so "moo-velous"? Ferdinand wears a brand-new pair of bib overalls, a striped shirt, and a jingle bell around his neck. Standing on his two hind legs, he measures 20½ inches. The spots on his muslin body are dry-brushed using acrylic paint.

AND CLARA

A miniature basket filled with dried flowers enhances Clara's pretty pink print dress. Loops of pearls, a tied bow for her horns, and contrasting fabric trims for her dress collar and pocket are the "cowgirl" fashion for Sunday gatherings and walks around the fields.

GENERAL INSTRUCTIONS

The following instructions are for sewing one cow body. Repeat these instructions to make the second cow. Directions for the clothing for each cow are given separately.

ARMS AND BODY

1. Sew the arms together in pairs, leaving the tops open. Clip the curves and trim the seam allowances around the hooves (hands) to ⅛ inch. Turn each arm right side out and stuff up to the topstitching line. Sew across the topstitching lines. (See the topstitching tip, *right*.) Lightly stuff the upper arms; baste the top edges closed.

2. Pin and sew two arms to one body piece between the small dots at the body sides. The arms should lie toward the center of the body with each thumb pointing up.

3. Sew the body pieces together along the shoulder and side seams, securing the arms. Leave the neck and bottom edges open. Do not turn the body right side out; set the body aside.

HEAD

1. Sew the ears together in pairs, leaving the bottoms open. Trim the seam allowances to ⅛ inch. Turn ears right side out and press.

2. Place a piece of paper inside each ear to prevent paint from bleeding through. Dry-brush one side of each ear with black acrylic paint. (To dry-brush, dip the fabric or stencil brush into the black paint and stroke it on a paper towel until most of the paint has been removed. When the brush is almost clean, dab the ears with it.) Allow the paint to dry; remove the paper.

3. Fold each ear in half lengthwise with the painted side out. Pin each ear to a head side piece between the small dots with the painted side facing the back of the head. Sew the ears to the head, using ⅛-inch seams.

4. To fit the head center to the head side pieces, sew a gathering stitch along each long edge of the head center piece. Pin the head center to one side head, matching the large dots. Fit the two pieces together by easing the gathering stitches. Beginning at the front neckline, sew the head center piece to the two head side pieces.

5. Clip curves and turn the head right side out.

6. Insert the head into the body at the neck. Pin the head neck seam to the body neck seam, matching the center front and center back dots. Sew the neck seam, attaching the head to the body. For stability, sew around the neck again ⅛ inch from the first seam in the seam allowance.

7. Turn the body right side out. Set the piece aside for later use.

LEGS

1. Sew a hoof to each leg piece, matching dots. Sew the legs together in pairs, leaving the tops open. Trim the hoof seam allowances to ⅛ inch and clip the curves. Turn the legs right sides out.

2. Firmly stuff each leg with fiberfill to the topstitching line. Sew across the topstitching line to close the lower leg. Loosely stuff the upper leg and baste the top edges closed.

3. Sew each leg to the body front between the dots, keeping the raw edges even.

4. Firmly stuff the head and neck, shaping the head as you work. Put extra fiberfill in the jowl area to make the sides of the head wider. Continue stuffing the body, making sure there is enough fiberfill in the neck and chest to support the head.

5. Turn the bottom edges of the body under ¼ inch. Hand-sew the body edges together, encasing the tops of the legs inside the body.

HORNS

1. Sew matching horn pieces together, leaving an opening between the dots. Trim the seam allowance to ⅛ inch, clip the curves, and turn the horns right side out. Firmly stuff the horns and hand-sew the openings closed.

2. Center and hand-sew the horns to the top of the head. Stitch along both the front and back of the head and horns for added stability.

FINISHING

1. Sew the button eyes to the head at the Xs, using two strands of black embroidery floss. Make two French knot nostrils at the small dots on the head center, using six strands of pink floss. (See page 7 for stitch diagram.)

2. Dry-brush random spots on the head with black acrylic paint (the method is described in Step 2 for the Head). Refer to the photo on pages 132 and 133 for painting ideas.

3. Brush a circle of blush on each nostril and on the inside of each ear.

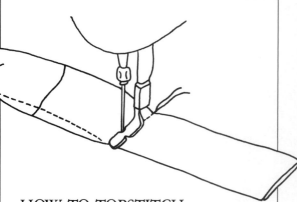

HOW TO TOPSTITCH ELBOW AND KNEE JOINTS

Knees and elbows that bend allow a doll to be posed in a variety of positions, which imparts a pleasing character and lifelike quality to a doll.

The zipper-foot attachment for your sewing machine makes this cumbersome joint construction easy. First, stuff the arm or leg up to the topstitching line to the firmness suggested in the pattern instructions. Position the zipper foot so that the wide part of the foot rests on the unstuffed leg or arm with the needle atop the stitching line. (The needle will be next to the stuffed portion.) Sew across the stitching line, forming the joint. Then follow the instructions to complete the arm or leg above the joint.

MATERIALS FOR FERDINAND'S AND CLARA'S CLOTHING

⅝ yard of print fabric for dress

⅓ yard of coordinating striped fabric for shirt, dress collar, and pocket

⅓ yard of muslin for pantaloons

½ yard of lightweight denim for overalls

⅔ yard of ⅛-inch-wide elastic

¼ yard of ⅛-inch-wide ribbon for collar

¼ yard of strung pearl beads

Two ³⁄₁₆-inch-diameter buttons for the shirt

Two nailhead brads or gripper snaps for overalls

Two ½-inch-wide cowbells

Two 9-inch lengths of string

Contrasting thread for overalls

◆

PREPARING THE PATTERNS

Trace the full-size clothing patterns on pages 138 and 139 onto tracing paper. Extend the bottom of the overalls pants leg 1 inch when you trace the pattern. Cut out the patterns.

◆

CUTTING THE FABRICS

The cutting instructions for pieces that have no patterns include ¼-inch seams.

From print fabric, cut:
- Two bodice pieces
- Two 6½x8-inch dress sleeves
- One 9¼x44-inch dress skirt
- One 2½x21-inch bow strip

From striped fabric, cut:
- Two dress pockets
- Two collars
- Two shirt fronts
- One shirt back
- One shirt facing
- Two 4½x6-inch shirt sleeves

From muslin, cut:
- Two 8½x11½-inch pantaloons

From denim, cut:
- Four overalls pants legs
- Two overalls front bibs
- Two overalls back bibs
- Two overalls bib pockets
- One ruler pocket
- One 2-inch-square pocket
- One 1¼x2½-inch hammer loop

CLARA'S PANTALOONS

Note: Refer to the box on page 130 for tips on making the pantaloons.

1. To establish the inside leg seams, fold one 8½x11½-inch pantaloons piece in half to form a 4¼x11½-inch rectangle. Use a pencil to make a dot ¼ inch from the fold on the bottom short edge on both layers of the fabric. Then, on the fold, make a dot 6 inches above the same edge. Unfold the piece and use a ruler to connect each edge dot to the fold dot, forming a narrow V shape. Place the marked rectangle on top of the unmarked rectangle. Stitch along the pencil lines to form the inseams. Cut between the stitching lines up to the dot.

2. Press under the bottom edge of each pantaloons leg 1¼ inches. Cut two 4-inch pieces of elastic. Sew the elastic on the wrong side of each bottom edge ¾ inch from the fold, stretching as you sew.

3. Sew the outside leg seams together. Press under the waist edge ¼ inch. Cut one 8-inch piece of elastic. Sew the elastic on the wrong side of the waist just below the folded edge, stretching as you sew. Slip pantaloons onto Clara.

CLARA'S DRESS

1. Cut along the fold of one bodice piece to form two back bodice pieces. Sew the two bodice back pieces to the bodice front at the shoulder seams. Stay-stitch the neck edge by sewing on the marked seam line. Clip the curves and press under the neck edge along the stay stitching. Press under ¼ inch along the bodice center back edges. Topstitch close to the neck and back bodice folds.

2. Press under one 6½-inch side of each sleeve 1 inch. Cut two 4-inch pieces of elastic. Sew the elastic on the wrong side of each edge ¾ inch from each fold, stretching as you sew. On the remaining 6½-inch side of each sleeve, use a pencil to mark 1½ inches from each long edge. Sew gathering stitches between the marks.

3. Pin the sleeves to the bodice armholes, pulling up the gathers to fit; sew the sleeves in place. Sew the underarm and side seams. Overlap the back bodice pieces ¼ inch and pin in place.

4. Sew the 9¼-inch edges of the skirt together for the center back seam. Turn under one of the 44-inch edges ¼ inch two times. Topstitch or hand-sew in place for the skirt hem. Sew gathering stitches on the remaining long edge. Pull up the gathers, fitting the skirt to the bodice waist. Pin in place, matching the skirt seam to the bodice back overlap, and distribute the gathers evenly. Sew the skirt to the bodice.

5. Sew the pocket pieces together, leaving an opening between the dots. Clip the curves, turn, and press. Hand-sew the pocket to the left side of the skirt, closing the opening as you sew.

6. Place the dress on the cow, and hand-sew the bodice back opening closed.

CLARA'S COLLAR

1. Cut the ribbon in half. Pin one end of each ribbon piece to the right side of one collar at the Xs with raw edges even and lengths of ribbon extending inside the collar. Place the remaining collar piece on top; stitch around the collar pieces encasing the ribbon ends, leaving an opening between the dots. Trim seams, turn, and press.

2. Place the collar around the neck and tie the ribbons into a bow.

FINISHING CLARA

1. Drape the pearl beads into two loops and tack them to the center front of the dress.

2. For a necklace, string a 9-inch length of string through one cowbell and tie it around the neck.

3. Fold the bow strip in half lengthwise and sew ends and sides, leaving a 2-inch opening in the center of the long side for turning. Angle the seams along the ends and trim the excess fabric. Turn the strip right side out, hand-sew the opening closed, and press. Tie the strip in a bow. Tack the bowknot to the center front of the horns.

FERDINAND'S SHIRT

1. Sew shirt fronts to shirt back at neck and shoulder seams. Clip corners and press open. Stay-stitch across the top opening; clip to stitching. Sew shirt facing to shirt, matching the small dots with the shoulder seams and the large dots with the dots on the shirt fronts. Clip curves and trim the corners. Turn the facing to the inside of the shirt and press. Turn remaining front edge under ¼ inch; press. Topstitch ⅛ inch from all edges around the shirt.

2. Turn one 4½-inch edge of each sleeve under ¼ inch and hem. Sew the opposite edge of each sleeve to an armhole opening between the dot. Sew underarm and side seams. Roll each sleeve back 1 inch two times to make cuffs.

3. For hem, press bottom edge of shirt under ¼ inch; stitch in place. Sew buttons to left front of shirt at Xs on pattern.

4. Place shirt on Ferdinand. With left front overlapping right front, hand-sew the shirt closed.

FERDINAND'S OVERALLS BIBS

1. Leaving the bottom edges open, sew the two bib front pieces together; sew the two back pieces together. Trim corners, turn, and press. Topstitch ⅛ inch from all seams on both pieces.

2. Sew the bib pocket pieces together, leaving an opening between the dots; turn and press. Hand-sew the opening closed. Position pocket on the front bib and topstitch in place. Topstitch the two vertical lines.

3. Topstitch the bib back along diagonal lines. (Do not topstitch the pocket line.)

continued

FERDINAND'S OVERALLS PANTS

1. Sew the pants legs together in pairs along the center seam. Set one unit aside for the front.

2. Press under the diagonal top edge of the ruler pocket ¼ inch. Topstitch ⅛ inch from the fold. Press under the side and bottom edges ¼ inch. Pin the wrong side of the pocket to the right side of the back of one leg in the position marked on the pattern; topstitch in place (do not topstitch the diagonal top edge of the pocket).

3. Press under one edge of the square pocket ¼ inch. Topstitch ⅛ inch from fold (top of pocket). Press under remaining edges ¼ inch. Pin wrong side of pocket to right side of overalls above the ruler pocket as marked on the pattern; topstitch in place (do not topstitch the top of pocket).

4. Press under long edges of hammer loop ¼ inch. Then fold the rectangle in half lengthwise. Topstitch the folded edges together. Fold the loop in half and sew it below the ruler pocket on the back overalls as marked on pattern.

FINISHING THE OVERALLS

1. Sew the bottom edge of the front bib to the top edge of the front pants. Press seam toward pants. Topstitch ⅛ inch above waist seam.

2. In same manner, sew back bib to back overalls.

3. Sew the side seams of the pants together, catching the edge of ruler pocket and the hammer loop into the seam. Sew the leg inseams. Turn overalls right side out. For cuffs, turn back each pants leg 1 inch two times.

4. Attach nailhead brads to front bib at the Xs on the pattern.

5. Place the overalls on Ferdinand. Tack each bib strap under a brad on the front bib. String a 9-inch length of string through one cowbell and tie it around Ferdinand's neck.

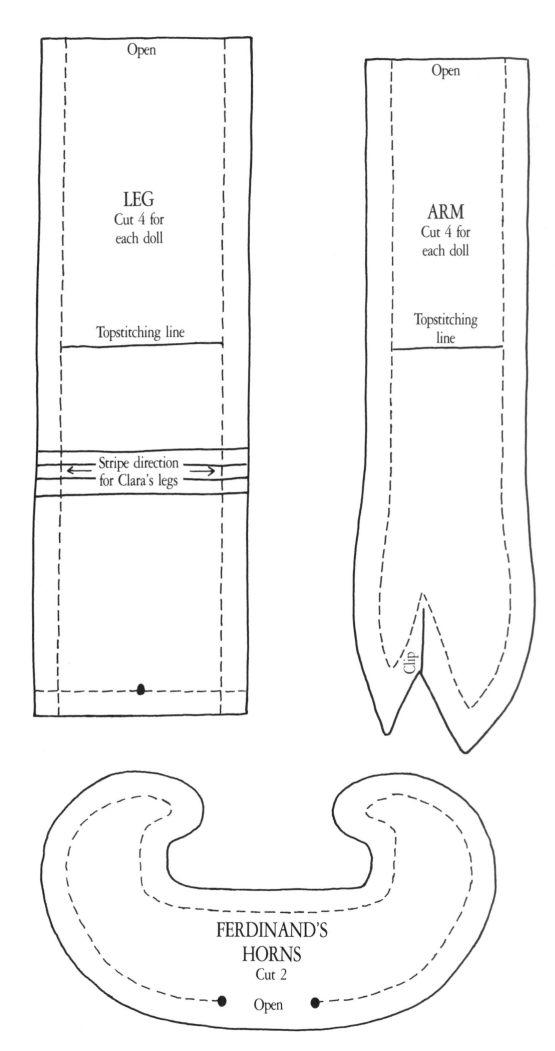

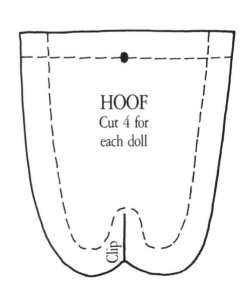

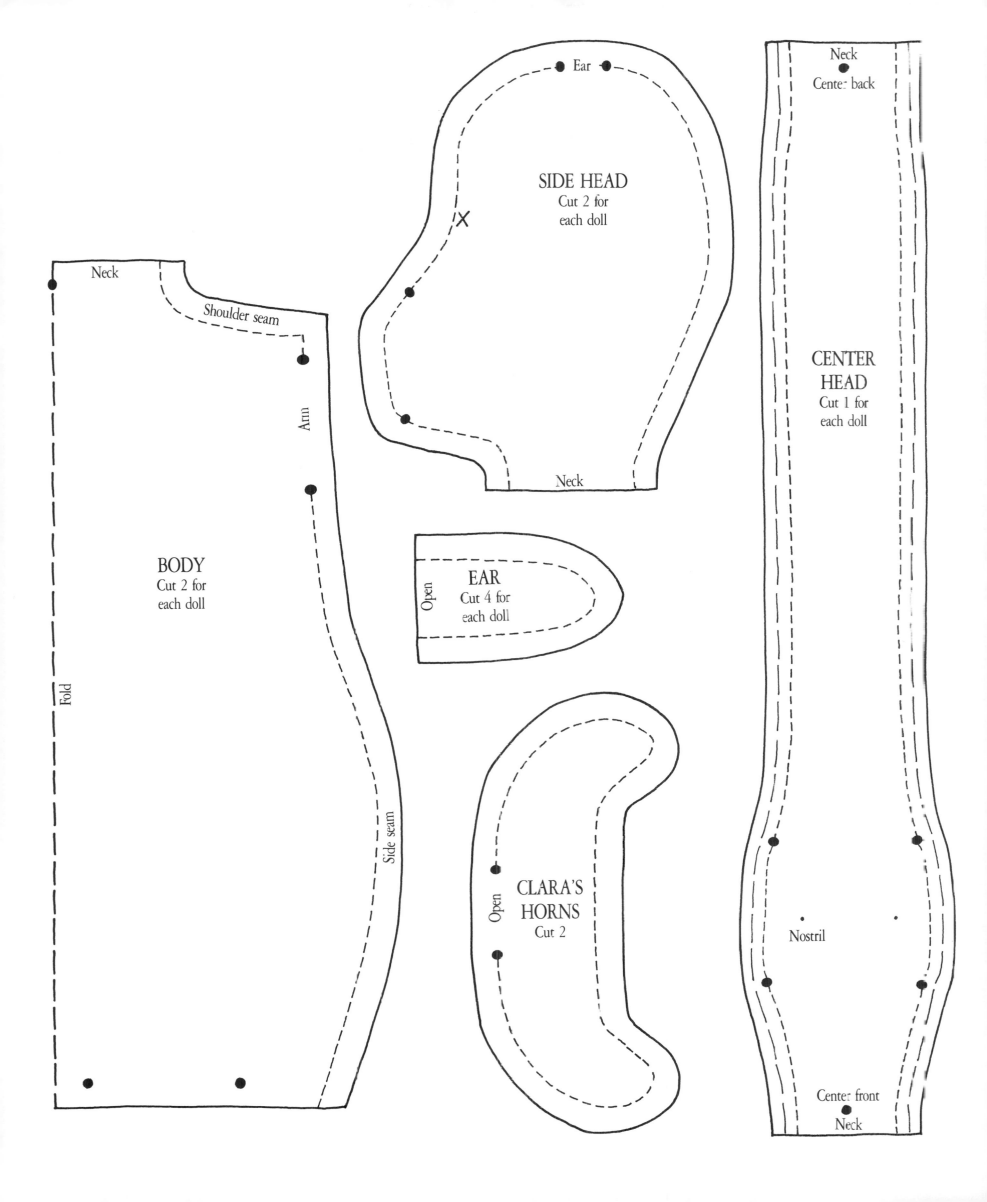

SIDE HEAD
Cut 2 for
each doll

Neck

Ear

Neck
Center back

CENTER
HEAD
Cut 1 for
each doll

Neck

Shoulder seam

Arm

BODY
Cut 2 for
each doll

Fold

Side seam

Open

EAR
Cut 4 for
each doll

Open

CLARA'S
HORNS
Cut 2

Nostril

Center front
Neck

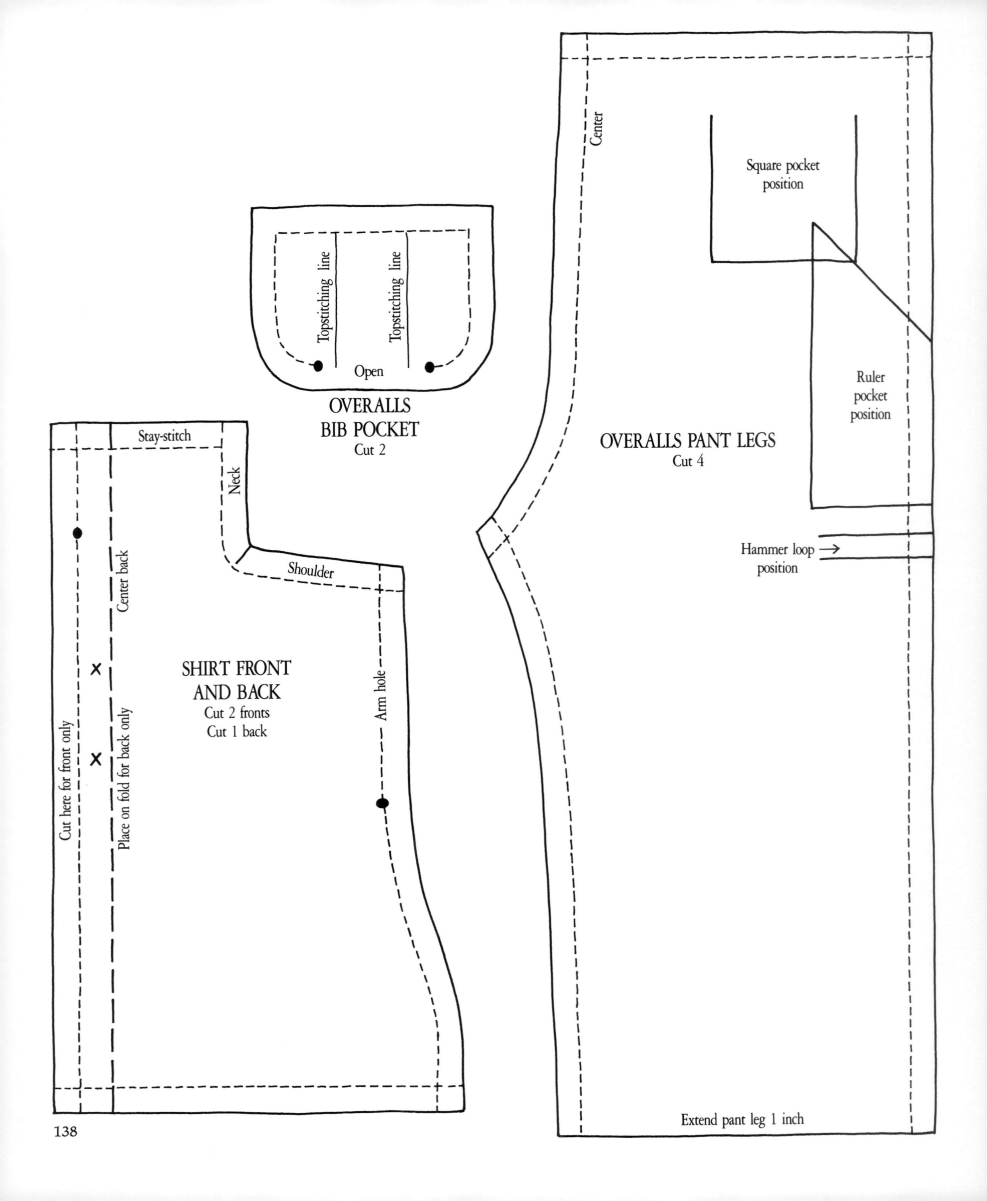

OVERALLS BIB POCKET
Cut 2

Topstitching line

Topstitching line

Open

OVERALLS PANT LEGS
Cut 4

Center

Square pocket position

Ruler pocket position

Hammer loop position

Extend pant leg 1 inch

Stay-stitch

Neck

Shoulder

Arm hole

Center back

Cut here for front only

Place on fold for back only

SHIRT FRONT AND BACK
Cut 2 fronts
Cut 1 back

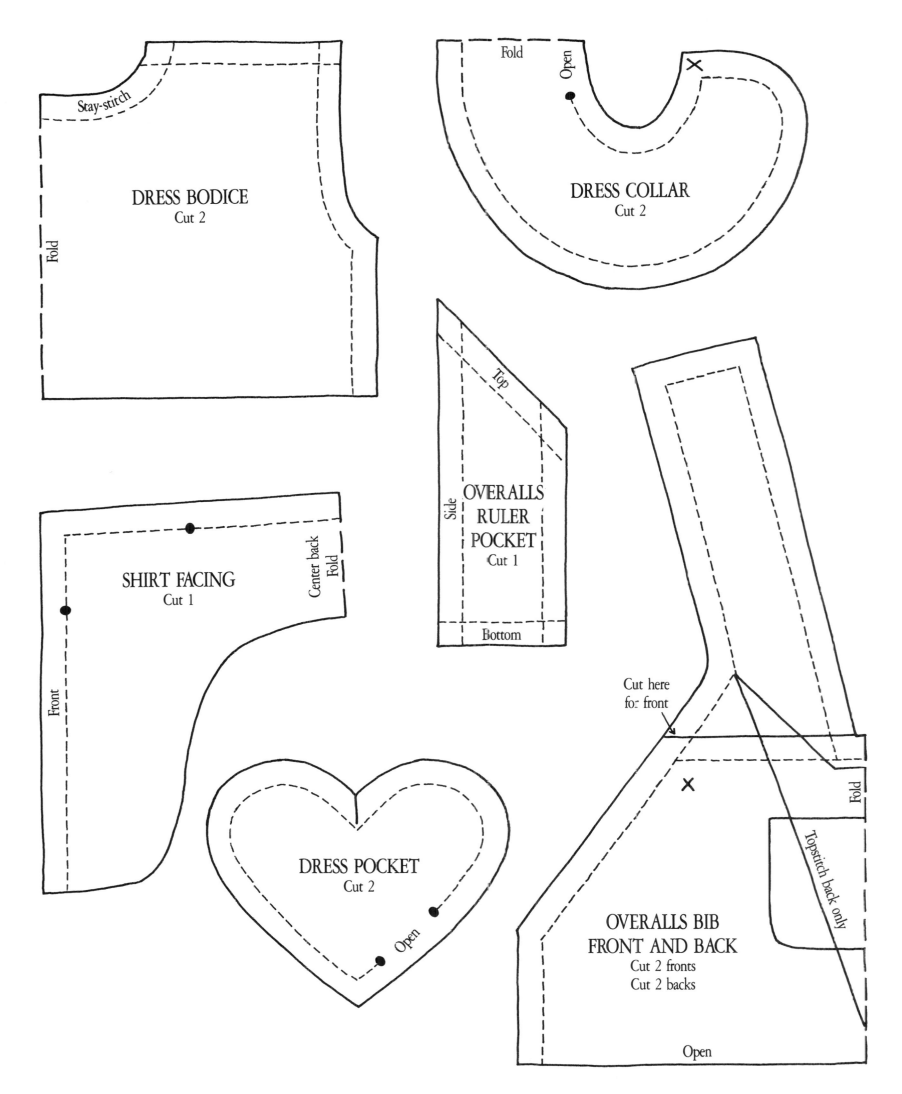

DRESS BODICE
Cut 2

Stay-stitch

Fold

DRESS COLLAR
Cut 2

Fold

Open

SHIRT FACING
Cut 1

Center back
Fold

Front

OVERALLS
RULER
POCKET
Cut 1

Side

Top

Bottom

DRESS POCKET
Cut 2

Open

Cut here
for front

Fold

Topstitch back only

OVERALLS BIB
FRONT AND BACK
Cut 2 fronts
Cut 2 backs

Open

139

DILLY AND DALLY

Clowning around in country shades of red, white, and blue, this pair of 12½-inch-tall silly bozos are costumed just right for

some surprising antics on a shelf full of Americana collectibles. To poke fun at die-hard party loyalists, make these clowns as

ingenious gifts and substitute political buttons or other memorabilia for the purchased ones on the coats.

GENERAL INSTRUCTIONS

The following instructions are for making one clown body and one set of clothing. Repeat the instructions to make a second clown.

FACE

1. Use a pencil to trace the facial features onto one of the muslin clown bodies.
2. Draw over the traced lines with the fabric marker. Do not draw the inside lip line of the mouth. Let the marker lines dry thoroughly.
3. To achieve the white highlights in the eyes and mouth, dry-brush both areas with acrylic paint. (To dry-brush, apply a small amount of paint to the brush. Stroke the brush on a paper towel to remove most of the paint. Work the paint remaining on the brush into the eye rims and mouth. Allow the paint to dry.)
4. With the fabric marker, draw the mouth's center lip line.

BODY

1. Sew the body piece with the face to one unmarked body piece, leaving the bottom edges open.
2. Clip the seams at the ears and around the curves. Turn the body right side out.
3. Lightly stuff each ear with fiberfill. Sew across the topstitching lines to close the ears. (See the box on page 134 for topstitching tips.)

LEGS

1. Sew gathering stitches along the bottom of each leg piece. Pull up the gathers to fit across the top of the shoe. Matching the dots, pin, then sew each shoe to each leg.
2. Sew the leg units together in pairs. Clip the shoe curves; turn each leg right side out.
3. Firmly stuff the shoes with fiberfill up to the ankle seam. Do not stuff the legs.
4. Referring to the photo, *opposite*, trim the shoes as follows: Wrap two ⅜x15-inch strips of fabric around the ankles and tie them into bows. Or, wrap bundles of three 15-inch-long pieces of string around each ankle; knot and tie bows at the center of each ankle.
5. Sew gathering stitches through both layers of fabric along the top edges of each leg. Pull up the gathers to fit both legs between the dots on the body. Pin, then sew the legs, with toes pointing outward, to *one* of the body pieces.
6. Firmly stuff the body with fiberfill. Turn under ¼ inch the bottom of the unsewn body edge. Hand-sew the bottom edges of the body together, encasing the leg seams inside the body.
7. Hot-glue a red pom-pom nose to the face.
8. Apply blush to the cheeks and tops of the ears.

COAT

1. Sew one hand to each arm at the wrists. Sew the arm units together in pairs, leaving the diagonal top seam open. Clip the curves and turn each arm right side out.
2. Lightly stuff each hand with fiberfill up to the wrist seam. Do not stuff the arms.
3. Trim the wrists in the same manner as the ankles (see Legs, Step 4, *left*).
4. Sew gathering stitches through both layers of fabric along each diagonal arm seam.
5. Sew the coat front lining and coat front together along the bottom edges between the dots. Clip the points. Turn the coat right side out and press.
6. Fold the pleat in the front of the coat, matching the left pleat line to the right pleat line (see pleat drawing on the pattern piece); press. Tack the pleat in place at the neck and bottom edges.
7. Turn under a ¼-inch hem along the bottom edge of the coat back and topstitch it in place.
8. Matching the raw edges, pin, then sew the arms to the coat back between the dots, pulling up the gathers to fit.
9. Sew the coat front to the coat back at the side seams, sewing through the arm seams. Do not turn the coat right side out.
10. Slip the neckline edge of the coat over the clown's head and position the neck of the clown inside the neck of the coat. Center the front of the coat with the front of the clown. Tie the coat to the neck with a piece of string, adjusting the gathers so they are evenly spaced around the clown's neck. Turning the coat to the right side, pull it down over the clown's body.

HAIR

1. Machine-sew through the center of a 2-inch piece of wool roving several times to make a part. Glue the part of the hair to the top of the head with the hot-glue gun.
2. Shape the hair and trim it to the desired length.

ACCESSORIES

1. To make the collar, sew running stitches with six strands of embroidery floss ¼ inch from one of the 18-inch sides of the collar strip. Leave enough floss to gather the collar to fit around the neck and tie into a bow at the back of the head. Leave the collar frayed around the edges.
2. For the bow tie, fold the rectangle in half to make a square. Sew together the edges that are opposite the fold; press the seam open. Place the seam in the center of the square. Sew the remaining two sides together, leaving an opening on one side for turning; turn right side out and sew the opening closed. Pinch the center to form a bow tie and tack it together to hold the shape. Hot-glue a ¾-inch-wide torn strip around the center of the bow. Glue the bow to the neck of the coat.

continued

3. To make the flower hat, sew the two hat pieces together. Cut a 1-inch slit in the center of one thickness of the fabric; clip curves and turn the hat right side out through the slit. Pleat the center of the hat, following the dot and arrow markings on the pattern; tack the pleats in place. Glue the silk flower over the pleat; glue the hat to the head.
4. For the straw hat, paint the hat with blue acrylic paint and glue it to the top of a clown's head.
5. To make the covered button for one coat, follow the manufacturer's directions on the button package. Cut out a star shape from a fabric scrap, using the pattern on page 143. Glue it to the covered button with crafts glue. Sew the button to the coat front at the X, through the pleat.

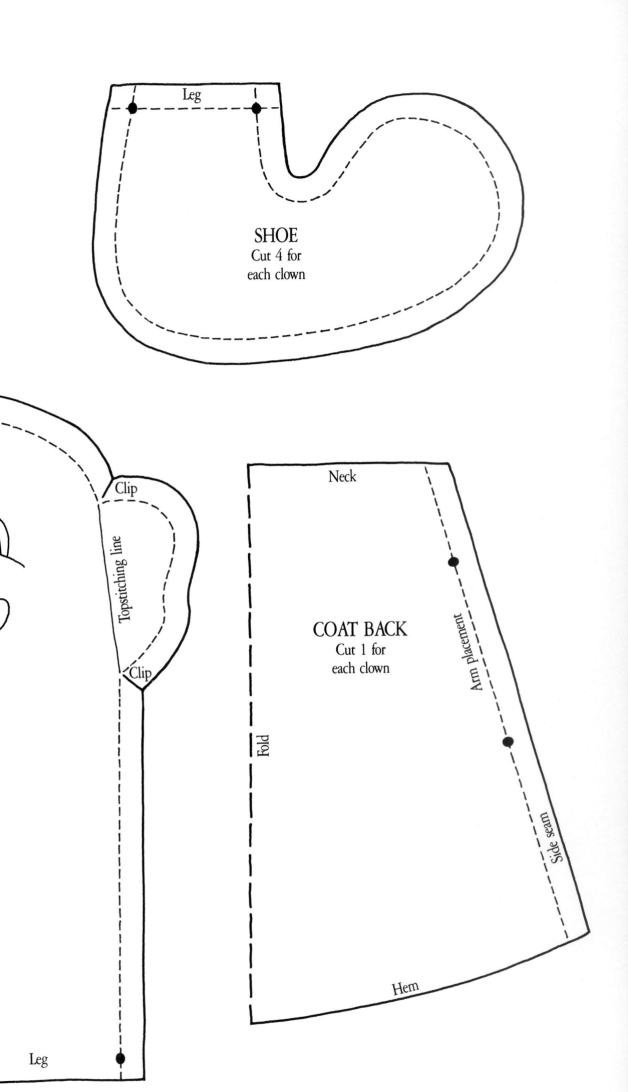

SHOE
Cut 4 for
each clown

BODY
Cut 2 for
each clown

Clip

Clip

Clip

Clip

Topstitching line

Topstitching line

Leg

Leg

COAT BACK
Cut 1 for
each clown

Neck

Fold

Arm placement

Side seam

Hem

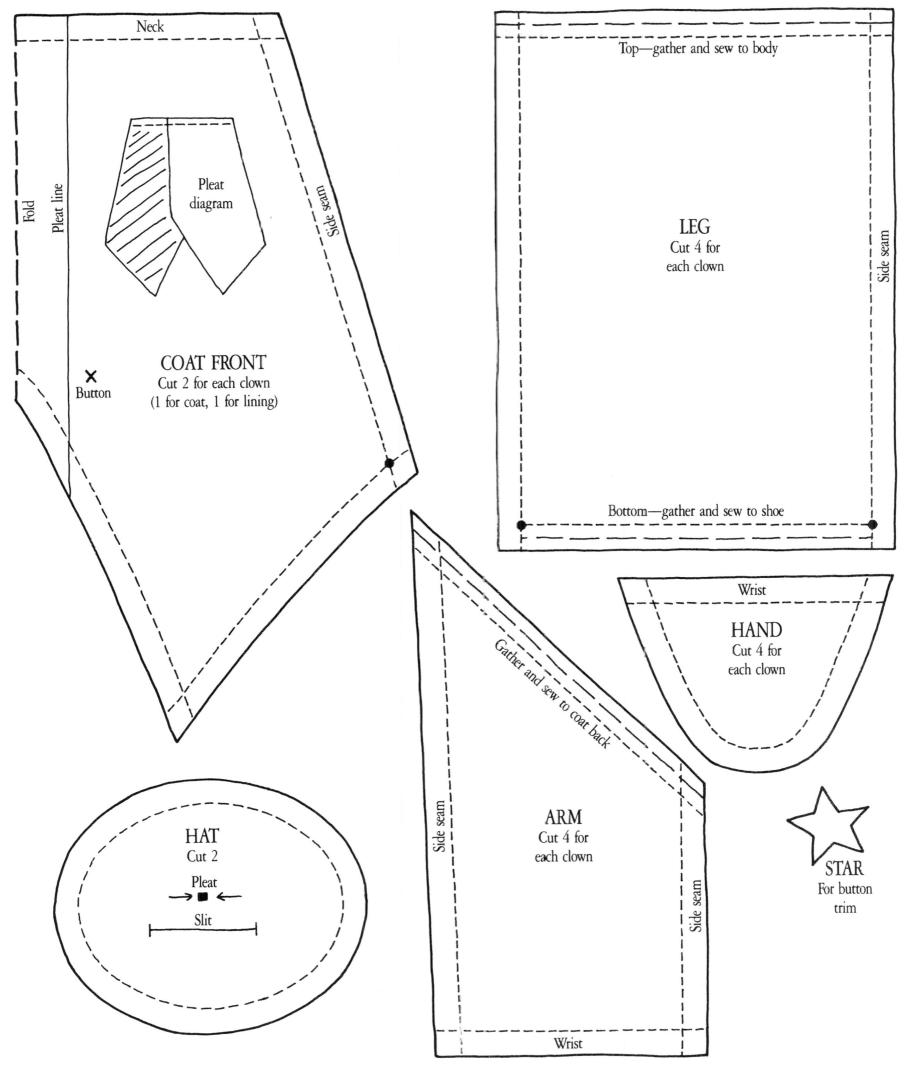

Neck

Fold

Pleat line

Pleat diagram

✗
Button

COAT FRONT
Cut 2 for each clown
(1 for coat, 1 for lining)

Side seam

Top—gather and sew to body

LEG
Cut 4 for
each clown

Side seam

Bottom—gather and sew to shoe

Wrist

HAND
Cut 4 for
each clown

HAT
Cut 2

Pleat
→ ■ ←

Slit

Gather and sew to coat back

Side seam

ARM
Cut 4 for
each clown

Side seam

Wrist

STAR
For button
trim

143

BARNUM

Toymakers, long captivated by the magic of the circus, crafted toys that inspired children to pretend they were performers with great skills and accomplish daring feats with wild animals. *Above,* the giant corduroy elephant, dressed in ruffles and a star-spangled hat, will dazzle a rider with hobbyhorse capers.

BAILEY

Decked in feathers, jewels, and a gold trim braid harness, the white plush hobbyhorse, *above,* is ready to prance about on his broomstick handle. Adjust the lengths of the broomsticks to fit the sizes of the high-spirited riders for whom you make these toys.

PREPARING THE PATTERNS

Trace the full-size head, tusk, and ear patterns on pages 148 and 149 and the hat patterns on pages 150 and 151 onto tracing paper. Cut out the patterns. Tape together the A/B lines and the C/D lines of the pattern pieces to make one head pattern. (See the Elephant Head diagram on page 148.)

———◆———

CUTTING THE FABRICS

The cutting instructions for pieces that have no patterns include ¼-inch seam allowances.

From gray upholstery fabric, cut:
◆ Two heads
◆ Two ears

From gray lining fabric, cut:
◆ Two ears

From white felt, cut:
◆ Four tusks

From red cotton fabric, cut:
◆ One 14x42-inch ruffle
◆ Two hat brims
◆ One hat side
◆ One 3½-inch-diameter circle for top of hat

From poster board, cut:
◆ One hat brim
◆ One hat side

HEAD

1. Sew the head pieces together, leaving the bottom open. Clip curves; turn head right side out.
2. Press under ¼ inch on the bottom edge of the head. Topstitch close to the folded edge.
3. Firmly stuff the head with fiberfill. Begin the stuffing at the trunk, using the handle of a wooden spoon to pack the fiberfill into the curves of the trunk. Insert the cardboard tube into the head. Continue stuffing the head and neck up to the gathering line, keeping the tube centered in the neck. (See the drawing of the horse head on the opposite page.)
4. Double-thread a needle with 2 yards of carpet thread, knotting the ends. Sew running stitches on the gathering line. Spread glue over the top 10 inches of the broom handle. Insert the broom handle into the cardboard tube. Remove the cardboard tube from the head by sliding it over the broom handle. Tightly pull the gathering threads, closing the neck opening around the broom handle. Wrap the extra length of thread around the neck several times and knot the ends.
5. Apply glue inside the neck gathers and around the broom handle. Let the glue dry.
6. Use a long needle double-threaded with carpet thread to sew the eyes to the head. Insert the needle at one of the X markings and pull it out at the opposite X. Thread a button onto the needle, and return the needle to the first X. Thread the second button onto the needle and repeat the stitch. Pull the thread to indent the eyes; knot thread.

EARS

1. Matching each lining ear with an upholstery fabric ear, sew the ears together in pairs, leaving openings as marked. Clip the curves and turn each ear right side out; press.
2. Turn under the open edges ¼ inch and hand-sew the openings closed. With the linings facing the back of the head, pin an ear to each side of the head along the ear placement lines. Hand-sew the ears to the head.
3. Tack the front of each ear to a cheek, matching the large dots.

TUSKS

1. Sew the tusks together in pairs, leaving openings as marked. Clip the curves and turn each tusk right side out.
2. Turn under the open edges ¼ inch and baste in place. Firmly stuff each tusk with fiberfill. Pin each tusk to the head at the markings, curving each one toward the trunk. Hand-sew the tusks in place.

NECK RUFFLE

1. Draw a horizontal line across the length of the ruffle strip 6 inches from one edge. Mark the 6-inch side with pins to designate it as the top of the ruffle.
2. Sew the 14-inch edges of the ruffle together, forming a tube. Press the seam to one side and machine-zigzag over the raw edges.
3. Hem both raw edges of the ruffle by pressing the fabric under ¼ inch two times; topstitch the hem. Sew gold rickrack to the *wrong* side of the hem of the top ruffle, and to the *right* side of the bottom hem.
4. To prepare the ruffle for gathering, lay the pearl cotton thread over the drawn line. Machine-zigzag over the thread, taking care not to catch it in the sewing. Begin the sewing at the seam.
5. Fold the top of the ruffle over the bottom ruffle, using the zigzag stitching as a guide. The rickrack will face to the right side on both edges.
6. Slip the ruffle onto the elephant's neck. Pull up the pearl cotton thread to gather the ruffle, adjusting the fullness around the neck. Knot the thread. Wrap the extra length around the neck several times, and knot it again.

HAT

1. Glue the ends of the poster-board hat side piece together, overlapping the ends ¼ inch.
2. Run a band of glue around the top edge (crown) of the poster board. Center the 3½-inch-diameter fabric circle over the crown opening, pressing the edges into the glue.
3. Press the top edge and one end of the red fabric side piece under ¼ inch. Run a band of glue around the top edge of the poster-board hat side. Fasten the folded fabric edge to the glued edge of the hat. Overlap and glue the fabric ends, keeping the folded edge on top of the raw edge.
4. Fold the fabric along the brim side to the inside of the hat and glue it in place.
5. Sew the fabric hat brim pieces together along the outer edge. Clip the curve; turn right side out and press. Slip the poster-board brim into the fabric brim. Sew along the inner curve, encasing the poster-board brim. Clip the seam allowance to the stitching line, forming tabs.
6. Position the brim between the dots on the bottom sides of the hat. Fold the tabs inside the hat and glue them in place.
7. Referring to the photo on page 144, glue silver metallic stars around the side of the hat. Glue gold rickrack around the brim and around the top and bottom edges of the hat side. Use a needle to punch a hole in opposite sides of the hat above the rickrack trim. Insert each end of the gold elastic cord inside the hat through the punched holes. Make an overhand knot in each end to secure the cord. Slip the hat onto the elephant's head.

MATERIALS FOR BAILEY

½ yard of white short-nap fur
for head

⅛ yard of white corduroy for ears

Two ⅝-inch-diameter half-dome shanked
buttons for eyes

1¼ yards of braid trim for harness

1 yard of braid trim for reins

1¼ yards of 1½-inch-wide white cotton
fringe for mane

Two 1½-inch-diameter brass rings

Two 1½-inch-diameter gold plastic coins or
disks

Two 1-inch red plastic jewels

Red fluffy feathers

One 4-foot broom handle

Carpet thread

Clear plastic tape

Polyester fiberfill

Cardboard tube

Crafts glue

Hot-glue gun

———◆———

PREPARING THE PATTERNS

Trace the full-size head and ear patterns
on pages 150 and 151 onto tracing paper.
Cut out the patterns. Tape the A/B lines
on the pattern pieces together to make
one head pattern.

———◆———

CUTTING THE FABRICS

When working with fur, cut *each* piece
individually from a single layer of the fur.
Trace each pattern onto the wrong side of
the fur, reversing the pieces as indicated
and following the nap direction arrows.
Cut the pieces from the fur working from
the back of the fabric. Take small snips
with the scissors to avoid cutting the pile.

From the fur, cut:
◆ Two heads

From the corduroy, cut:
◆ Four ears

SPECIAL INSTRUCTIONS

1. After cutting the fabrics, transfer the X placement markings to the fur side of the fabric using
brightly colored tailor's tacks (see the tip for tailor
tacks on page 31). The remaining construction
markings can be transferred to the wrong side of
the fur.

2. Before sewing fur pieces together, brush the fur
away from the seam line. After sewing, use a
straight pin to pull the fur from the seam. This
technique blends the fur and conceals the seams.
Trim the fur remaining in the seam allowance to
reduce the bulk.

HEAD

1. Sew the head pieces together, leaving the bottom open. Clip curves; turn head right side out.

2. Firmly stuff the face portion of the horse's head
with fiberfill. Insert the cardboard tube into the
neck. Continue stuffing the head and neck up to
the gathering line, keeping the tube centered in
the neck. (See the drawing of the horse head,
right.)

3. Double-thread a needle with 2 yards of carpet
thread, knotting the ends. Sew running stitches
on the gathering line. Spread glue over the top 10
inches of the broom handle. Insert the broom
handle into the cardboard tube. Remove the cardboard tube from the head by sliding it over the
broom handle. Tightly pull the gathering threads,
closing the neck opening around the broom handle. Wrap the extra length of thread around the
neck several times and knot the ends.

4. Apply glue inside the neck gathers and around
the broom handle. Let the glue dry.

5. Use a long needle double-threaded with carpet
thread to sew the eyes to the head. Insert the
needle at one of the X markings and push it out at
the opposite X. Thread a button onto the needle,
and return the needle to the first X. Thread the
second button onto the needle and repeat the
stitch. Pull the threads to indent the eyes; knot
the thread.

EARS

1. Sew the ears together in pairs, leaving openings
as marked. Clip the curves and turn each ear right
side out; press. Slip-stitch the openings closed.

2. Shape each ear by making a small tuck on the
fold line; tack the tuck in place. Pin the ears to the
head along the placement lines, hand-sew the ears
to the head.

MANE

1. Fold the fringe into fourths. Whipstitch the
bottom edges (unfringed edges) together to make
one strip for the mane.

2. Hot-glue the whipstitched edge of the mane to
the head between the dots.

FINISHING

1. For the harness, cut two pieces of braid trim,
one for the nose and one for the upper head; use
the horse head pattern to measure the length of
each piece and add ¼ inch to each end for seams.

2. Sew the ends of each piece together to form two
circles. Slip each circle into place on the head.
Then cut two straight pieces of trim to join the
circles on each side of the head. Tack the straight
pieces in place.

3. Sew a brass ring to each side of the harness at
the Xs.

4. Hot-glue a jewel to the center of each disk.
Hot-glue the disks to the harness at the medallion
markings. Hot-glue feathers behind the disks as
shown in the photo on page 145.

5. Tie the reins to the brass rings.

HOBBY TOY TIP

In the process of developing our hobby
toys, we discovered a good method for
stuffing the animals' heads. After stuffing
the face portion with fiberfill, insert a
cardboard (paper towel) tube into the neck
and add fiberfill around it. This makes the
head easy to handle and maintains a center
opening in the neck for the broom handle.
When the toy is completely stuffed, slide
the broom handle in the cardboard tube to
check the angle of the stick, making cer-
tain it is correct for the toy. Once the angle
is correct, remove the handle, dab glue
over the portion of the handle that will be
inside the head, slip the handle back into
the tube, and pull the cardboard tube out
of the head, sliding it over the length of the
handle.

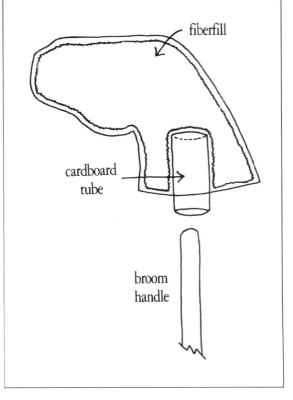

fiberfill

cardboard
tube

broom
handle

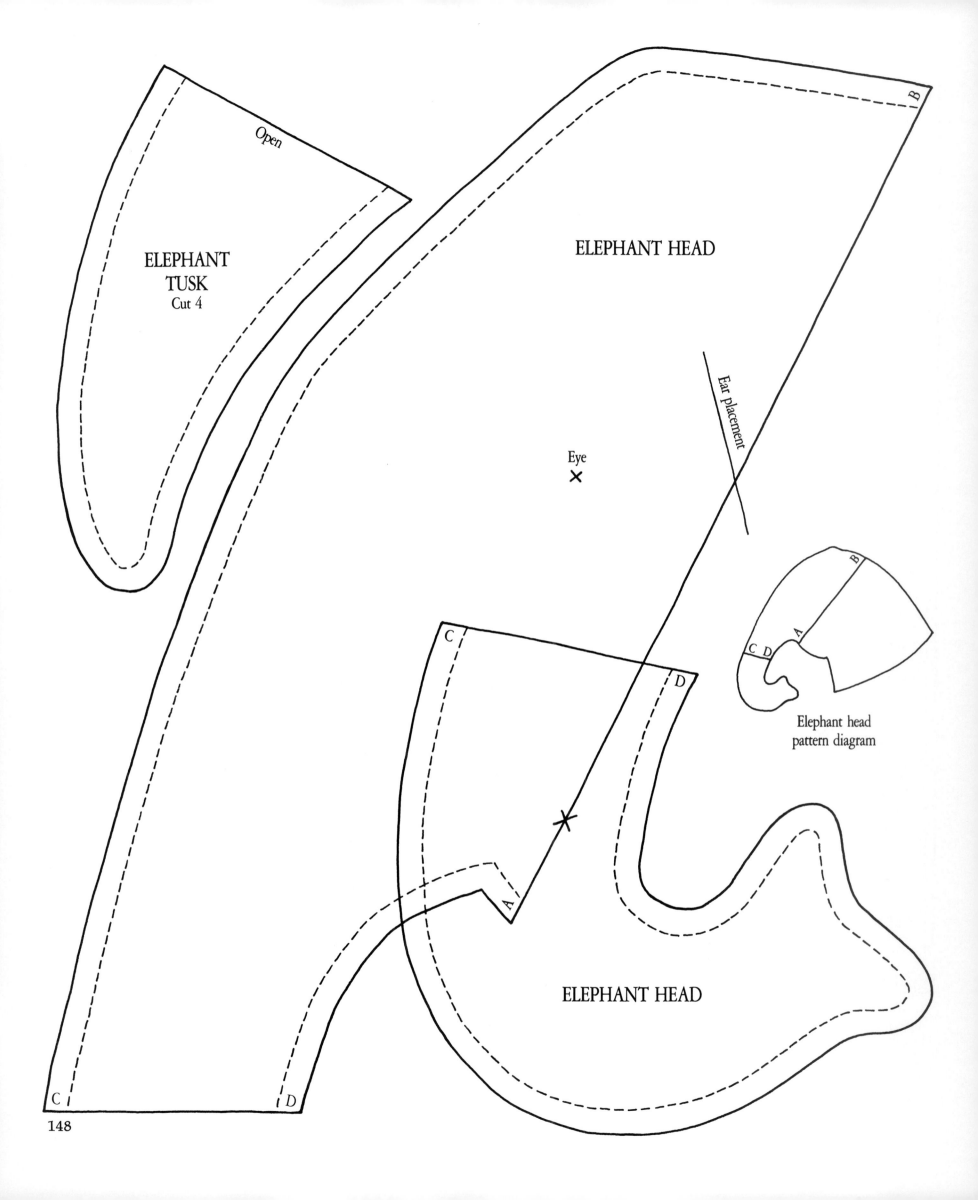

ELEPHANT TUSK
Cut 4

Open

ELEPHANT HEAD

Eye

Ear placement

ELEPHANT HEAD

Elephant head
pattern diagram

148

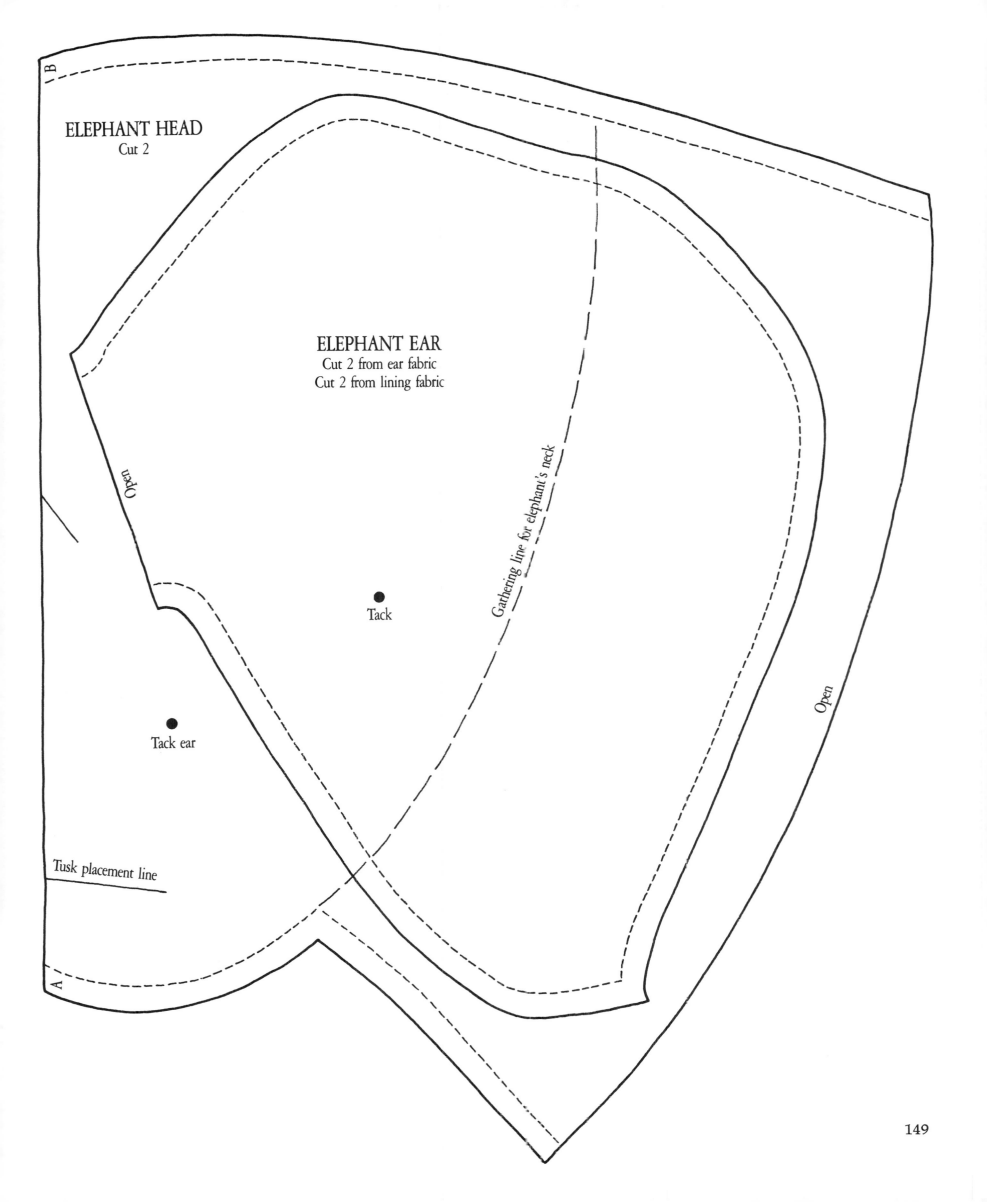

ELEPHANT HEAD
Cut 2

ELEPHANT EAR
Cut 2 from ear fabric
Cut 2 from lining fabric

Open

Tack

Gathering line for elephant's neck

Open

Tack ear

Tusk placement line

B

A

149

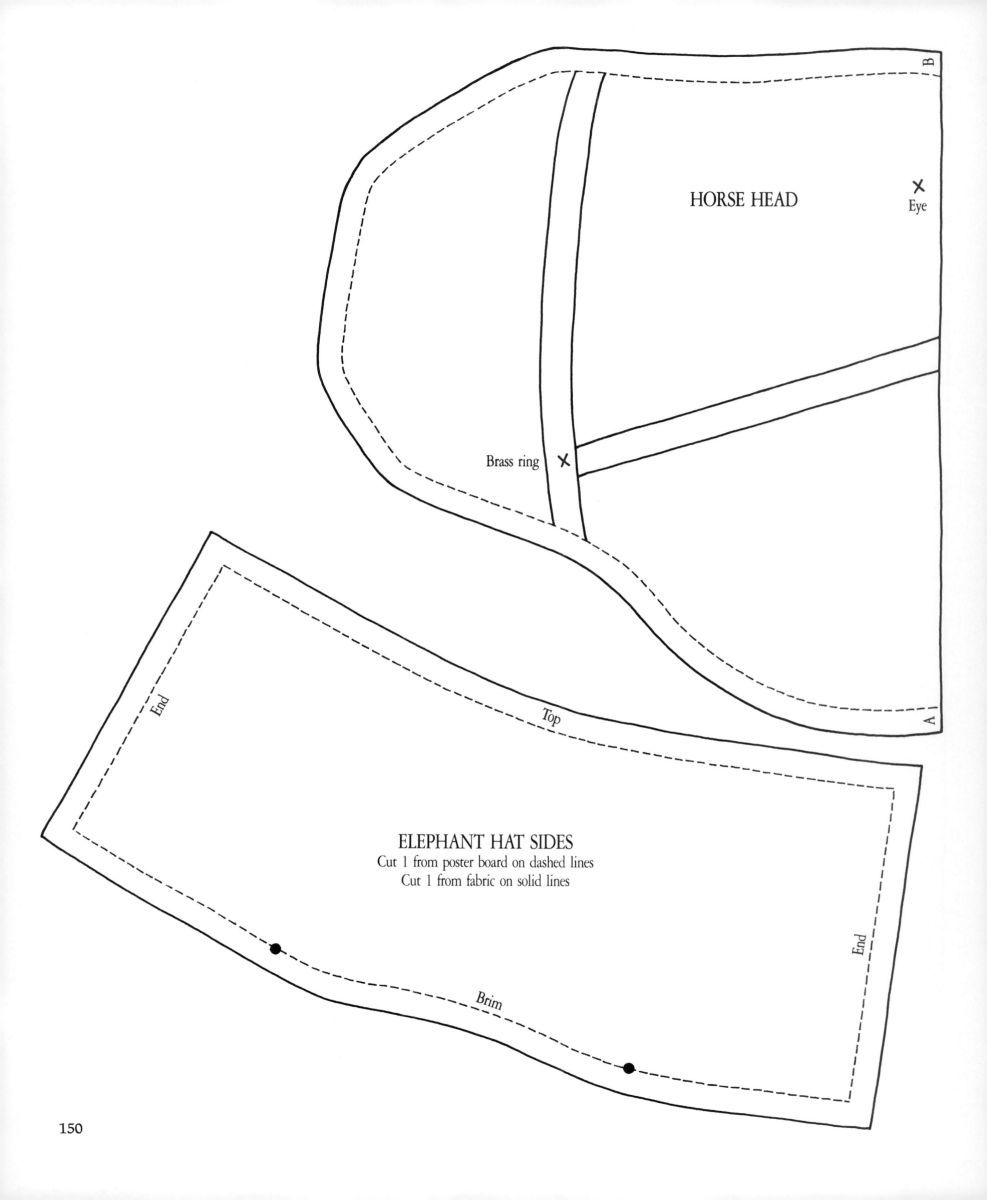

HORSE HEAD

✗
Eye

Brass ring **✗**

ELEPHANT HAT SIDES
Cut 1 from poster board on dashed lines
Cut 1 from fabric on solid lines

End

Top

End

Brim

B

A

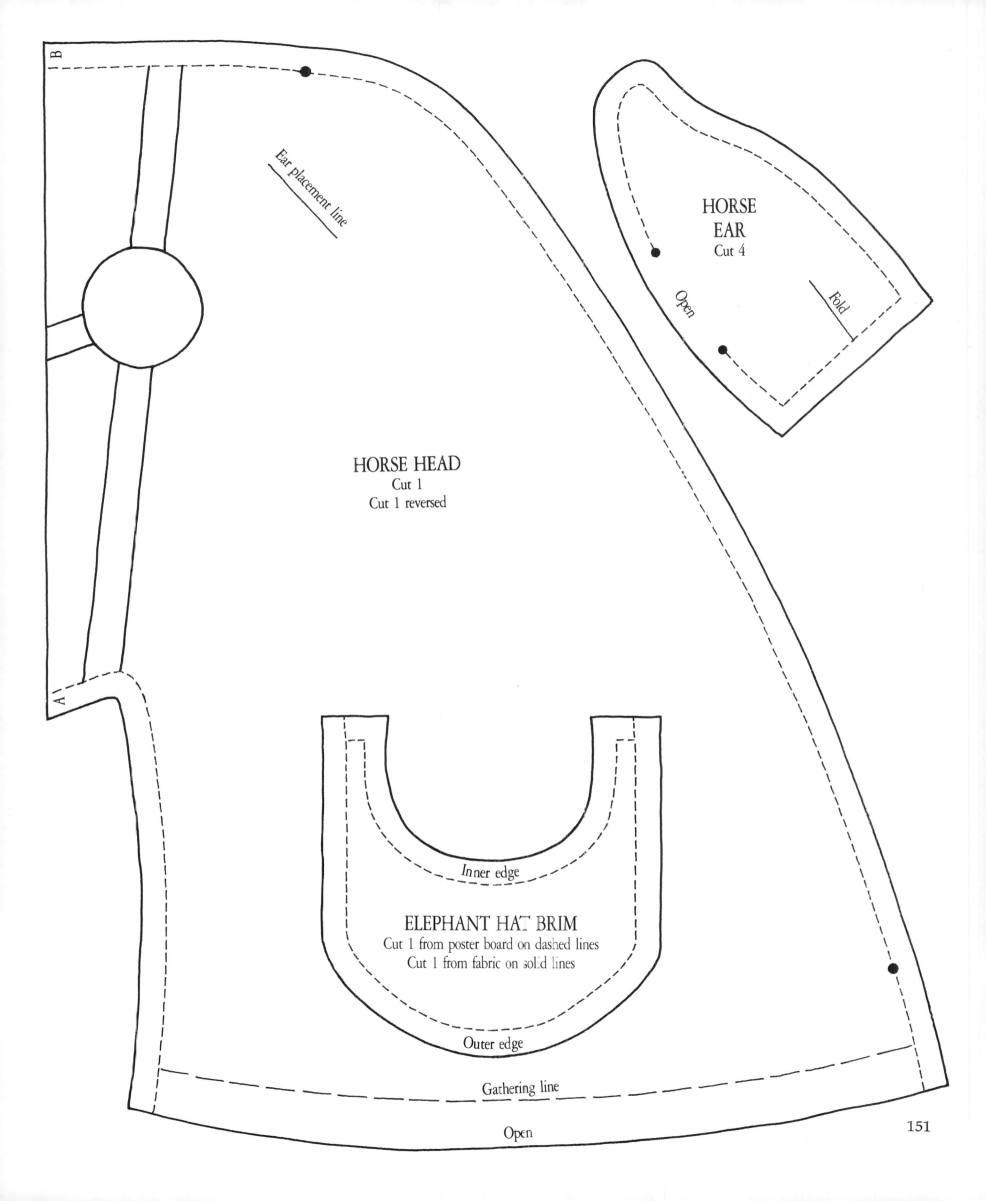

B

Ear placement line

HORSE
EAR
Cut 4

Open

Fold

HORSE HEAD
Cut 1
Cut 1 reversed

A

Inner edge

ELEPHANT HAT BRIM
Cut 1 from poster board on dashed lines
Cut 1 from fabric on solid lines

Outer edge

Gathering line

Open

JACK-IN-THE-BOX

• • •

Tucked away in a black foam core box that's 6½ inches high and covered with storybook illustrations, this impish Jack springs from a dryer tubing body when the lid is raised. He's smartly dressed in a knit fabric suit, puffy neck ruffles, and a gold lamé crown that's trimmed with bells.

HEAD

1. Sew the head side pieces together at the center back seam. Sew darts matching the dots. Trim the dart seams to ⅛ inch.

2. Sew the face pieces together from the dot to the neck edge along the center front seam. Trim the seam to ⅛ inch; clip curves, and turn face right side out.

3. Sew the face to each of the head sides at the cheek seams. Press the seam allowances away from the face. Topstitch ⅛ inch from the cheek seam through all fabric thicknesses, creating a ridge around the face.

4. Stuff the nose with fiberfill. Referring to the photo on page 152, use a pencil to draw a smile onto the face. Embroider the smile using outline stitches and black carpet thread. (See stitch diagram on page 7.)

5. Glue the felt head over the plastic foam ball using the hot-glue gun. Stretch the felt while gluing. The head piece will cover slightly more than one-half of the ball.

6. For the eyes, cut two circles of black felt slightly larger than the sequins. Glue the felt eye circles to the head as shown on the pattern. For lower eye rims, use the black marker to draw a thin line along half of the outer edge of each sequin. Dip the pointed ends of two glass-top pins in crafts glue. Push each pin through a sequin and into the foam head, keeping the eye rim along the lower edge of the eye and the felt piece slightly above the sequin.

7. Using the line on the pattern as a guide, embroider two short straight stitches for eyebrows with black carpet thread.

8. Paint cheeks with red acrylic paint that is diluted with water.

9. Pin the crafts fur to the head. Clip notches along the fur edges to shape and fit it over the curves of the head. Remove the pins and glue the fur to the head. Finger-comb and trim the hair as desired.

CROWN

1. Sew the crown pieces together between the dots along the pointed edges. Open the fabric at each end seam to make one fabric thickness. Sew the two end seams together, forming a circle. Trim the seams to ⅛ inch around the points and clip the curves. Turn the crown right side out; press. Turn under the bottom edge ¼ inch; topstitch close to the fold.

2. Hand-sew a jingle bell to each point.

3. Place the crown on Jack's head. To hold the crown in place, dip the points of several straight pins in crafts glue. Insert the pins through the topstitched edge of the crown and into the plastic foam head.

BODY

1. Count 40 rings on the dryer exhaust tubing. Cut off the extra tubing and discard it.

2. Draw a 3¼-inch-diameter circle in the center of the mat board. Use the nail to punch eight holes evenly spaced around the circle. With a double length of carpet thread, sew the bottom ring of the dryer tube to the mat board through the punched holes. Sew around the tube three times; knot the thread.

3. Fold the body piece in half to measure 15x4 inches. Sew the 15-inch sides together with ¼-inch seams. Turn the piece right side out; slip the body over the tubing.

4. Hand-sew the top edge of the body fabric to the top ring of the tube. Glue the bottom ½ inch of the fabric body to the mat board close to the tubing with crafts glue.

5. Glue the felt hands together in pairs. With the black marker draw finger lines on both sides of the hands as marked on the pattern.

6. Center and pin a hand inside each folded arm with the raw edges matching. Sew the side and hand seams together, encasing the hands in the seams; turn each arm right side out.

7. To trim the sleeves, glue gold braid ⅝ inch from the bottom of each wrist edge.

8. Baste the top edges of each arm together. Fold the top edges over the top ring of opposite sides of the tubing. Hand-sew the arms to the tube.

9. Fold the neck ruffle in half to measure 29x3 inches. Sew each of the short ends with ¼-inch seams; turn the ruffle right side out. Sew the long edges of the ruffle together with a double row of gathering stitches. Gather the ruffle to measure 10¼ inches long; knot the threads to secure.

10. Tack the short ends of the ruffle together. Insert the gathered edge into the top of the tubing. Hand-sew the ruffle to the tube with a double row of running stitches; knot to secure.

JACK'S BOX

1. Referring to the drawing, *below,* use crafts glue to fasten the four foam core sides on top of the base piece. Position the front and back pieces so

continued

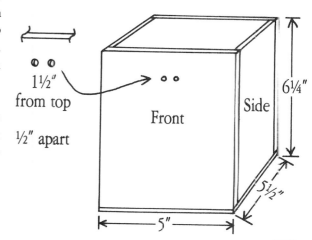

they measure 5 inches across; position the two sides so they measure 5½ inches across when assembled. The height of the glued box will measure 6¼ inches. Tie a piece of string around the box to hold the box together while the glue dries.

2. Following the manufacturer's instructions on the rubber cement, glue a picture to each of the sides and base of the box as follows. Glue one 5x5½-inch picture to the base; glue the two 5x6¼-inch pictures to the front and back of the box; glue the 5½x6¼-inch pictures to the remaining two sides. Glue the last picture to the remaining piece of foam core (top side of box lid).

3. Referring to the drawing on page 153 and using a nail, pierce two holes in the box front. Place the holes ½ inch apart and 1½ inches down from the top edge. Sew the bead to the box with a double length of carpet thread, sewing through the punched holes. Knot the threads inside the box and cover the knot with black plastic tape.

4. Cover all edges of the box and lid with strips of black plastic tape.

5. Place the lid on top of the box with the picture facing toward the front of the box. Mark and pierce two holes in the front edge of the lid with a nail. Place the holes ¼ inch apart, ½ inch from the edge, and centered on the 5-inch edge.

6. Thread each end of the gold elastic cord through each of the holes from the top side (picture side). Keeping the ends even, make an overhand knot in the cord to form a 1½-inch-long loop on the top of the lid. Tie a second knot close to the ends of the cord.

7. Fasten the back of the lid to the box along the inside and outside edges with strips of black tape.

8. Use crafts glue to fasten the bottom of the mat board with the body tube inside the box with the thumbs facing the front of the box. Allow the glue to dry.

9. Hot-glue the head to the top of the body tube with the head slightly angled so the nose points to a box corner.

10. Cover the point of a glass-headed pin with crafts glue. Insert the pin through the knot at the end of the gold cord and into the foam head behind the crown.

11. Close the lid by pushing the head down into the box and pulling the elastic loop over the bead.

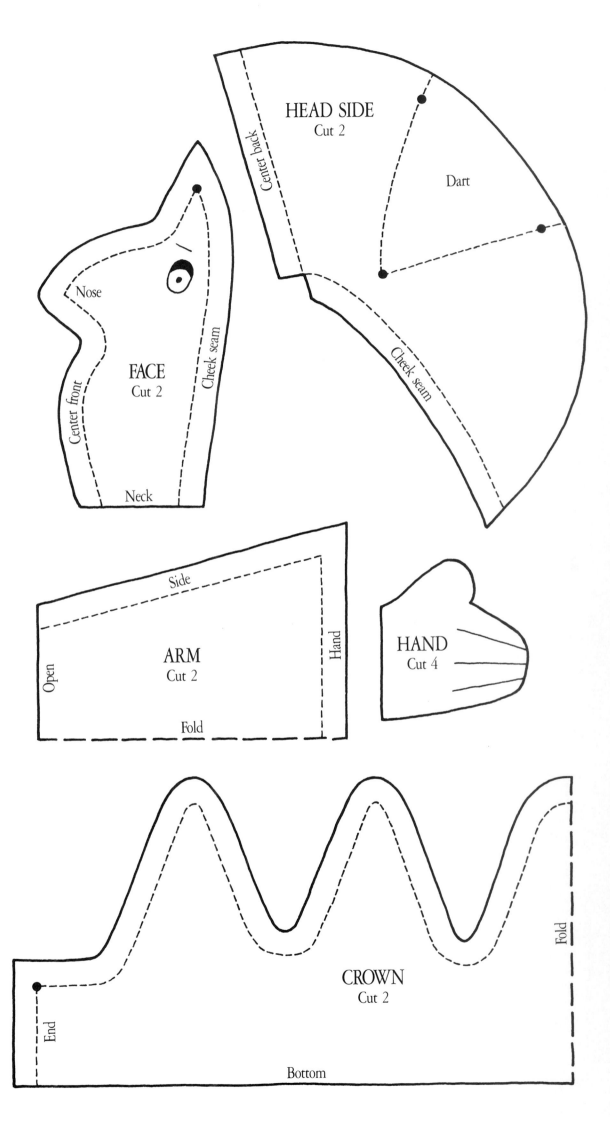

154

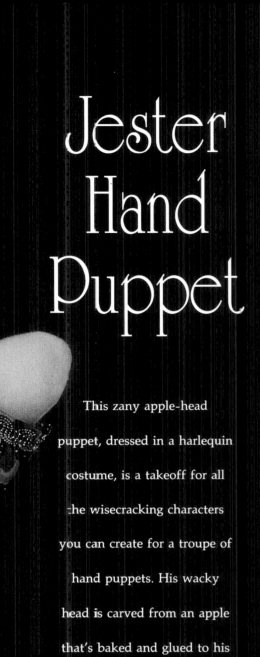

Jester
Hand
Puppet

This zany apple-head puppet, dressed in a harlequin costume, is a takeoff for all the wisecracking characters you can create for a troupe of hand puppets. His wacky head is carved from an apple that's baked and glued to his mitten body. From the top of his tassel to the soles of his shoes, he measures about 12 inches long.

PREPARING THE PATTERNS

Trace the full-size patterns on page 157 onto tracing paper. Cut out the patterns.

◆

CUTTING THE FABRICS

Cutting instructions for pieces without patterns include ¼-inch seams.

From knit fabric, cut:
- Two gloves
- Four 4½x1½-inch legs

From print cotton, cut:
- Two shirts

From lamé, cut:
- Two 2½x9-inch ruffle strips

From chintz, cut:
- Two hats
- Four shoes

From velveteen, cut:
- Two 3x4-inch pants

From interfacing, cut:
- Two hats

GENERAL INSTRUCTIONS

The puppet glove fits either the left or right hand. Because the puppet has a front and back, determine the hand on which you want to use your puppet before sewing the head and clothing to the glove.

CARVING THE APPLE HEAD

1. Referring to the drawing, *below,* and using the melon baller and paring knife, hollow out a 2-inch-diameter cavity from the apple. Start at the stem end of the apple and hollow the cavity so it is slightly off center and extends almost to the blossom end.

2. Peel the skin from the apple.

3. Dissolve the salt in the lemon juice in the glass bowl. Soak the apple for 15 minutes in the lemon solution, turning it occasionally so all portions of the apple absorb some of the liquid.

4. Remove the apple from the liquid. Referring to the drawing, *below,* use the paring knife to carve facial features into the thicker side of the apple. The features should be exaggerated to allow for shrinkage during the drying process.

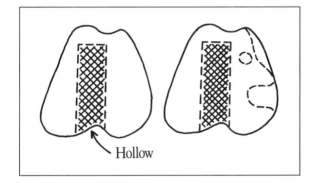

Hollow

5. Soak the apple for an additional 15 minutes in the lemon solution.

6. Place the apple on the pie plate and bake it in a 170-degree oven until it turns brown and is about one-half of its original size. Turn the apple occasionally to promote even drying. The baking process will take 10 to 15 hours. If the apple remains sticky after baking, air-dry it for several days.

PUPPET GLOVE

1. Sew the glove pieces together leaving the bottom edges open. Clip the corners; turn the glove right side out.

2. Lightly stuff the hands of the glove with fiberfill. Turn under the bottom edge ¼ inch; machine- or hand-sew it in place for the hem.

LEGS AND PANTS

1. Sew the short edge of each leg piece to the top edge of each shoe piece. Sew the leg units together in pairs. Clip curves; turn the legs right side out.

2. Firmly stuff the shoes with fiberfill. Lightly stuff the legs with fiberfill to within 1 inch of the top. Align the seams and baste the tops together.

3. Referring to the pantaloon tip on page 130, fold one of the pants pieces with the 3-inch edges together. Mark ¼ inch on each side of the fold along one of the raw edges on both sides of the fabric. Make a second mark on the fold 1¼ inches above the first marks. Unfold the piece; using a pencil, connect the marks to form a narrow V shape. Place the marked piece on top of the unmarked piece and sew along the V-shape lines. Cut along the fold between the sewing lines to the point of the V. Press the seams open.

4. Press under the bottom edge of each pants leg ¼ inch. Topstitch close to the fold for the hem. Sew the side seams together; turn the pants right side out.

5. Insert a leg unit into each pants leg. Align the top edges of the legs with the top edges of the pants (waist) and baste the edges together. Sew the assembled pants/legs to one side of the glove at the placement line as shown on the pattern.

SHIRT

1. Sew each shoulder seam from the dot to the sleeve opening. Clip to each dot; press the seams open.

2. Press under ¼ inch along the neck and sleeve openings. Topstitch braid atop each sleeve edge.

3. Stay-stitch ¼ inch along the bottom edge of the shirt. Press under the fabric along the stay-stitching line, clipping the top points and mitering the bottom points to make the fabric lie flat. Topstitch braid along the bottom edge, overlapping and easing the braid at the points so it lies flat.

4. Slip the shirt over the glove. Tack the neckline of the shirt to the glove at the placement line.

5. Sew the ruffle strips together to form one 2½x17½-inch strip. Turn under the long edges ¼ inch and topstitch them in place. Machine-sew two rows of gathering stitches down the center of the strip. Pull up the gathers to fit the ruffle around the neck. Tack the ruffle to the neck of the shirt, overlapping the ends at the back of the shirt.

HAT

1. Trim the seam allowance from the two hat interfacing pieces. Do not cut away the interfacing along the bottom edge. With the bottom edges even, fuse the interfacing to the chintz pieces, following the manufacturer's instructions.

2. Sew the hat pieces together, keeping the stitching at the edge of the interfacing and leaving the bottom edges open. Trim the seam allowance to ⅛ inch. Clip curves; turn hat right side out.

3. Slip the hat onto the puppet's head. Pinch and pin together the corners on both sides of the hat at the Xs, adjusting the positions of the pins so the

the Xs, adjusting the positions of the pins so the hat fits the head. With a double-threaded needle, tack the sides of the hat together; knot the thread.

4. Glue braid along the outside edges on one side of the hat. Sew the tassel to the top of the hat. Glue the hat to the apple head with the braid side facing the front.

FINISHING

1. Glue the wiggle eyes in place on the head. Apply powder blush to the cheeks. Glue the pearl cotton in the mouth cavity, shaping the thread into a small circle.

2. Spread crafts glue over the head portion of the glove. Place the glove on your hand and slip the apple head over the glove and fasten it to the glove. Add more glue to the head or glove to secure the fit.

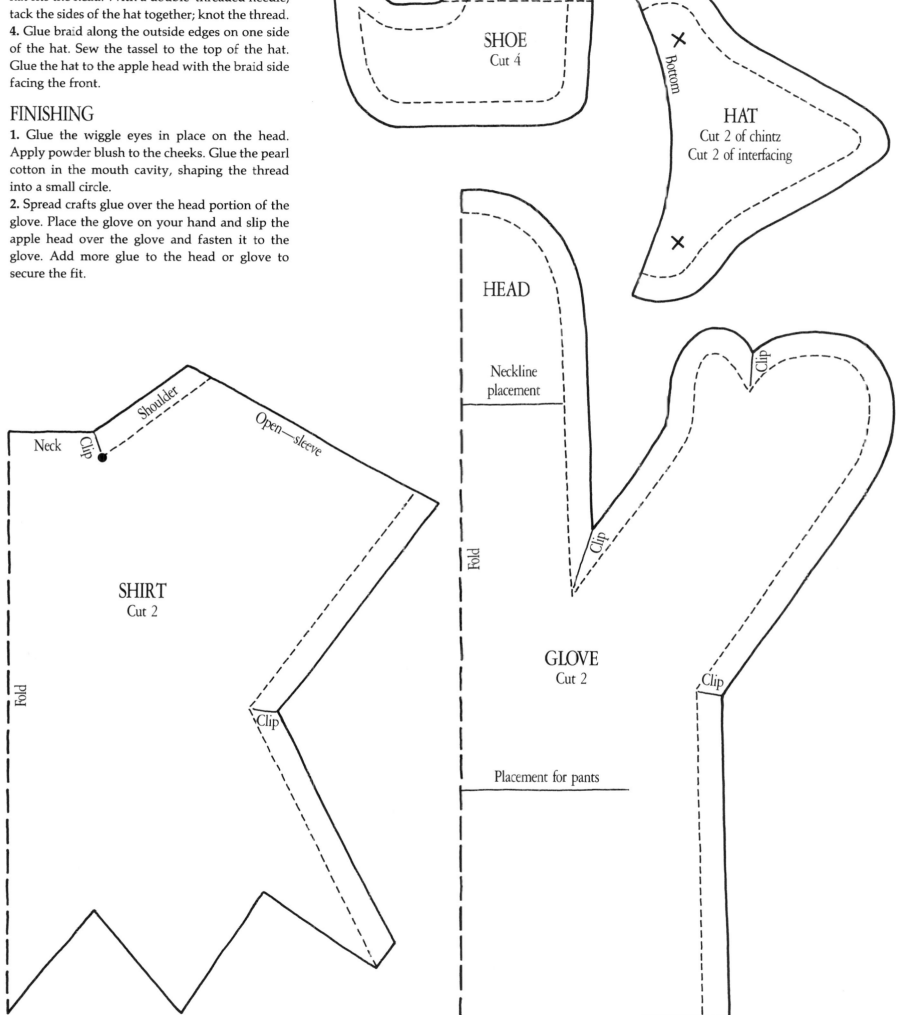

Acknowledgments

We express our gratitude and appreciation to the many people who helped produce this book. Our heartfelt thanks go to each of the artisans and designers who enthusiastically contributed designs, ideas, and projects.

Kathy Bast—Nursery rhyme pull toys on pages 24 and 25; farm puzzles on pages 46 and 47

Heidi Boyd—Frog doll on page 96

Phyllis Dunstan—Victorian dolls on pages 56 and 57; rabbit on pages 74 and 75; topsy-turvy doll on pages 110 and 111; shoe and dolls on page 116; hobby-horse toys on pages 144 and 145; jack-in-the-box on page 152

JoAnn Gummere—Long-legged cats and rabbits on pages 18 and 19; angel dolls on pages 82 and 83; bear on pages 3 and 106

Barbara J. Hickey—Bears on pages 28 and 29

Cindi Hurlbut—Uncle Sam doll on page 42; giraffe dolls on pages 122 and 123; girlfriend dolls on page 128

Donna Kozera—Raggedy kids on page 14; bunny and kitten toys on pages 88 and 89; clown dolls on page 140

Lois Liden—Doll on cover and on pages 34 and 35

Karen Logsdon—Twin dolls on page 70; cow dolls on pages 132 and 133

Eve Mahr—Hand puppet on page 155

Eitha Myhand—Noah's Ark on pages 100 and 101

Warren Neubauer—Picture puzzle blocks on pages 12 and 13

Linda Stueve—Calico cat and gingham dog on pages 52 and 53

Doll Supply Sources

Most of the supplies for making dolls and toys can be purchased at your local fabric and crafts supply stores. If you cannot find the items you are looking for, write to the companies listed below for information or a catalogue.

All Cooped Up
560 South State Street, B-1
Orem, UT 84059
Send $1.00 for catalogue

Donna Gallagher
Creative NeedleArts, Inc.
994 South Sunbury Road
Westerville, OH 43081
Send $1.00 for catalogue

INDEX

Page numbers in **bold** type indicate photographs. The remaining numbers refer to how-to instructions.

A-C

D-F